Steve Bruce is Professor of Sociology at the University of Aberdeen. His books include *God Save Ulster!: The Religion and Politics of Paisleyism* (Clarendon Press, 1986), *The Rise and Fall of the New Christian Right: Protestant Politics in America, 1978–88* (Clarendon Press, 1987), and *A House Divided: Protestantism, Schism and Secularization* (1990).

RELIGION AND MODERNIZATION

RELIGION AND MODERNIZATION

Sociologists and Historians Debate the
Secularization Thesis

Edited By
STEVE BRUCE

CLARENDON PRESS · OXFORD

1992

Oxford University Press, Walton Street, Oxford OX2 6DP
Oxford New York Toronto
Delhi Bombay Calcutta Madras Karachi
Petaling Jaya Singapore Hong Kong Tokyo
Nairobi Dar es Salaam Cape Town
Melbourne Auckland
and associated companies in
Berlin Ibadan

Oxford is a trade mark of Oxford University Press

Published in the United States
by Oxford University Press, New York

British Library Cataloguing in Publication Data
Data available

Library of Congress Cataloging in Publication Data
Religion and modernization: sociologists and historians debate the
secularization thesis / edited by Steve Bruce.
Includes bibliographical references and index.
1. Secularism.   I. Bruce, Steve, 1954- .
BL2747.8.R45 1992 306.6'09'034—dc20 92—15171
ISBN 0-19-827369-X

Typeset by Pentacor PLC, High Wycombe, Bucks.
Printed and bound in
Great Britain by Biddles Ltd.,
Guildford and King's Lynn

Preface

THIS collection had its origins in an argument between two sociologists of religion. For more than a decade I have been interested in the fate of religion in the modern world. In *A House Divided: Protestantism, Schism, and Secularization*, I tried to bring together a number of themes in a general explanation of the career of Protestantism in modern industrial societies. Although not originally conceived as a restatement of the secularization thesis, it began by trying to establish that among the major changes in the position of Protestantism was the brute fact of decline. As my own original research was concerned only with recent changes, much of the material was drawn from the work of historians of religion. In that context I was introduced to the work of Hugh McLeod, Callum Brown, Alan Gilbert, David Hempton, and others. At the same time, a number of historians, including some of those just mentioned, were attacking the poor historical foundations of much sociological writing on secularization. Roy Wallis, who was then head of the Department of Social Studies at The Queen's University of Belfast, was a sympathetic but earnest critic of my work and, although we agreed enough to co-author a number of essays on secularization, we often found important points of disagreement in our discussion of some of the mechanics of what we saw as the decline in the social significance of religion in the western world. Always of an empiricist bent, Wallis suggested that we try to move our arguments forward by hosting a small symposium of sociologists and historians who had a detailed knowledge of patterns of religious adherence to exchange ideas and information.

Professor Wallis died suddenly on 6 May 1990, just a fortnight before the symposium was due to convene. The symposium was cancelled but I resolved to press on with the editing of the papers into a collection. Hugh McLeod and John Wolffe of the University of York decided to arrange a meeting in September. David Bebbington and Edward Royle joined us and made valuable contributions to the discussions.

Although the symposium never met in Belfast, the willingness of The Queen's University to make funds available for it was an essential stimulus and I would like to thank the university's senior officers. I would also like to thank John Wolffe and Edward Royle of the University of York for organizing our meeting.

S. B.

Contents

The Contributors

STEVE BRUCE is Professor of Sociology, University of Aberdeen.

ROY WALLIS was, until his death in 1990, Professor of Sociology, The Queen's University of Belfast.

CALLUM G. BROWN is Senior Lecturer in History, University of Strathclyde.

HUGH MCLEOD is Senior Lecturer in History, University of Birmingham.

ROBIN GILL is William Leech Professorial Research Fellow in Applied Christian Theology, University of Newcastle.

MICHAEL P. HORNSBY-SMITH is Senior Lecturer in Sociology, University of Surrey.

ROGER FINKE is Assistant Professor of Sociology, Purdue University.

BRYAN WILSON is Reader in Sociology, University of Oxford, and a Fellow of All Souls College.

I

Introduction

STEVE BRUCE

As the first essay in this collection notes, 'the secularization thesis is one of sociology's most enduring research programmes and like many other long-standing theoretical frameworks it has generated a multitude of criticisms'. Before introducing the items in what I hope will be seen as a useful contribution to an evaluation of the secularization thesis, I want to address and answer the challenge that the thesis is not worthy of evaluation because it is part of an ideological project. The secularization thesis has at least some of its roots in *secularism*. Comte was certainly more influenced by his desire to see the disappearance of the unhealthy superstitions of religion from the modern world than by an 'objective' assessment that such changes were taking place. But one might have expected that the rise of ideologically 'neutered' (if not entirely neutral) social science would have killed dead the argument that the secularization thesis should be judged by the values of its proponents. Failing that, one might have expected the argument to trip over the contemporary absence of avowed secularists in the ranks of the documenters of secularization. Yet the author of a recent study of fundamentalism casually rejects the secularization thesis on the grounds that, like Marxist identifiers of 'increasing class struggle', the desires of 'secularizationists' cloud their judgments.[1] Although element-ary, this is an important point and I want to examine the claim that the identification of secularization is a distortion of secularism.

Although it is not often presented as starkly as I have summarized it, the 'secularist' objection to secularization is an *ad hominem* argument. It is thus proper to answer it by considering what is known about the values of those most often associated with the Anglo-Saxon literature on seculariza-tion: David Martin, Bryan Wilson, and Peter Berger. Contrary to what one might expect from closet secularists, in their different ways all have made it very clear that they expect a secular world to be rather unpleasant. In his Hobhouse Memorial Lecture Wilson extended his writings on secularization to consider the consequences of a loss of value consensus and common morality and concluded:

if the civic space is peopled by those whose emotions are uneducated, who are fed on hedonism and cynicism, and who are untrammelled by inner restraints, shall we escape new forms of oppressive social control to contain the latent hostilities between a people which does not trust the system and a system which cannot trust the people?[2]

This is hardly the view of someone who welcomes what he describes. Like Wilson, Martin has a clear 'small "c"' conservative dislike for the hedonism and liberality of the modern secular world and he adds a further reason for finding the secular world uncongenial: he is an ordained Anglican who has given considerable effort, not only to exploring the relationship between sociology and theology, but also to doing the latter. Similar observations could be made about Berger. Those who accuse him of secularism must have overlooked *A Rumour of Angels* and *The Heretical Imperative*, books in which he tries to reconcile his Lutheran faith and theology with his calling as a sociologist by finding in the natural conditions of human life 'signals of transcendence' which indicate a background of the supernatural. In view of what they have actually written about secularization, it is hard to believe Lawrence when he describes Berger and Wilson as two 'Advocates of the post-traditional world [who] want to believe in "secularization" '.[3]

Fortunately, I can establish my point without getting bogged down in that favourite of undergraduate essay topics 'Can sociology be ideologically neutral?'. That two of three proponents of secularization are Christians who regret the changes they describe and the third is, for different reasons, equally unenthusiastic about a secular society seems good grounds for arguing for the more restricted position that, even if scholars cannot leave aside entirely their own preferences, there is no regular relationship between how they describe and explain the past and what they wish for the future. Establishing that clears the way for the approach underlying this collection.

However much one may regret it there can be little doubt that most changes in the status of theories and perspectives in the social sciences and humanities owe more to fickle intellectual fashion than to advances in knowledge. Despite the popularity in sociology of continental philosophers,[4] I remain committed to the view that the way to improve our understanding is not through radical leaps of perspective (stimulating though such leaps may be) but through examining the elements of the competing positions in order that we can agree on what would count as evidence for one position but not another, and searching for such evidence. Incrementally improving knowledge by bringing together evidence and competing explanations may not be easy but it remains the only way forward for an empirical discipline. That is the assumption which informed the choice of contributors to this collection.

In Chapter 2, Wallis and Bruce clarify the 'secularization' thesis by outlining its main elements and by countering some of the least useful criticisms of it. Hence the main purpose of their contribution is to present the parts of the story in such a way that they can be challenged by the appropriate evidence. Even when such evidence is not yet available, clarification remains important because it allows us to identify what sorts of research still need to be done.

In addition to their particular merits, the remaining essays share the common virtue of representing an advance in the discovery and presentation of data pertinent to one aspect of the debate. It is no fault of previous sociologists and historians of religion that their evidence was often weak and impressionistic. The social and human sciences generally have seen major steps forward in data collection and analysis. Rather than criticize Weber or Wilson for the 'lightness' of their evidence, what is important is that the advances seen in other fields be now repeated in the study of religious change. Brown, in support of a trenchant attack on secularization, offers impressively substantial data on changes in church membership in Britain and the USA during the period of industrialization and urbanization.

Like Brown, McLeod focuses on the city but instead of considering the evidence for very broad trends, he concentrates on a detailed examination of the central period in the history of London, New York, and Berlin, the major cities of the three industrial nations of the nineteenth century. His comparisons lead him to conclude that the search for some 'master factor' cause of secularization is mistaken. Although less dismissive of the work of sociologists than Brown, McLeod argues that:

in the short run at least, historical factors—events and experiences specific to particular countries, regions, ethnic groups—were of considerable importance, and should not be neglected in the search for more general explanations of secularization.[5]

Gill's work, although still in its early stages, represents a major step forward in the use of the main data source for students of nineteenth-century British religion: the 1851 census of church attendance. By recomputing figures from the original census returns, Gill has been able to resolve a number of problems well-known to those who have tried to use the data and has extracted genuinely comparable statistics. He has also brought together a number of surprisingly neglected sources to produce time-series statistics of church capacity and church attendance. The conclusion of his research is the novel one that, contrary to what has previously been believed, over-provision, rather than under-provision of places for worship, was a major factor in church decline. In a neat inversion of the orthodoxy, he offers the possibility that a decline in religious belief did not cause empty churches; empty churches undermined religious belief.

Roman Catholicism has usually played one of two minor 'character parts' in the secularization debate. The apparent strength of the Catholic Church amongst the Victorian working class is usually presented as an exception to generalizations about the secularizing effects of industrialization. The recent decline in various indices of vitality is offered as evidence that secularization gets to all religions eventually. Whatever the truth of these and related images of Catholicism, they have very rarely been rooted in any good evidence. The recent studies of Michael Hornsby-Smith and his colleagues have begun to remedy the omission and in this essay he considers the extent to which recent changes in English Catholicism should be seen as evidence of secularization. Usefully, he recognizes that secularization is a multi-faceted notion and presents the data as they bear on different aspects of the thesis.

The history of religious change in the USA has always posed a major difficulty for the secularization thesis. Although it is possible to discern a slight downturn on some indices of religious involvement, it is still the case that the people of the nation usually regarded by sociologists as the most modern, remain church-going. Finke argues that, contrary to the secularization thesis, pluralism is associated with increased religious adherence. The point is not new but there has recently been an advance in the quality of statistical evidence used in discussions of American church membership. Working with Rodney Stark, Finke has made important contributions to that improvement in the evidential base and in this essay summarizes his findings. Bruce's discussion of pluralism in the contrast of religion in Europe and USA argues that Finke's approach remains too simple and that improvements in the quality of data need to be matched by increased sophistication in thinking about how such 'variables' as pluralism and urbanization are supposed to affect individual choices about church involvement. Although the issue of the impact of pluralism thus remains unresolved (at least between these authors), the two essays together will allow others to take the argument forward and find the evidence to bring it closer to resolution.

Although the discussion was not initially planned as a concerted critique of the work of Bryan Wilson, his pre-eminence in the field is recognized by the prominence given to his writings in the opening summary of the thesis and in subsequent chapters. It seemed fitting then to give him the opportunity to reply to his critics and this he has ably done, quite sensibly eschewing the option of a line-by-line refutation and instead reminding us of the big themes in the thesis that tend to get overlooked in the concentration on statistical material.

CONCLUSION

Although it is possible to conceptualize it in other ways, secularization primarily refers to the beliefs of people. The core of what we mean when we talk about this society being more 'secular' than that is that the lives of fewer people in the former than in the latter are influenced by religious beliefs. Given the level of abstraction at which they commonly work, it is always possible for sociologists to forget that simple fact. Although clearly I am using 'choose' in a loose sense, we need to explain why some people choose to be or to remain religious while others do not. A compounding danger for sociologists is the ecological fallacy. As Bruce argues in his essay on pluralism, it is all too easy to impute to one group of people the characteristics of another or to suppose that a property of an abstraction such as 'society' also accurately describes the everyday lifeworld of the people who make up the society. We may miss the possibility that the characteristic of the abstraction is an aggregate of two conflicting tendencies at a lower level. For example, one may miss the fact that a decline in the productivity of an economy may make some people richer and others poorer. This reminds us of the obvious need for caution in moving from describing broad social patterns to explaining them, if the explanation involves assumptions about the behaviour of specific groups or individuals.

If, to put it bluntly, we take the 'bottom line' of secularization to be changes in the religious beliefs and behaviour of individuals, we have to build our general explanations of secularization on a more detailed knowledge of religious belief and behaviour than we have at present. For times other than the present, that requires the work of historians. At the same time, historians draw on often unstated and unexamined generalizations in describing and explaining their particular cases. Often without being too clear about it, they use the work of sociologists.

The conclusion of these observations is the obvious but often insufficiently followed injunction that sociologists and historians must continue to debate, must pool their expertise, and must challenge each others' disciplinary assumptions. I hope this collection is a useful step in that direction.

NOTES

1. B. B. Lawrence, *Defenders of God: The Fundamentalist Revolt Against the Modern Age* (London, 1990).
2. B. R. Wilson, 'Morality in the Evolution of the Modern Social System', *British Journal of Sociology* 36 (1985), 315–32.
3. Lawrence, *Defenders*, 63.
4. Two works by British sociologists—B. S. Turner, *Religion and Social Theory* (London, 1983) and J. Beckford, *Religion and Advanced Industrial Society* (London, 1989)—have suggested that the sociology of religion is in the doldrums because it has failed to pay sufficient attention to the work of various continental social theorists and philosophers. The pointlessness of their proposed method is inadvertently evidenced in Turner's list of the neglected great, which now seems very dated.
5. See Ch. 4 of this volume.

Secularization: The Orthodox Model

ROY WALLIS AND STEVE BRUCE

THE secularization thesis is one of sociology's most enduring research programmes and like many other long-standing theoretical frameworks it has generated a multitude of criticisms. Most critics have been satisfied with presenting by way of refutation such anomalies as evidence of enduring religiosity or countervailing trends. Few have attempted to erect a comprehensive alternative theory. The only compelling recent contender has been the self-equilibrating model of relatively constant religious 'demand' which Stark and Bainbridge have founded on exchange theory.

In this opening chapter we will make some general remarks about theory in relation to broad patterns of social change, present the skeleton of the secularization thesis within that context, consider some of the alleged countervailing evidence, and reflect briefly on the only serious alternative paradigm.

SOCIAL CHANGE

Experience should by now tell us that history moves along nudged and deflected by a multitude of contingencies. Sociologists seeking to discern general trends and comparative patterns should not deceive themselves that they will discover deterministic laws underlying the manifest empirical diversity. What they may hope to find are explanatory models, representing typical patterns in ideal–typical circumstances. The use of such models will facilitate the interpretation of historical data in the light of the particular contingencies operating in that setting. The secularization thesis is a research programme with, at its core, an explanatory model. This model, as presented below, asserts that the social significance of religion diminishes in response to the operation of three salient features of modernization (another ideal–typical model), namely (1) social differentiation, (2) societalization, and (3) rationalization.

It recognizes, however, that social change is a multiply contingent process and that ideal–typical conditions often may not be met. There may be countervailing factors, sometimes generated by the same process of modernization. We believe that two such processes, which we call cultural defence and cultural transition, are especially relevant.

THE THESIS

The secularization thesis is contentious, in part because it has important social implications but also because secularization is a multi-faceted notion which does not lend itself readily to definitive quantitative test.

The difficulties in arriving at simple measures of secularization begin with the corresponding difficulty of defining *religion*. A distinction is often made between functional and substantive definitions of religion. Functional definitions identify religion in terms of what it does. For example, religion may be that which provides solutions to 'ultimate problems' or answers fundamental questions of the human existential condition. Substantive definitions identify religion in terms of what it is. For example, religion may be that clutch of beliefs and actions predicated upon the assumption of the existence of supernatural beings or powers.

Both kinds of definitions pose problems. First, functional definitions count as religious things that on the face of it do not look very religious (political ideologies or secular therapies, for example) and that are typically regarded as secular by their adherents. For that reason functional definitions tend not to accord well with the understandings of ordinary people. Secondly, it is not at all clear just what is an 'ultimate' question or in whose mind it is ultimate. Proponents of such an approach often fall back on the examination of beliefs and institutions which are conceived as religious in some other, substantive, sense and the phenomenon they describe seems at times to have little to do with issues of 'ultimacy'. Thirdly, while we readily concede the value of exploring similarities between religious institutions and other patterns of behaviour that at times seem to serve similar purposes, calling them all religious gains very little except some contentious theoretical baggage and loses much analytical clarity. A legitimate interest in exploring 'functional' equivalents of religion can be pursued as readily with a substantive definition of religion as with a functional one. Fourthly, the functional definition involves the danger of inappropriately establishing by definition what needs to be argued for and demonstrated: that this or that is indeed the functional equivalent of religion. Finally, a functional definition has the disadvantage of foreclosing on the issue which interests us in this volume of essays. Given that by definition humans always have *ultimate* questions, functional definitions of religion do not allow us to talk of secularization at all, only of 'religious' change.

Substantive definitions also pose difficulties. They may be closer to what the average Westerner understands by 'religion' but when we seek to unpack the notion of 'supernatural', we find difficulties in relation to non-western or traditional cultures. A world in which one daily communes with ancestors or takes steps to avoid ubiquitous witchcraft may not be one in which it is easy for the actors themselves to discriminate the natural from the supernatural. If the actors are not making the distinction then a substantive definition which can be applied across cultures has to be an observer's rather than an actor's concept.

However, a definition which articulates with broad, contemporary, common-sense reflection on the matter is usually not a bad place to start. Moreover the usefulness of any conceptualization depends not upon who makes the distinctions it entails but upon their success in the explanatory endeavour in which they are deployed. We use a substantive definition because it seems to permit the formulation of a theory which has considerable explanatory scope.

Religion for us consists of actions, beliefs, and institutions predicated upon the assumption of the existence of either supernatural entities with powers of agency, or impersonal powers or processes possessed of moral purpose, which have the capacity to set the conditions of, or to intervene in, human affairs. Further, the central claims to the operation of such entities or impersonal powers are either not susceptible to, or are systematically protected from, refutation.

On the basis of this definition we can begin to spell out what is involved in the notion of secularization. Some commentators mean by secularization the decline of religion.[1] This is awkward. It is perfectly coherent to argue that a diminishing public role for religion and declining involvement in religious institutions leave untouched the extent of 'true religion'. On this account, all that is lost is nominal adherence, social performance of religious rites, shallow acceptance of prevailing dominant ideas, and unnecessary entanglement of religious roles and institutions with secular matters, leaving behind a firm or even firmer religiosity in those who continue to practise or believe (and this is the argument of Hornsby-Smith in Chapter 6). We have no brief for a definition of 'true religion' and little worthwhile evidence of the 'depth' of faith amongst the faithful. Hence with Wilson we set a more restricted test of secularization, namely that of the diminishing social significance of religion.[2]

The social significance of religion is clearly a multidimensional notion. Broadly it seeks to capture the extent to which religion *makes a difference* to the operation and standing of social roles and institutions (including those roles and institutions conventionally labelled religious) and to the beliefs and actions of the individual. Because the notion is multidimensional we should not assume that the dimensions will all vary at the same rate or even in the same direction. This is an unfortunate complication but then social life is unfortunately complicated.

Stated briefly the secularization thesis asserts that modernization[3] (itself no simple concept) brings in its wake (and may itself be accelerated by) 'the diminution of the social significance of religion'. What features of modernization are involved? There seem to be three that are particularly salient: social differentiation, societalization and rationalization.

SOCIAL DIFFERENTIATION

Social differentiation is the process by which specialized roles and institutions are developed or arise to handle specific features or functions previously embodied in, or carried out by, one role or institution. For example, specialist institutions arise to provide education, health care, welfare, and social control, all once in the domain of religious institutions. An obvious early site of such specialization is the family, which cedes most of its roles as a unit of production, education and social control to factories, schools and police forces. In addition to religious offices, the eighteenth-century Church of Scotland provided education, social welfare, and social control. Although the specialist secular institutions which adopt these roles may continue to be dominated by religious professionals, in time clerics are eclipsed as specialist professionals are trained and new bodies of knowledge or skill are generated, areas of expertise in which religious officials will not be as highly trained as lay professionals.

The notion of social differentiation also embodies another element: the economic growth implicit in modernization leads to the emergence of an ever-greater range of occupation and life situation. This plurality of life experience may be seen in the emergence of classes (which, particularly during the early stages of capital accumulation, may often be enmeshed in conflict with each other). The plausibility of a single moral universe in which all manner and conditions of persons have a place in some grand design is subverted.[4] Traditional integrated organic conceptions of the moral and supernatural order begin to fragment. Depending on the nature of the society and the religious culture, fragmentation may take the form of the rise of a plurality of competing conceptions or, where the traditional order is more resilient and the religious tradition less open, fracture across sharp social divisions between those who remain within the religious tradition and those who openly oppose it. The differentiation of lifeworlds encourages a differentiation of metaphysical and salvational systems along lines more suited to each class or social fragment.[5]

SOCIETALIZATION

The second element, identified by Bryan Wilson, is that of societalization, the process by which 'life is increasingly enmeshed and organized, not locally but societally (that society being most evidently, but not uniquely, the nation state)'.[6] By this Wilson means the attenuation of close-knit, integrated, small-scale communities as a result of the growth of large-scale industrial and commercial enterprise, the emergence of modern states co-ordinated through massive, impersonal bureaucracies, and the development of anonymous urban agglomerations as the typical residential setting.

Religion, Wilson argues, has its source in, and draws strength from, the community. As the *society* rather than the community has increasingly become the locus of the individual's life, so religion has been shorn of its functions. Religion has traditionally celebrated and legitimated local life.[7] When the total, all-embracing community of like-situated people working and playing together gives way to the dormitory town or suburb, there is little held in common left to celebrate. The societal system relies less on the inculcation of a shared moral order and more on the utilization of efficient technical means of eliciting and monitoring appropriate behaviour.

The consequence of differentiation and societalization is that the plausibility of any single overarching moral and religious system declines, to be displaced by competing conceptions which have less connection to role performance in an anonymous and impersonal public domain and more to privatized, individual experience. Religion may retain subjective plausibility, but it does so at the price of its objective taken-for-grantedness. Religion becomes privatized and is pushed to the margins and interstices of the social order. It is no longer a matter of necessity but, in the term found on many American forms, is a matter of 'preference', a leisure activity. To borrow the phrase coined by American conservative critics of what they regard as a too rigorous separation of Church and State, the public world becomes a 'naked public square'.[8]

RATIONALIZATION

While differentiation and societalization are essentially changes in the structure of societies, a third significant process is that of rationalization, which largely involves changes in the way people think and consequentially in the way they act. Weber and Berger suggest that the Judaeo-Christian tradition was peculiarly susceptible to secularization.[9] In brief, Judaism postulated a transcendent god. The projection of the divine at one remove from the world allowed people to see the world as secular and permitted its rational and empirical exploration more freely than would be possible in a world immanently pervaded by the supernatural. Judaism also postulated a single god. Monotheism encouraged ethical rationalization— the attempt to reduce theology and ethics to a consistent rational system of ideas and to eliminate magical means of salvation—in a way likely to be impeded where a culture (such as that of ancient Greece) can attribute worldly outcomes to a plurality of supernatural entities sometimes operating at cross-purposes. The development of a healthy tradition of rationalistic scrutiny may, of course, in time, subvert what it was first embarked upon to render impregnable.

Judaeo-Christianity, in the view of Weber and Berger, sowed the seeds of its own destruction by freeing the way for empirical enquiry, pragmatic and instrumental treatment of this world, and by encouraging rationalization of theology (and after theology of economics, politics, and public life generally). Rationalization involved the pursuit of technically efficient means of securing this-worldly ends. One of its most potent forms was the development of technology. Technically efficient machinery and procedures reduced uncertainty and thereby reliance upon faith. The domain over which religion offered the most compelling explanations and the most predictable outcomes shrank. The growth of technical rationality gradually displaced supernatural influence and moral considerations from ever-wider areas of public life, replacing them by considerations of objective performance and practical expedience.

The Weber–Berger thesis argues that Catholicism marked an interruption, even reversal, of the process of rationalization which was reinstated on course by the Reformation. However, the fact that the Reformation introduced a *variety* of forms of theology and of relationships between Church and State, poses a major problem for analysis thereafter in the vastly increased complexity of the religious situation in modern western societies.

THE BASIC PATTERNS

To the underlying causes, we must add the variations which result from differences in theology, ecclesiology, Church-State relations and the role of religion in ethnic conflict. We can discern the following broad patterns which were set by the role played by, and the position of the Church during, the course of modernization.[10]

First, Catholicism remained dominant—which also largely coincided with late industrialization—and a monolithic organic ideology was supported by national élites resisting the rising forces of liberalism and socialism, which through confrontation generated strong opposing organic secularist ideologies with an anti-clerical bent. The society divided into clerical and anti-clerical blocks. In this category fall the cases of Catholic western and southern European states.

Secondly, Protestantism became dominant and latitud-inarian state churches allied with national élites faced rising liberalism and socialism, which were none the less able to draw upon dissenting variants or strands within the Protestant faith. That social fragments could develop deviant interpreta-tions of the dominant religious tradition to legitimate their concerns and criticize the social position, political power, and mores of superior groups meant that religion *itself* did not become a central focus of conflict, only the particular privileges of its forms. The masses dropped away in the course of major social dislocations (in the English case, during the Civil War, the Restoration, rural–urban migration, and the First and Second World Wars) in indifference rather than outright hostility to organized religion. In this category fall the northern European states of Britain and Scandinavia.

Thirdly, the greater the plurality of religious expressions available, that is the greater the variety of dissent, the stronger the continued involvement of the masses in religious institutions in Protestant-dominated settings. The extreme case here is the USA, which represents the 'universalisation of dissent',[11] where no one religious expression was uniquely identified with the social élite, and a multiplicity of forms was imported or invented to appeal to all manner and condition of persons. In this case, religious freedom represents a central value of the nation. Religious adherence is thus an aspect of commitment to the national identity, but religious expressions themselves tend to undergo adaptation to the secular values of the society.[12] All the Protestant-dominated immigrant-based societies (the USA, Canada, Australia, and New Zealand) display this pattern to a greater or lesser extent, depending on the degree of priority retained by the Anglican Church. The stronger the Anglican Church, the greater the decline in church involvement over recent decades.[13]

Fourthly, in dual societies, divided between large blocs of Catholics and Protestants, 'pillarization' occurred as each confession sought to encapsulate its own people and to provide a distinctive body of institutions to serve their social and political needs. While religious attachments remained relatively high, Catholics and Protestants had increasingly to collaborate to retain a Christian character to the society in the face of liberal and secularist forces.[14] Such collaboration however, could only take place where both Catholics and Protestants had come to agree on the issue of national sovereignty—often in the course of securing freedom from imperialistic domination (as in Switzerland and Holland). Where the issue of national sovereignty remained unresolved, however, religion was likely to be the basis of divergent national aspirations, and thus to remain a symbolic focus of dispute. The obvious case is that of Ulster.

Finally, to cover the broad territory of western Europe, there are the Catholic states in which class formation and social differentiation have not issued in widespread sharp antagonism towards the Church, because the Church has provided a central focus of cultural identity in opposition to an imperialistic neighbour which sought to impose an alien set of cultural values and identities upon a reluctant populace. Religious adherence remained strong as an expression of protest, of rejection of alien values and domination, and as an expression of cultural and social integrity. The obvious cases here are Poland and the Irish Republic.[15]

These specific historical and cultural patterns suggest a simple heuristic principle, namely that social differentiation, societalization, and rationalization generate secularization except where religion finds or retains work to do other than relating individuals to the supernatural. This principle helps explain not only some of the patterns outlined above, but also some of those to be found *within* particular societies. We might say that religion diminishes in social significance except in two broad contexts, those of *cultural defence* and of *cultural transition*.

CULTURAL DEFENCE

Where culture, identity, and sense of worth are challenged by a source promoting either an alien religion or rampant secularism and that source is negatively valued, secularization will be inhibited. Religion can provide resources for the defence of a national, local, ethnic, or status-group culture. Again, Poland and the Irish Republic are prime examples, but Ulster can also be included, as in more attenuated form can other 'dual' societies, or the peripheries of secularizing societies, resistant to the alien encroachment of the centre.

In the United Kingdom, for example, the greater attachment to their religious institutions of the Welsh and still more of the Scots evidences this factor.[16] The national culture and identity are associated with presbytery and chapel against the attempted cultural domination of English Anglicanism or metropolitan secularity. In Northern Ireland, rates of church involvement are high not only amongst Catholics but also amongst Protestants, who feel threatened by them.[17]

In the USA, the greater attachment of southern and mid-western states to traditional Protestant religious forms has represented an element of a nativist defence of the culture of native-born Anglo-Saxon Protestants. Influxes of Catholics and Jews and the attempts of a secularistic establishment in the north and east to impose unwanted social and cultural patterns throughout the Republic provoked cultural defences from the peripheries.

The more socially peripheral and culturally distinct the region, the more likely religion is to provide a focus of resistance, particularly when language no longer provides a viable basis for the assertion of cultural difference.

CULTURAL TRANSITION

Where identity is threatened in the course of major cultural transitions, religion may provide resources for negotiating such transitions or asserting a new claim to a sense of worth. The Herberg thesis argues that religious institutions provided resources for the assimilation of immigrants into American society.[18] Ethnic religious groups provided a mechanism for easing the transition between homeland and the new identity in the USA. The Church offered a supportive group which spoke one's language, shared one's assumptions and values, but which also had experience of, and contacts within, the new social and cultural milieu.

A similar pattern is evident amongst Asian immigrants to Britain.[19] They congregate where others have gone before. They establish a religious community and its appropriate institutions and roles as soon as they can, and within that community they can reassert their cultural integrity, their commitment to its values, and sense of the worth of the identity which it has created in them. They may often fall away from observance before families and cultural institutions are established, but they often become more observant—perhaps even more observant than they were at home—when these are in place.

There is another important manifestation of this counter-vailing tendency for religion to retain significance, even temporarily to grow in significance, where it comes to play a role in cultural transition, and that is in the course of modernization itself.

Modernization disrupts communities and traditional employment patterns and status hierarchies. By extending the range of communication, it makes the social peripheries and hinterlands more aware of the manners and mores, lifestyles and values, of the centre and metropolis, and vice versa. Sectors of the centre are motivated to missionize the hinterland and periphery, seeking to assimilate them, by educating their dwellers and socializing them to the centrally approved standards of performance in 'respectable' beliefs and practices. They are moved to 'improve' and elevate the masses in the rural areas and those who move to the fringes of the cities and there pose the threat of an undisciplined or radical rabble on the doorstep. Sectors of the social periphery in turn are motivated to embrace the models of respectable performance offered to them, especially when they are already in the process of upward mobility and self-improvement. Industrialization and urbanization therefore tend to give rise to movements of revival and reform, drawing the lapsed and heterodox into the orbit of orthodoxy. The new converts and the practices of the revivalists might not always be acceptable to the dominant religious organizations. The awkwardness of their position is then solved by secession (or expulsion) and the formation of new sects and denominations. Methodism and the Evangelical Revival in Britain are prominent examples.

Commitment to Nonconformity marked a withdrawal from the old system of dependency on parson and squire, an assertion of autonomy and independence by the formerly deferential middling and lower orders, and the acceptance of religious values and practices which endorsed recently acquired socio-economic and democratic aspirations. Evangelicalism gave a spiritual legitimation to the desire for improvement within these strata, while inculcating the values and habits of thrift, conscientious hard work, self-discipline, sobriety, and the deferral of gratification which would assist them to the realization of those values.

Although industrialization and urbanization tend, then, in the long term to undermine traditional community and thereby to subvert the basis on which religion can most readily flourish, in the short term they can be associated with an *increase* in attachment to religious bodies. This is the point forcefully argued by Callum Brown.[20]

However, the increase in organized religious activity was short-lived. As the figures in Brown's essay amply demonstrate there has been a major decline in British church adherence since the 1950s.

In America, there is no evidence of long-term decline in church membership, and weekly attendance appears over the period 1939–71 to have risen to a peak in the mid-1950s and then gently fallen back to around 40 per cent of the adult population. However, while these rates show considerable stability, various studies show signs of the substantial modification of religious belief, and the attenuation of supernaturalism.[21]

As well as there being fewer churchly people, the lives of those who retain some organized religious connection seem less dominated by religion: they attend church less (the pattern of twice-Sabbath attendance and mid-week prayer or Bible-Study meetings has declined except amongst the smaller and more fundamentalist bodies). A smaller proportion of all reading matter is religious and there can be little doubt that that is so for the churchly as well as the unchurched.[22] Those who attend church today are less knowledgeable concerning the doctrines and scriptures. Being church members distinguishes them relatively little in belief and behaviour from those who are not.

America is the paradigm case of such attenuation of distinctive belief, amounting in some liberal denominations to a virtual evacuation of the supernatural from religion, where what remains for the majority of attenders of liberal denominations at least is a practice predominantly serving social and psychological functions. Most importantly, the sense of necessity appears to be disappearing from American religion. Gallup and Poling conclude a review of recent surveys by saying:

Many young people seem quite comfortable with a solitary, personal approach to matters of faith—so much so that three out of every four state that they believe a person can be a good Christian even if he or she does not attend church. Should that attitude prevail for long, it means an absolute goodbye to the present religious arrangement in North America.[23]

Although the authors miss the point and assert that little has changed, the restudy of religion in the Lynds' 'Middletown' is also instructive. Between 1924 and 1977 the given reasons for church attendance and involvement shifted markedly from obedience to pleasure. Middletownians now go to church because it is personally rewarding rather than because God commands it.[24]

To summarize, it is no part of this argument that religion will disappear from the modern world. Religion is a singularly resilient phenomenon which is likely to survive as privatized belief and practice, at society's margins or in its interstices, and may even revive in times of trauma or major social transformation which may give it new work to do. Where it survives as a widespread practice it will tend to do so on the basis of an attenuation of what is specifically religious about it; that is at the expense of supernaturalism. Otherwise it will survive and be transmitted best in the private subjectivity of individuals and families, or in tight-knit sectarian groups which can cut themselves off from the world to varying degrees. It is in those settings where 'societalization' is held at bay by the creation of an insulated sub-society which preserves a distinctive sub-culture that 'sectarian' religion persists and grows.[25]

It must be said, however, that not every commentator would accept the above analysis. Some argue that there is more religion around today than our account gives credit for; others that the past was less religious then we suppose.

COMMON AND IMPLICIT RELIGION

Those who wish to challenge our description of the present as largely secular distinguish between the 'official' religion of orthodox institutional belief and practice, and common or folk religion which 'may be described as those beliefs and practices of an overtly religious nature which are not under the domination of a prevailing religious institution'.[26] It is, therefore, an amorphous category, the more so because it cannot be entirely distinguished from official religion, since it also involves the adaptation or utilization of official religious beliefs and practices in unofficial ways.

That there is widespread evidence of religion beyond its institutional forms is incontrovertible. Stated belief in God is widespread: 94 per cent of Americans, 65 per cent of Scandinavians, and 76 per cent of the population of the United Kingdom, affirm a belief in God.[27] An Independent Television Authority survey conducted in 1968 showed that 37 per cent of the UK population held a personalized image of God, while a further 42 per cent believed in the existence of a Life Force, Spirit, or Principle underlying events in the world. Belief in life after death is held by about 69 per cent of Americans, and 43 per cent of the UK population.[28] One half of all Americans and one fifth of all English people were found to believe in Satan in the early 1970s.[29] The reading of horoscopes seems widespread. A 1976 survey in Great Britain found that rather more than a third of all adults give a positive response to the question of whether they were 'aware of, or influenced by a presence or power, whether referred to as God or not, which is different from their every day selves'.[30]

Thus, we must agree that there is a good deal of common religion about but what does this entail for the secularization thesis? We would argue that remarkably little follows, particularly from responses to such leading questions as those just cited. It is, indeed, precisely the claim of the secularization thesis that religious belief and practice will tend to become more individualized, fragmented, and privatized, as this sort of evidence seems to show. Moreover, although trend data in this area are not readily available, we would argue that the evidence is clear of a decline of belief in diverse supernatural beings: witches, demons, ghosts, fairies; the power of supernaturalistically charged talismans and amulets; in the Devil and Hell; and in superstitious ideas and practices.

Perhaps centrally for the secularization thesis, the case that these diffuse, varied, and fluid beliefs and practices compensate *in their social significance* for the declining power and influence of institutional religion has clearly not been made. Indeed, their very individualized and privatized character seems precisely to contradict any such claim.

We might note two further grounds for arguing that we underestimate the present strength of religion. The first of these is substantive and concerns the supposed re-introduction of religious ideas and symbols into political life. The claim is sometimes made that the rise of the new Christian right in the USA in the early 1980s and its much slighter shadow in Britain are significant counters to our assessment of the present social significance of religion. One of us has argued at length that the new Christian right in the USA was of little significance and that such very small successes as the movement did enjoy were ironically based on subordinating religious particularism to an appeal to universal secular values of fairness.[31] Further, the claim that 'examples of resistance to secularization are not confined to marginal movements, immigrants, "residues" and protest movements' is made by Thompson with what he calls:

just one, but very relevant, contemporary example . . . the efforts of Mrs Thatcher and the head of her Policy Unit, Professor Brian Griffiths, in blending together religious and other values in the ideology of Thatcherism.[32]

Within a month of that gem of socio-political insight being published, Margaret Thatcher had resigned and an entirely conventional civil servant had replaced Professor Griffiths. It is always possible to identify one or two minor British politicians or academic advisers who wish to promote some sort of new Christian right in Britain. What has not been established is that their ideas are popular or have any influence.

The second ground on which our analysis of present religiosity can be faulted is the less obviously substantive claim that other activities are the functional equivalents of religion and that religiosity is demonstrating itself in new ways. It may well be that support for a football club serves some of the same social and psychological needs which were once served by participation in organized religion but even if this can be shown to be the case, it confirms rather than contradicts our analysis and we see no harm in calling the process of moving from organized religion to politics, football or some other functional equivalent, 'secularization'.

A GOLDEN AGE?

The converse of the view that there is more religion today than proponents of the secularization thesis recognize is that there was less in the past than they claim. This view draws some support from early essays on the topic by David Martin and others,[33] who seemed to think that the secularization thesis required a prior 'Age of Faith' in which virtually all members of a society were orthodox believers and regular participants in the prevailing Church.

The historical record is ambiguous. Laslett asserts 'All our ancestors were literal Christian believers, all of the time' and then adds:

Not everyone was equally devout, of course, and it would be simple-minded to suppose that none of these villagers ever had their doubts. Much of their devotion must have been formal, and some of it mere conformity. But their world was a Christian world and their religious activity was spontaneous, not forced on them from above.[34]

Sources such as Ladourie[35] and Thomas[36] show that there was often considerable laxity in practice in medieval and post-medieval Europe but Clark insists that the constant references to the supernatural in the literature of the seventeenth century cannot be dismissed 'merely as common form':

On the contrary, it is more often necessary to remind ourselves that these words were then seldom used without their accompaniment of meaning, and that their use did generally imply a heightened intensity of feeling. This sense of closeness of God and the devil to every act and fact of daily life is an integral part of the century.[37]

There are, of course, problems of appropriate comparison. Members of the congregation at the various choral offices of Lincoln Cathedral are handed a card which politely points out that the choir seeks perfection in worship and that, while silent prayers and thoughts will be appreciated, the audience should not sing along. In many of the religious forms that dominated pre-modern societies, lay participation was rarely encouraged and sometimes prohibited. God was properly served by the regular performance of the appropriate religious rituals by religious professionals. There is no point in comparing popular participation in that form of religion with the 'classes' of Methodism. As we are unable in this brief review to present a detailed summary of the historical record we will simply note that our reading leads us to regard as judicious the work of Peter Collinson, who concludes that most inhabitants of Elizabethan and Jacobean England were active in support of the Church, even if they were sometimes poorly informed about the details of their faith.[38] Finally we would add an important point. It is often missed by those critics of 'the age of faith' who draw on records of churchmen complaining how irreligious was their flock that the complaints very often mention promiscuous flirtation with non-orthodox religion. Outside the organized Church there was widespread supernaturalism.

We readily concede that it is possible to exaggerate the religiosity of the past and underestimate that of the present. We fully recognize the point made by Brown and others that the early stages of industrialization were accompanied by increased personal involvement in religious activities and, for those so involved, increased knowledge in the beliefs that informed such activities. However, nothing in our extensive reading of the history of religion and of studies of present-day 'implicit' religion leads us (or many other people) to doubt that there has been a major change in the importance and popularity of religion and that the term 'secularization' is as good a way of describing it as any.

THE STARK–BAINBRIDGE THEORY OF RELIGION

The major theoretical challenge to the secularization thesis comes from scholars who suppose that religion performs social or psychological functions sufficiently vital that it cannot disappear and hence the appearance of decline must either mask some process of substitution or be merely temporary. The most elaborate recent version of this sort of argument is the functional-for-the-individual thesis of Stark and Bainbridge.

Stark and Bainbridge develop an 'exchange theory' model of religion based on the familiar postulate that people seek rewards. Some rewards are scarce or unavailable even though highly desired. When highly desired rewards are not available directly, people may instead accept *compensators*: 'intangible substitutes for a desired reward'.[39] Some desired rewards are 'of such a magnitude and scarcity that only by assuming the existence of an active supernatural can credible compensators be created'.[40]

The theory postulates a persisting demand for such rewards and therefore a constant demand for credible intangible substitutes (for example, the promise of eternal life in the hereafter in compensation for the lack of guaranteed immortality here and now below). For the complex of reasons known as the Niebuhr thesis[41], organizations offering supernatural-istically derived compensators will gradually tend to shift away from their earlier supernaturalistic tradition. As the tradition itself loses credibility, and thus the ability to generate credible compensators, so new forms of religion based on imported or culturally innovative beliefs and practices—informed by a stronger version of the super-natural—will emerge as cults, some of which may provide the basis of a new religious tradition. Thus, Stark and Bainbridge propose a relatively constant religious economy: the desire for great and scarce rewards being met by different forms of religious belief and organization. The decline of the leading churches in the tradition will first be replaced by growth in sectarian variants, and then later by growth in cultic innovations. Secularization is thus self-limiting.

Elsewhere we have presented a detailed analytical critique of the Stark–Bainbridge thesis and we will not repeat it here but will confine ourselves to considering the evidence for the thesis.[42] It is certainly the case that conservative churches and sects within the prevailing tradition have grown as the leading churches have become more liberal and less supernaturalistic. However, the British conservative churches and sects have not grown at anything like the rate that would be required to replace the losses sustained by the mainstream churches. The Protestant churches in Britain lost over half a million members between 1970 and 1975 alone. The conservative churches that were growing gained about 14,000 new mem-bers in the same period, making little impact upon the overall loss. As Brierley points out, over the last fifteen years British church membership overall has declined by around 1.5 million.[43] There has been a decrease of 4,000 in the number of full-time ministers and around 3,000 church buildings have closed. Losses to the mainstream churches and denominations have not been made up by the increases experienced by sects and conservative churches, nor have they been made up by the culturally imported or innovative 'cults'. Brierley shows a decline in Unification Church members (or 'Moonies') in Britain in 1980–5 from 570 to 350.[44] The Mormons lost about 10,000 in the same period. Losses were also experienced by Spiritualism and Theosophy. While the Church of Scientology has shown a pattern of growth from an estimated 10,000 in 1970 to an estimated 46,000 in 1985, statistics relating to that body should be viewed with some suspicion but even if they are accurate they do not make much of an impression upon the losses of the mainline churches.

The British evidence, then, does not lend support to the Stark–Bainbridge theory of religion or to the consequential claim that secularization is a self-limiting process. The Canadian studies by Bibby similarly offer no support.[45]

CONCLUSIONS

Like many influential research paradigms, the secularization thesis has been much caricatured and misunderstood. For example, one still finds opponents arguing against it on the grounds that its earliest proponents strongly *desired* a secular society. We take the view that while the reasons why a particular scholar promotes a thesis may be of biographical or historical interest they are not germane to its testing. That must rest solely on its accuracy and analytical utility.

One also finds the thesis being represented as postulating even and irreversible decline. We hope that the above summary, condensed as it has had to be, will have made it clear that there is no necessity for such an assumption; nothing in the social world is irreversible or inevitable. However, we find the basic themes of the secularization thesis sufficiently convincing to believe that it is a paradigm which can continue to support worthwhile research and explanation and which is not yet in need of replacement.

NOTES

1. P. Foster, 'Secularization in the English Context: Some Conceptual and Empirical Problems', *Sociological Review* 20 (1972), 153–68.
2. B. R. Wilson, *Religion in Secular Society* (London, 1966).
3. Our conceptualization of modernization is that of Levy in P. L. Berger, *Facing Up to Modernity* (Harmondsworth, 1979), 101. See also A. Giddens, *Consequences of Modernity* (London, 1991).
4. A. MacIntyre, *Secularization and Moral Change* (London, 1967).
5. P. L. Berger, *The Social Reality of Religion* (London, 1969).
6. B. R. Wilson, *Religion in Sociological Perspective* (Oxford, 1982), 154.
7. Ibid. 159.
8. The phrase was coined by R. Neuhaus, *The Naked Public Square: Religion and Democracy in America* (Grand Rapids, Mich., 1984).
9. M. Weber, *Ancient Judaism* (New York, 1967); Berger, *Social Reality of Religion*.
10. This section follows but simplifies the patterns described in D. Martin, *A General Theory of Secularization* (Oxford, 1978).
11. Ibid. 30.
12. W. Herberg, *Protestant-Catholic-Jew* (New York, 1959); B. R. Wilson, *Religion in Secular Society*; Martin, *General Theory*.
13. Data are presented in R. Wallis and S. Bruce, 'Secularization: Trends, Data and Theory', *Research in the Social Scientific Study of Religion* 3 (1991), 1–31.
14. J. Goudsblom, *Dutch Society* (New York, 1967). It is interesting to note that as religious adherence has declined so the Protestant and Catholic pillars have become more integrated. In the early 1980s Catholic and Calvinist political parties and trade union organizations united to form single 'Christian Democratic' institutions; see T. R. Rochon, 'The Creation of Political Institutions: Two Cases From the Netherlands', *International Journal of Comparative Sociology* 25 (1984), 173–88.
15. On Poland, see M. Pomian-Srzednicki, *Religious Change in Contemporary Poland: Secularization and Politics* (London, 1982). On Ireland, see J. Fulton, *The Tragedy of Belief* (Oxford, 1990).
16. The church membership proportions of the adult population of the parts of the United Kingdom in 1980 were as follows:

England—13%, Wales—23%, Scotland—37% and Northern Ireland—80%; see P. W. Brierley, *UK Christian Handbook
(1985/86 Edition)* (London, 1984).

17. For an analysis of the importance of evangelical Protestantism
for the ethnic identity of Ulster Protestants, see S. Bruce, *God
Save Ulster! The Religion and Politics of Paisleyism* (Oxford, 1986).

18. Herberg, *Protestant-Catholic-Jew*.

19. R. Ballard and C. Ballard, 'The Sikhs: The Development of
Southern Asian Settlements in Britain', 21–56 in J. L. Watson
(ed.), *Between Two Cultures* (Oxford, 1977); on West Indian
immigrants, see K. Pryce, *Endless Pressure* (Harmondsworth,
1979).

20. C. G. Brown, 'Did Urbanization Secularize Britain?', *Urban
History Yearbook* (1988), 1–14 and his essay in Ch. 3 of this vol.

21. See J. D. Hunter, *Evangelicalism: The Coming Generation* (Chicago,
1989) and S. Bruce, *A House Divided: Protestantism, Schism and
Secularization* (London, 1987), Ch. 8.

22. L. Schneider and S. M. Dornbusch, 'Inspirational Religious
Literature: From Latent to Manifest Functions', *American Journal
of Sociology* 62 (1957), 476–81.

23. G. Gallup Jr. and D. Poling, *The Search for America's Faith*
(Nashville, 1980). It is important to note that we do not see
ourselves here entering an argument about what is 'real' religion
but merely commenting on objectively available data. We
should be able to agree on what counts as the 'supernatural' and
assess the relative presence and importance of beliefs about it.
That such identification and evaluation is difficult does not
mean that it is impossible.

24. Bruce, *A House Divided*, 200.

25. This case is argued at length in Bruce, *A Home Divided* and in S.
Bruce, 'Modernity and Fundamentalism: The New Christian
Right in America', *British Journal of Sociology* 41 (1990), 477–96.

26. R. Towler, *Homo Religiosus: Sociological Problems in the Study of
Religion* (London, 1974), 148.

27. J. Wilson, *Religion in American Society* (Englewood Cliffs, NJ,
1978), 34.

28. Ibid. 35–8.

29. Our listing of such figures does not mean that we are insensible
to the possibility that they are largely an artefact of the research
process. All the usual cautions about the significance of survey
data need to be inserted *a fortiori* here.

30. D. Hay and A. Morrisey, 'Reports of Ecstatic, Paranormal and
Religious Experience in Great Britain and the United States: A

Comparison of Trends', *Journal for the Scientific Study of Religion* 17 (1978), 255–68.

31. S. Bruce, *The Rise and Fall of the New Christian Right: Conservative Protestant Politics in America 1978–1988* (Oxford, 1988) and *Pray TV: Televangelism in America* (London, 1990), Chs. 8 and 9.

32. K. Thompson, 'Religion: The British Contribution', *British Journal of Sociology* 41 (1990), 535.

33. D. Martin, 'Towards Eliminating the Concept of Secularization', in J. Gould (ed.), *Penguin Survey of the Social Sciences* (Harmondsworth, 1965); R. M. Goodridge, '"The Ages of Faith": Romance or Reality?', *Sociological Review* 23 (1975), 381–96.

34. P. W. Laslett, *The World We Have Lost* (London, 1971), 74.

35. E. LeR. Ladourie, *Montaillou: Cathars and Catholics in a French Village, 1294–1324* (Harmondsworth, 1980).

36. K. Thomas, *Religion and the Decline of Magic* (London, 1973).

37. Quoted in R. K. Merton, *The Sociology of Science: Theoretical and Empirical Investigations* (Chicago, 1973), 233.

38. P. Collinson, *The Religion of Protestants: The Church in English Society 1559–1625* (Oxford, 1982) and *Godly People: Essays on English Protestantism and Puritanism* (London, 1985).

39. R. Stark and W. S. Bainbridge, 'Towards a Theory of Religion: Religious Commitment', *Journal for the Scientific Study of Religion* 19 (1980), 121.

40. R. Stark, 'Must All Religions be Supernatural?', in B. R. Wilson (ed.), *The Social Impact of New Religious Movements* (New York, 1981), 162.

41. H. R. Niebuhr, *The Social Sources of Denominationalism* (New York, 1962).

42. R. Wallis and S. Bruce, *Sociological Theory, Religion, and Collective Action* (Belfast, 1986). Stark and Bainbridge present the most elaborate versions of their theory in *The Future of Religion: Secularization, Revival and Cult Formation* (Berkeley, Calif., 1985) and *The Theory of Religion* (New York, 1987).

43. P. W. Brierley, 'Religion', in A. H. Halsey (ed.), *British Social Trends Since 1900* (London, 1988), 518–60.

44. Ibid. 549.

45. R. Bibby, 'Religious Encasement in Canada', *Social Compass* 32 (1985), 287–303; R. Bibby and H. R. Weaver, 'Cult Consumption in Canada: A Further Critique of Stark and Bainbridge', *Sociological Analysis* 35 (1985), 189–200.

3

A Revisionist Approach to Religious Change

CALLUM G. BROWN

SOCIAL-SCIENTIFIC study of religion has been dominated by the theory of secularization—the assumption of the inevitability of the decline of religion in modern societies. The contention of this chapter is that secularization theory is deficient both as a workable hypothesis of historical change and as an explanation of the available evidence on the growth and decline of religion in the world's first two industrial-urban nations—Britain and the USA.

An alternative approach to religious change is proposed—an approach which is non-linear in its description of historical change, refutes inevitability but allows prophecy, and seeks a greater degree of consistency with the historical evidence. Initially, the chapter does not propose alternative theories of religious change, though a brief sample of how these might develop from historical analysis is given. Rather, it dwells on the shortcomings of secularization theory, deriving from these an approach which offers a flexibility to both change and continuity in the social experience of religion, and an adaptability to different historical and national contexts. In short, the alternative approach would permit the conception of religion undergoing both decline (secularization) and growth (religionization) in modern societies.

THE THEORETICAL CONTEXT

In their recent review of the British contribution to the sociology of religion, Wallis and Bruce observed that:

Whatever the differences in their approach to religion, Marx, Durkheim and Weber all foresaw a major decline in its role in the modern world. Religion's ability to provide a single, integrated and generally held conception of meaning had been fatally eroded by the emergence of a plurality of life experiences deriving from widely differing relationships to a rapidly changing social order, by the increasingly rationalistic organization of an industrialised, mass market economy, and by more universalistic conceptions of citizenship.

The British contribution, they noted, had been made largely within these assumptions, focusing on the extent of secularization in Britain, its consequences for religious institutions, and the extent of 'resistance' to it.[1]

These observations are unquestionably true. Not only the sociology of religion in Britain but the profession as a whole has rested its work on the same foundation. Even when religious growth has been examined, it has been placed within the context of secularization. Thus, Stark and Bainbridge wrote in 1985 that secularization 'is the primary dynamic of religious economies, a self-limiting process that engenders revival (sect formation) and innovation (cult formation).'[2] The most influential British contribution to the sociology of religion, Wilson's *Religion in Secular Society*, gave the profession both its short-hand definition of secularization (the declining social significance of religion) and the apparent statistical backing to the theory of religious decline in both England and the USA.[3] For all the qualifications and academic queasiness which the theory aroused, generations of students and researchers accepted the textbook descriptions of 'a firm, inexorable series of secularization processes'.[4] Even one of the principal critics, David Martin, did not attack the fundamental hypothesis, but initially tried (unwisely) to suggest that 1960s' British culture contained enough religious belief and practice as to be 'far from secular', and subsequently provided a complex 'General Theory' which explained international differentiation in the survival of religion.[5]

If we accept the Wallis and Bruce review as accurate, the sociology of religion appears little further forward than it was in the mid-1960s. Yet, because their essay dealt only with British sociology, it did not mention Cox's 1982 book, *The English Churches in a Secular Society: Lambeth 1870–1930*.

Though the title suggests similarity with many other books on the theme of religious decline, Cox in his first and last chapters mounts an assault on the very foundations of secularization theory. He attacks the irrationality of the *idea* of the theory—its presumption of inevitability and inexorability to religious decline which, in Cox's view, deprives it of any meaning as a theory of historical change. Of Martin's contribution, Cox writes: 'But Martin leaves us with a logical difficulty. His general theory only explains decline. Growth or revival is explained by "something else", usually "history" . . . The general theory serves as a substitute for serious scholarly inquiry.'[6] He concludes:

What I object to is the air of inevitability which results from wrapping all of these changes up unto a package called 'the process of secularization' and using that package as an explanation of social change in the modern world.[7]

In historiographical terms, any theory which seeks to explain the totality of overall religious change in modern society solely in terms of secularization (that is decline) is improperly imbalanced as an interpretation of history. It is historicist (in the Popperian sense) to an extent that sees every manifestation of empirical contradiction to the theory as aberrant, or as an historical survival, or as temporary.

Secularization theory has long infected the disciplines of Church history and religious (that is Church) sociology. For Church historians, it seemed to fit well with the crumbling of religious adherence in 1950s' and 1960s' Britain, and Victorian clergy provided the anecdotal backing for the supposed nineteenth-century origins of religious decay in urban and industrial society. To the early work of Wickham and Inglis was added in the 1960s and 1970s the more profoundly pro-secularization history-writing of Robert Currie and, especially, Alan Gilbert.[8] In order to fit secularization theory (which places great emphasis on the decline of religion in industrial cities), Gilbert had to explain away the evident church growth of the last century:

religion enjoyed continuing social prominence because, fortuitously, the conflicts, tensions, and political alignments precipitated during Britain's transition to urban society and liberal democracy coincided precisely with inherited religious confrontations between 'Church' and 'chapel'.

In this way, Gilbert was able to argue that 'religion's inherited social prominence and continuing involvement in mainstream politics masked the impact of secularization because it guaranteed, at least temporarily, the Churches' institutional significance'. Confronted by his own statistical evidence of increasing church adherence *per capita* during most of the nineteenth century, Gilbert stated that 'growth ceased to be progressive and became marginal',[9] thus echoing an argument of American sociologists and Bryan Wilson (to which I shall return) that secularization can occur despite church growth. Of this tendency of historians to accept unquestioningly secularization theory, Cox comments: 'It is difficult to overstate the extent to which the very best historians of Victorian religion are addicted to the language of inevitable and irreversible decline, decay and failure, and explain that historical change with references to an underlying "process" of secularization.'[10] The argument here, as it is that of Cox, is that any theory of historical change which presumes inevitability and unidirectionality is implausible at a conceptual level and deficient as a basis for empirical research.

It is worth observing that the attractiveness of secularization theory in the 1960s and 1970s was enhanced for sociologists by the growth of new religious movements in America and western Europe. The social dynamics of the time emphasized the decline of traditional religious adherence amongst the young of the western industrial nations, and the appearance amongst them of quixotic, sometimes imported religions and quasi-religions provided a spur to sociologists. As Robin Gill has observed, 'If sociologists have given considerable attention to sects and to new religious movements over the last twenty years, they have seldom studied churches or denominations with the same level of scholarship. Instead, they have tended to make sweeping generalizations about such phenomena as church decline.'[11] A preoccupation with the exotic rather than the ordinary overtook the sociology of religion, to the extent that some suggested that the new religious movements in the USA constituted an inevitable 'compensating' reversal of secularization. Even when that idea was effectively refuted, the arguments of sociologists continued to presume, not to question or prove, secularization.[12]

Returning to the conceptual shortcomings of secularization theory, there is one major problem which sociologists and historians have been sidestepping for decades—the American experience. It has been accepted by generations of sociologists of American religion that secularization has proceeded during this century despite rapid church growth during its first six or seven decades.[13] Even those like Robert Wuthnow, who provides a well-researched and deeply thoughtful analysis of changes in organized religion in the USA since 1945, overlook the fundamental significance of two events in that period: in the late 1950s the first downturn in the proportion of population attending church, and in the early 1970s the first downturn in church adherence *per capita*.[14] Because of the pervasive effect of secularization theory in neutralizing seminal research, such fundamental historical changes in the social experience of religion pass with virtually no remark in standard works on the history of American religion.

Robin Gill, the leading British religious sociologist to criticize secularization theory, has commented on the 'odd asymmetry' which has produced this line of thinking. Taking Wilson to task, he criticizes the illogicality of reasoning which has created a consensus that American churches have this century performed social rather than religious functions, and as such were part of 'the secularization process'. Gill notes that by 1974 Wilson was evading the full statistical evidence on church growth and decline in Britain and the USA because the downturn in church adherence in North America was by then making redundant the argument of church growth being part of secularization.[15]

The fact is that American sociologists of religion have been mishandling the statistics for generations, arguably failing to face up squarely to the social processes they delineate with great quantitative clarity. They produce regression equations relating church adherence and religious diversity scores in one-date 'snapshot' analyses to levels of literacy, ethnic composition, and a myriad of other data, but do not consider the time-series figures for *per capita* church adherence. The latter clearly show church growth until around 1970. This does not fit with secularization theory. The first reaction has been to denigrate the accuracy of the figures; Glock and Stark in 1965 actually cited all the relevant data stretching from 1850 to 1962, but spent nine pages questioning their accuracy, and then concluded:

This exploration into the long-term evidence on the religiousness of Americans does not lead us to any firm conclusions even within the limited perspectives of the observations discussed. Perhaps the confusion may be dissipated as we now go on to examine the alternative proposition that the long-term trend in America has been toward the increasing secularization of religion.[16]

The 'confusion' was in their minds; the quantitative evidence they studied was unequivocal on the issue of the growing social significance of religion in church membership.

Glock and Stark's second response is the one so ably put forward by Wilson in *Religion in Secular Society*—namely that the statistics of American religion conceal the true, downward course of the social significance of religion. Because religion is (or perhaps was until comparatively recently) the cement in American community life, is the agent of much political discourse and public and political ceremony (the National Prayer Breakfast, St Patrick's Day parades, and Thanksgiving), and is an important element in the ethnic structure of American society, its 'true' significance in the conventional terms of European and less-developed societies is much diminished. Wilson feels able to comment that 'though religious practice has increased, the vacuousness of popular religious ideals has also increased'.[17]

This line of argument produces what may be in practical terms an untestable and unfalsifiable hypothesis, impervious to whatever 'objective' evidence may seem to challenge it. True, statistics of religious adherence and practice are not and should not be the only measures of the social significance of religion, but they are vital evidence which cannot be discarded at the dictates of a hegemonic theory which tends to suppress critical enquiry. They are important indicators of key changes in social behaviour—there are probably none better to be had in the realms of religion. They must be taken seriously.

To the empirical weakness of the theory of secularization must be added doubts about the value of the sub-themes of social differentiation, societalization, and rationalization (see Wallis and Bruce in Chapter 2). These concepts start from the proposition (1) that the disintegration of 'a single moral universe', supposedly evident in pre-industrial society, undermined the social significance of religion. This became evident in (2) the drift from a 'community'-based organization to a 'society'-based one in which 'religion has been shorn of its functions'. At the same time, there was (3) the increasing rationalization of people's thinking: 'technically efficient machinery and procedures reduced uncertainty and thereby reliance upon faith'. In those many countries and regions where the social significance of religion evidently survived these changes during industrialization, 'religion finds or retains other work to do than relating individuals to the supernatural': that is the 'cultural defence' of national, ethnic, or status groups which are under threat from alien cultures or religions, and the 'cultural transition' of peoples migrating to alien places where the maintenance of religious attachments may have eased assimilation or offset its more profound initial impact.

The problem here is with the proposition that the social significance of religion has as its sourcespring 'a single moral universe'. A plurality of conceptions of world-view does not undermine the power of religion to provide unifying succour within that very plurality, inculcating moral and social values that retain allegiance across denominational divides and across the divide between the secular and the profane. It is the very power of religion to generate powerful social concepts despite, rather than because of, a diversity of churches that has fomented so much interest amongst social historians of industrial society in recent years. The study of the concept of 'respectability', for instance, has produced a sophisticated literature of British social mores in the nineteenth and early twentieth centuries when, during the very period of maturation of the industrial economy, the immense religious diversity of the nation was counterpointed by the unanimity of a religious-based social morality nurtured within the Sunday schools and churches of competing denominations.[18] Equally, sociologists have themselves studied in great detail the power of religion to unite American society in social mores and national consciousness despite an even greater diversity of competing denominations. The sociology of religion is not acknowledging the issue of what it purports to analyse if it does not see the power of pluralistic religion to unify in very important ways.

We may also doubt that 'religion . . . has its source in, and draws strength from the community' rather than from 'society'. The evidence for the reverse proposition may be just as strong. Religion can and has retained its social significance across the change from pre-industrial to industrial society. But leaving the evidence aside, why should religion be stronger in a 'community' than in a 'society'? The power of religion in some of the most advanced economies of the world, and in the (different) most rapidly advancing countries, is manifestly apparent in the late twentieth century. More fundamentally, doubts can be expressed concerning the rigidity implied in the dichotomy between 'community' and 'society'.

Underlying this, often unsaid, is the notion that the monopoly or near-monopoly of denominational provision in pre-industrial society (usually by an established Church) meant a greater degree of religious adherence and practice than was evident in later religiously pluralistic societies. The twin notions of pre-industrial piety and industrial secularity, expressed in extreme form in Peter Laslett's dictum that 'All our ancestors were literal Christian believers, all of the time',[19] has a pervasive effect upon both social history and sociology. There is no room here to tackle pre-industrial religion in detail. What can be said is that the patchy evidence shows little of the universality of religious practice long assumed by so many historians and sociologists. In many parts of Britain, the paucity of churches and problems of transport made high levels of church attendance impracticable, and levels of church accommodation (pew seats *per capita*) in industrial cities were comparable with provisions in pre-industrial town or country parishes. In any event, as Spufford so ably argues, when comparing religion in pre-industrial and industrial society we are not comparing like with like.[20] In the former religion was an agency of central and local government, the Church by law established to uphold good order and prompt payment of taxes. Church membership was an alien concept, and church-going was only periodically enforced during times of political and constitutional strife. In industrial society, religion became pluralistic and legally optional for the people. It remained an agency of the State, but in new, usually more subtle ways. It was as a diffusive rather than an enforced religion that Christianity in Britain and the USA became so important to social mores, law-making and organized leisure in the nineteenth and early twentieth centuries.

Wallis and Bruce's exempting factors in secularization, which may be summarized collectively as 'ethnic defence', are in fact those functions which religion has found in industrial society (as, to a lesser extent, in pre-industrial society) to result from migration. But although they mention them, they do not give sufficient weight to other factors which make religion relevant in industrial society: notably religion as group identity for social or occupational strata (what might be called 'class defence'), and the interconnected social-mobility function of religion (where the socially aspiring can affirm the religious basis for shedding their social—and also ethnic—roots in favour of upward mobility). It is when we fail to fully acknowledge that religion can acquire new ways in which to find social significance that the plausibility of secularization is undermined as a theory of explanation in industrial society.

To restate in different terms a point made by Cox, religion is not a human failing that was born in ignorance and that is dying in knowledge. There was no 'ideal state' in which religion grasped the total world-view of the people, and which has been dissipating for the history of humankind. Religion adapts to different social and economic contexts. It is not static, unchanging and unyielding to different situations. Such changes that churches undergo do not necessarily mean secularization. A change from pre-industrial to industrial society can mean the loss of some forms in which religion had previously had social significance (such as state monopoly), but it can acquire new ways—such as vigorous Dissent and chapel-building, which actually mean at the end of the day increased church provision *per capita* and higher levels of church-going, and new agencies of a diffusive Christianity such as Sunday schools, missions to the working classes, and organized revivalism which can create new forms of church connection. The conditions which promoted such adaptation can rightly be seen by the historian as a threat of secularization, but its successful overcoming should also be acknowledged—in the first instance as a theoretical possibility. It is in this context that secularization theory is deficient as a workable account of historical change.

SOME STATISTICAL EVIDENCE

To a great extent, secularization theory has survived for so long because the quality and quantity of empirical research into the history of religious growth and decay has been rather poor. Case studies and overviews abound in the social history of religion, but few if any have seriously sought to *test* the theory of secularization. Traditionally, evidence has been gathered to *demonstrate* the workings of secularization, not to confirm or falsify it.

The simplest way to begin testing secularization theory is to examine the available statistics of religious adherence and practice. Some defenders of secularization theory may argue that such quantitative sources may provide evidence of church growth and decay, but that this does not equate directly with secularization or its reverse. In addition, American advocates of secularization theory will suggest—as they have for decades—that church growth can occur during secularization. As I have already argued, this position is unreasonable as a general proposition. Religious adherence and practice are the most obvious outward measures of the social significance of religion, after which such other measures as the institutional role of religion in the state, the ideological role of religion in politics and popular culture, and so on must come. For, in general terms, the wider social significance of religion can only rest upon *some* basis of popular acceptance, enthusiasm, or acquiescence in religion, as demonstrated by some significant degree of religious adherence and practice.

In this context, it is not only legitimate but necessary to assess whether secularization has occurred at all in industrial societies, and if so when it occurred, by looking first at the long-term trends of religious adherence and practice. This should form the base from which any examination of religionization and secularization proceeds.

The availability, reliability, and comparability of statistics of church adherence and practice are notoriously fraught. But this should not stop us from attempting to make serious use of them. For most countries, usable historical statistics of religious adherence and/or practice exist. It is one of the most remarkable gaps in the social-scientific study of religion that long-term time-series statistics have not—to the best of my knowledge—been compiled and used for sustained analysis. In American sociology of religion generally, there seems to be a long-established habit of using 'snapshot' statistics only.[21] In at least one case, an investigator has used two 'snapshot' points only sixteen years apart to provide pairs of regression equations in an attempt to seek relationships between religious adherence and religious diversity on the one hand, and literacy, ethnic composition, industrial structure, etc. on the other; it would have been simpler, more logical, and (given the failure of the enterprise to show any meaningful relationships) more likely to be successful if time-series data had been used over a longer period.[22]

Clearly, 'snapshot' data are important in a field of enquiry into historical change where statistics can be discontinuous and problematic. In many cases, there may only be complete or near-complete data from one or two years during a nation's industrial history, and such data sets can provide useful analysis of the effect of urbanization on church-going.[23] But data which may demonstrate causal relationships over the long-term are infinitely more desirable.

Compiling long-run time-series can only really be undertaken from the middle of the nineteenth century. The type of statistics we need are religious adherence and/or church attendance *per capita*. To undertake this in religiously diverse societies like Britain and the USA, we require to have membership or attendance data from as many different denominations as possible. This only becomes a reasonable proposition in the case of Britain after about 1840–60, and after about 1880 in the United States. With this kind of data, secularization theory's case that the social significance of religion was adversely affected by urbanization and industrialization becomes statistically testable. Figures 3.1 to 3.3 show church adherence *per capita* and the extent of urbanization in Scotland during 1840–1986, England and Wales during 1840–1964, and in the USA during 1890–1984. Considering church adherence alone for the moment, it should be noted that the US graph was compiled from episodic data (from twelve points) taken directly from the Bureau of the Census compilation (a compilation used by, *inter alia*, Glock and Stark up to the mid-1960s). By contrast, Figures 3.1 and 3.2 show church adherence figures for *every year* between the boundary dates, compiled by arduous manipulation of extant data which requires some explanation.

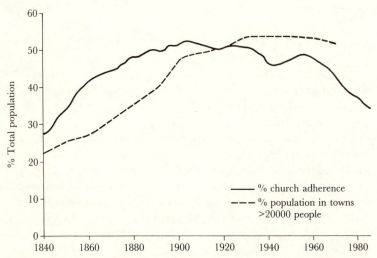

Sources: R. Currie, A. Gilbert, and L. Horsley, *Churches and Churchgoers*, 128, 132–4, 137 (n.7, n.8), 141–4, 149–50, 153, 154 (n.3), 169, 172–3; British Parliamentary Papers, *Religious Worship and Education, Scotland, Report and Tables* (London, 1854); P. Flora *et al.*, *State, Economy and Society in Western Europe 1815–1975*, ii (Frankfurt, 1987), 280.

FIG. 3.1. *Church adherence and urbanization: Scotland 1840–1986*

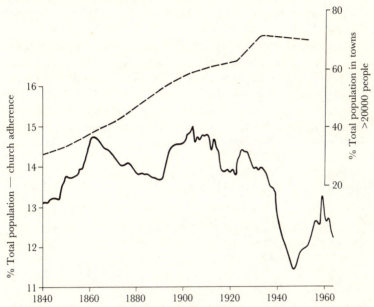

Sources: R. Currie, A. Gilbert, and L. Horsley, *Churches and Churchgoers*, 128–9, 139–44, 145 (n.4, n.5), 147–51, 153; P. Flora *et al.*, *State*, 279.

FIG. 3.2. *Church adherence and urbanization: England and Wales 1840–1963*

In both of the British graphs, the principal source of information was the compilation of church statistics by Robert Currie, Alan Gilbert, and Lee Horsley.[24] In the Scottish graph, the data include church membership/adherence for all Presbyterian churches, the Baptist, Catholic, Congregationalist, Scottish Episcopal, and Methodist churches, and Presbyterian Sunday-school enrolment. Most of the figures were based on actual church-collected figures for 1870–1986, but for 1840–69 they were derived from sporadic figures and estimates which have been denominationally weighted by me at 1851 according to denominational alignments as revealed by aggregate attendances at the religious census of that year. Estimates of Catholic population (in both this and Figure 3.2) have been divided by a factor of 1.75 to produce a series of notional mass attenders, and the figure 120,000 was substituted for the rather high estimate of 190,000 Catholics for Scotland in 1841. Communicant data of the United Presbyterian, United Free, and antecedent churches for the period 1840–1914 were multiplied by a factor of 1.39 to create a series compatible with Church of Scotland communicants' rolls and Free Church members/adherents. All gaps in annual data for each denomination were then filled by linear extrapolation, the figures totalled for each year, and expressed as a percentage of total population for each year (with annual population figures similarly calculated by linear extrapolation from the decennial censuses).

Figure 3.2 covering England and Wales incorporates church membership/adherence/Easter communicant figures only (excluding Sunday-school enrolments) for the Church of England, the Church in Wales, all Methodist churches, and the Baptist, Catholic, Congregationalist, and Presbyterian churches (including the Presbyterian Church of Wales). Apart from Catholic data (see above paragraph), no attempt has been made at denominational weighting to take into account the differences in measures (notably the underscoring by Church of England communicant data). Figures have been calculated for every church at every date for 1900–64, but for 1840–99 three new sets of data enter: Church of England (including Wales) in 1885, Baptists in 1891, and Congregationalists in 1900.

It is important to be clear about the value of the data that result. Although the church adherence data used to compile Figure 3.1 have been employed in publishing elsewhere two graphs which provide rough estimates of percentage church adherence *per capita*, the church adherence graphlines in Figures 3.1 and 3.2 cannot be used to estimate the level of religious adherence at any one point.[25] Their value lies solely in providing an illustration of *trends* in religious adherence— as a set of figures whose *changes* are of significance, and which can be compared with each other (and possibly for regression against other time-series data in tests for causal relationships). This value is greatest with the Scottish data because of its inclusion of estimates for every church over the whole period, and because of the weighting of data to provide a fair indication of relative denominational strengths.

The English and Welsh graph is satisfactory for its denominational coverage after 1900, but becomes progressively less satisfactory as it moves backwards—especially before 1885 when there are no Anglican data. In general terms, the data for England and Wales for 1840–84 are Dissenting data only, and for this reason probably overstate the decline in adherence during 1862–84. (Indeed, it may be conjectured that the decline in Dissenting adherence *per capita* during these years was balanced by a growth in Anglican adherence *per capita*, though it is perplexing that once Anglican data do commence in 1885, there is a five-year period of modest decline in aggregate adherence *per capita*.)

Clearly, the statistical problems with these graphs restrict their use. None the less, it is argued that the construction of them is valid, and that it is legitimate to make proper, restricted, and qualified use of them. So, what do they show? Let us examine the Scottish and English and Welsh graphs first. They display a similar general shape—of overall upward trend followed by overall downward trend. The peak index figures for adherence *per capita* are 1905 for Scotland and 1904 for England and Wales. In the post–1900 period (when the graphs are most reliable), a downward trend accelerates with the outbreak of the First World War, followed by a growth to an inter-war peak in 1924 in Scotland and 1925 in England and Wales, followed by a steady decline which again accelerates with the effects of world war in 1940. This is then followed by a rise from the middle of the war to post-war peaks of 1956 in Scotland and 1959 in England and Wales, after which steep and thus far unremitting decline sets in. This similarity in trend in the two British graphs after 1900 is very suggestive of a common twentieth-century experience in the social significance of church adherence.

Turning to the 1840–1900 period, the church adherence graphlines in Figures 3.1 and 3.2 show significant net increases in church adherence *per capita*. However, there is the problem of apparently contradictory trends in 1863–91. In England the trend was downward during 1863–74, 1878–81 and 1883–90, whilst in Scotland it was generally upward during these years. It seems clear, as has already been stated, that the absence of Anglican data sharpens the downward gradient of the England and Welsh data, and indeed may well reverse the trend entirely. In this regard, it is interesting in the Scottish data that the periods 1864–75 and 1880–3 show significant decelerations in growth (and, in the latter of these, actual decline), perhaps mirroring the situation south of the border. Overall, the Scottish data suggest that the annual growth rate lessened after 1863, starting to fluctuate in the 1880s and 1890s between growth and decline as it neared the peak in 1905.

A fair conclusion here may be that if there were usable Anglican data to include pre–1885, the two graphs would show strikingly similar trends in annual fluctuations and in long-term change over the entire piece 1840 to 1964.

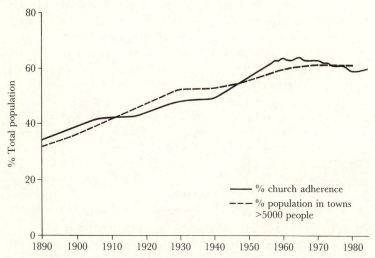

Sources: Bureau of the Census, *Historical Statistics of the United States, Bicentennial Edition, Part I* (Washington, DC, 1970), 9, 391–2; Bureau of the Census, *Statistical Abstract of the United States*, 1972–88.

Fig. 3.3. *Church adherence and urbanization: USA 1890–1985.*

Turning now to Figure 3.3 on the USA, what is immediately striking is the sharp and, with the exception of the period from the mid-1900s to the late 1910s, sustained rise in church membership *per capita* right through until the peak in 1970, after which decline set in. This presents a clear difference from the British experience, when the peak was some sixty-five years earlier.

A number of preliminary conclusions are in order here. Religious adherence grew significantly in mainland Britain over the course of the last sixty years of the nineteenth century, and only peaked in 1904–5. This reinforces a large body of research conducted since the 1960s which has pinpointed the period 1890–1914 as a turning-point for the social significance of religion in British urban life.[26] However, the data show that the level and continuity of decline in religious adherence thereafter has been considerably overstated. The net level of decline only became appreciable after the 1950s, and was preceded by great fluctuation (the downward shifts being most accentuated by the world wars).[27] Church-membership decline, as the Scottish graph shows, really only became very steep after 1963.

By contrast, the graphline of US church membership in Figure 3.3 demonstrates what has long been known, though perhaps what has been little appreciated—the tremendous growth in church connection *per capita* from the late nineteenth century down to 1970. Despite some decline, the level of church membership in the 1980s remained higher than at *any time* before the 1950s. Taken in absolute terms, church membership has been around or over 60 per cent of total population since the mid-1960s. By contrast, the absolute figures for Scottish church adherence (the most reliable from mainland Britain) show that at the all-time peak in 1904 around 50 per cent of population were church members or Sunday-school enrollees, and that in 1956 (the post-1905 peak) the figure was around 47 per cent.

Despite these interesting points, the central objective of this chapter is to place these data alongside the theory of secularization. In respect of the notion that urbanization and industrialization instigate the decline of religion, these data seriously erode it and, arguably, negate it. It is not merely a case (as Bryan Wilson thought in 1966) of explaining away the rise of US religious adherence during the advance of urban and industrial society. Figures 3.1 and 3.2 show that the USA is not an aberration but the norm; all three graphs show that church membership *per capita* grew in the world's first pair of industrialized nations.

The position in the world's third industrial nation, Germany, still leaves room for parallel statistical consideration. Both McLeod and Hölscher, who have studied nineteenth- and twentieth-century German religion generally, and the position in Berlin and Hanover respectively in detail, conclude that the social (and political) significance of religion declined during the era of industrial city growth.[28] However, statistical evidence gathered by Hölscher suggests that in Hanover the evening communion rate for the *Landeskirche* (Lutheran Church), by far the largest denomination in the city, fell until the 1880s and then stayed roughly static during the period of rapid urban growth that ensued. Moreover, statistics Hölscher has compiled for states in the Federal Republic of Germany show a steep rise in the evening communion rate in the period since the Second World War. Given the later start to German urbanization in the late nineteenth and early twentieth centuries, and given the profound transformation wrought on the Federal Republic by the post-war 'economic miracle', detailed statistical analysis of the pace and timing of urban development may yet allow a case to be made for German inclusion in the Britain–USA model posited above.

Figures 3.1 to 3.3 suggest something further: that historians and sociologists should give consideration to the argument that urbanization and industrialization can *cause* church growth. They may not be the only causes, and they may not cause church growth evenly or universally but the evidence from the USA and Britain makes it worth contemplating this possibility.

This case can be put into sharper relief by examining the graphlines on the percentage of population living in urban areas also given in Figures 3.1 to 3.3. (Though the measures differ, their directions of change and gradients constitute reasonable data for the present purpose.) An assessment of the three urbanization graphlines shows a striking similarity between Scotland and England and Wales, with sustained rises down to 1890–1910 when high plateaux of urbanization were attained and then sustained for the remainder of the period down to the 1980s. The graph for the USA, by contrast, indicates that the rise has been sustained until the 1980s, though with similar evidence of slowing down, probably prior to attaining a similar peak to that of Britain.

Comparing the urbanization rate with the church adherence rate in each country reveals an interesting correlation. Throughout most periods of church growth, urbanization was proceeding rapidly. However, church growth slowed down, stagnated and declined when urbanization was slowing down and stagnating. The quantitative evidence—however problematic it may be—sustains a strong case for the disintegration of secularization theory in urbanizing societies.

A REVISIONIST INTERPRETATION OF THE STATISTICS

Evidence in this chapter hints at an interaction between long-term industrial urbanization (with all the social and economic developments that entails) on the one hand and the growth of religious adherence on the other. This does not preclude short-term reversals for the social significance of religion. Indeed, I have suggested elsewhere that in Scotland and England the onset of the early Industrial Revolution in *c.*1750–*c.*1840 instigated a decline in church adherence resulting from inadequate ecclesiastical response to the changing location (rural to urban) and size of population; in other words, churchbuilding failed to keep pace with the growth of urban and industrial districts.[29] By contrast, the evidence from the USA suggests that churchbuilding must have been considerably stronger there during the parallel period of early industrial urbanization stretching into the 1910s. (The reason for this divergence was probably the peculiar legal and political constraints on the established Churches of England and Scotland in relation to church planting, and the absence of those constraints in the USA.) In any event, the relative shortage of church accommodation in Britain was probably reversed after *c.*1840—it certainly was in Scotland, especially in towns and cities—by the explosion of church construction by Dissenting denominations during the Victorian period. With this came rising church recruitment *per capita* during the rapid urbanization after the mid-nineteenth century. In the USA, church growth relative to population attained a very significant level after the 1880s.

The period when church growth ceases and decline commences is very important. That the dates of peak adherence in Scotland (1905) and England and Wales (1904) differ strikingly from that in the USA (1970) should focus attention on the different time frames of social and economic development. It was in 1851 that the decennial census first recorded that more than half of the British population lived in cities; the roughly equivalent date for the USA was 1920. The proportion of the population living in cities in Britain stabilized in 1911, whilst in the USA stabilization has yet to be attained. In other words, the urbanization of American society has been following about seventy to ninety years behind that of Britain. In a similar way, the data in this chapter show that the periodization of major church growth and decay in the USA follows about sixty-five years behind that of Britain. Moreover, stagnation and decay in church growth commenced in both nations at about the time when urbanization started to stagnate. This is not, of course, the whole story, but the correlation appears striking.

How might a 'religionization theory' explain such evidence of the growing social significance of religion, and how would a revised, scaled-down secularization theory then explain when decay did occur? One fruitful way to approach these related questions is through the experience of migrants to cities. The vast bulk of urban population growth during rapid city expansion has resulted from migration and not from natural increase. Preceding rural–urban migration, the ties between people and organized religion were often fraught. For some, the very cause of migration from their place of origin was to escape persecution and suppression of their churches. For such people, an increase in popular religiosity is perhaps an understandable and non-contentious product of migration.

But of more general importance to the religiosity of the majority of migrants to cities (especially those from the same country) was the emergence of class society and the role of Dissenting churches. To a great extent the emergence of

Dissent pre-dated migrants' arrival in urban centres. Fuelled in both Britain and North America by Protestant fervour, evangelical religion was growing in rural and semi-rural places of origin because it was there, not in large cities, that the bulk of eighteenth- and nineteenth-century people experienced the birth of an industrial class society. Early industrialization was characteristically located in rural areas, introduced on the one hand by the spread of textile out-working (especially weaving) and mills (especially spinning), extractive and metallurgical industries, and on the other hand (in Britain at least) by the erosion of the traditional paternalistic agrarian society and economy. As landownership became increasingly concentrated, and as subsistence and small-scale farming were marginalized by the growth of capitalistic farming based on waged labour, the economic fabric of pre-industrial society started to erode older forms of social relations. It was in this context that the power of the parish church was undermined as social and spatial mobility based on an industrializing society produced Dissenting churches (Methodism, Nonconformity, and Presbyterian churches) with which both the alienated and the aspiring identified. In the USA, a similar general trend may be identified in the evangelical, millenarian, and sect-forming developments stretching from the 'Great Awakening' of the eighteenth century through to the birth of 'new religions' in the nineteenth and twentieth centuries.

Despite the appearance of a sustained revivalist religious atmosphere in the emerging societies of the world's first two industrial nations, levels of church adherence and participation seem to have been adversely affected during the early stages.[30] It has been suggested already that the cause in Britain may be the difficulty in providing churches in new, populous urban areas. At the same time, there was a period of adjustment for religion to the new urban context of a class society, with a development period for new religious agencies—notably voluntary organizations such as Sunday schools, Bible classes, home missions and so on; arguably, there was a lengthy (perhaps 50–60 year) adjustment period for religion in the new social context. In addition, there may have been a tendency during rapid urban growth for existing congregations to fail to recruit, or to fail to retain, new migrant worshippers because of unrealistic occupational, financial, and social qualifications for church membership. More generally, the rapid process of social differentiation that was taking place may have led to a deliberate policy on the part of many congregations to be selective in whom they admitted to membership. Each of these factors may also have been evident in the USA, though we should note in addition that the strong ethnicity of American congregations, and the periodization of immigration waves of individual ethnic-religious groups, may have resulted in delays during which first-generation immigrants had to establish their churches and religious networks before being able to make significant inroads into their 'constituencies'.

Taken collectively, these and other factors may have induced a temporary period when the religiosity of the people, as measured by church adherence *per capita*, was in decline. However, sufficient evidence exists to suggest no absence of religious fervour and enthusiasm—especially in those industrializing districts.

More broadly, the position of the rural–urban migrant cannot present a full story. The social significance of religion in rising urban centres was also heightened by what might be described as the institutional and ideological roles of religion. At a simple level, urbanizing nations like Britain and the USA were characterized by the overt secularization of civil institutions: central government agencies, and, perhaps more importantly, local government agencies like education, poor relief, and the judiciary. 'Secular' issues of urban management, slum clearance, sanitary reform, and crime were increasingly put to the top of the urban agenda. Yet, the rise of civil agencies (especially *ad hoc* authorities to control these functions) was in Britain very much a product of the victory of Dissent. In short, the 'secularization' of social policy in the mid- and late-nineteenth century resulted from a rising religious fervour for democratic ecclesiastical influence in public policy—and not from religious decline. Indeed, as urban élites increasingly identified social problems, moral and religious agencies were heavily deployed in tackling them. Prostitution, drink, and gambling were confronted not only by such voluntary agencies as church missions, temperance societies, and so on but also by central and local government exerting 'moral force' upon the population—nowhere more apparent than in the prohibition movement in both the USA and Britain between the 1850s and the 1930s. But it must be emphasized that the temperance issue was only one element in a much broader and more profound religious grasp upon the philosophy and agencies of social redemption in urban society, perhaps best encapsulated in the varying concepts of 'respectability' which dominated the social mores of both proletarian and bourgeois.

In these ways, the social significance of religion acquired new forms of influence in the democratic institutions of the religiously-pluralistic societies on both sides of the Atlantic. Initial industrial urbanization certainly threatened secularization, but the danger was largely of a logistical nature—the transfer of ecclesiastical resources to growing population centres—rather than a crisis of popular faith. As new sects and denominations became established and acquired financial and membership stability, recruitment of new arrivals and of the 'unchurched' became very successful in the later stages of urbanization. Religious precepts—especially emanating from the large evangelical movement—became central to social policy responses in urban areas, generating considerable cross-fertilization between religious philanthropy and municipal enterprise.

What, then, induced the commencement of secularization when urbanization stagnated—in Britain in the years before 1914 and in the USA in the years from the late 1960s onwards? In the first instance, it should be emphasized that the process of decline was less sudden in Britain at the turn of the century than is conventionally acknowledged, and that it only became steep after 1960. In the USA, it may be too early to tell the present gradient of the decline in church membership *per capita*, but the British experience might suggest that steep decline will occur perhaps two or three decades after the 1970 peak.

Having said that, the watersheds of 1904–5 in Britain and 1970 in the USA are important. Amongst the causes, we might point to the disappearing role of the in-migrant— diminishing the 'new blood' to sustain church recruitment, links with rural 'piety' (even if mythical), and congregational vitality (especially in ethnic-based churches). Secondly, these peak years fall in the midst of periods—from Hyndman to Ramsay MacDonald in Britain (1880s–1930), and from the New Deal to Nixon's 'end of the urban crisis' in the USA (1932–1970)—which witnessed the rise of truly secular urban policy devoid of moral solutions to urban problems: comprehensive urban redevelopment, housing projects, and welfarism. (Interestingly, religious 'backlashes' to the perception of these 'secular' trends were evident in Scotland in the 1910s and early 1920s in the strong temperance lobby of the period, and in the USA in the late 1970s and 1980s in the form of the Moral Majority and allied movements.) Thirdly, the 1900s in Britain and the 1960s in the USA witnessed congregational disruption as suburbanization pushed the middle classes out, leaving emptying inner-city churches in financial insolvency and devoid of strong lay (and possibly clerical) leadership. This left a legacy of struggle for proletarian religion, and (perhaps more contentiously) a slow process of goal displacement for bourgeois religion as its perceived power to reform society dissipated.

After the initiation of church decline in Britain in the 1900s, it is less easy to account for the emergence of sharp secularization there in the 1960s. An easy approach is to point to the rise of the transatlantic youth culture—the hippie era, the liberalization of sexual mores, and the drugs revolution—which undermined conventional church adherence. However, this leaves a problem. For all that this culture emerged more strongly in the USA than in Britain, the level of church adherence in the former did not suffer the same degree of catastrophic fall as befell the latter. Though the direction of change is the same in both nations at the present (that is a secularizing trend), church decline in the one may not equate directly with the contemporaneous church decline in the other.

Indeed, the implication of these observations on religionization and secularization is that the pace of change, and the place within the overall social development of a country in which that decline occurs, are very significant to analysing causes. Replacing existing secularization theory cannot involve generating simple, monocausal theories of religious change. The primary task here has been to point to a correlation between urbanization and increasing social significance of religion—a phenomenon not limited to Britain and the USA in the nineteenth century, but one arguably evident today within the Islamic world, urbanizing Latin America and the Pacific Rim. Only as a secondary task have suggestions been made as to how to analyse the data with a view to developing theories of religionization and secularization. The emphasis here has been upon pinpointing the timeframes of urban and industrial development, and of avoiding the pitfalls of comparing—as Wilson did in the 1960s—the contemporaneous developments in Britain and the USA when those two nations were at very different stages in their economic, social, and religious evolution.

CONCLUSION

The argument here has been that existing secularization theory is logically deficient as a theory of historical change, and is insufficiently 'bedded down' in the empirical evidence of growth and decline in the social significance of religion in the world's first pair of industrial nations.

The observations made in the chapter do not in themselves constitute a substitute to that theory. Clearly, they seek to point the way towards the development of theories of religious change, and towards essentially *historical* as distinct from *sociological* ways of articulating them. As a starting point, I offer the following basic principles which might be regarded as vital to them. The social significance of religion (1) can rise and fall in any social and economic context—pre-industrial, industrial, post-industrial; (2) does not decay automatically or irreversibly with the growth of human knowledge, rationality or technology; (3) does not decay automatically or irreversibly with industrialization or urbanization; (4) is not to be measured by unity of religious belief or uniformity of religious adherence in a given nation/region; (5) can be challenged by fundamental social and economic change, and can suffer short to medium-term decay, but can adapt to the new context and can show significant long-term growth; (6) can change the ways, or the balance of the ways, in which it arises from one social and economic context to another. Whilst state monopoly of religion can create powerful significance for pre-industrial religion as tax-collector, community centre, law-giver and enforcer, welfare distributor, and so on, the loss of such significance can be compensated during industrialization by the appearance of new, or enhancement of other, forms of significance. This includes the interaction between on the one hand, increasing diversity (or Dissent) with the rise of religious revival and enthusiasm, class consciousness and class conflict, and on the other, new (evangelical) 'agencies' of religion (like Sunday schools, mission stations, the temperance movement, and so on). In short, the social significance of religion can be sustained or even increased during the transition from pre-industrial to industrial society by adaptation to a pluralist environment.

NOTES

1. R. Wallis and S. Bruce, 'Religion: The British Contribution', *British Journal of Sociology*, 40 (1989), 493.
2. Stark and Bainbridge, *Future of Religion*, 429–30.
3. B. R. Wilson, *Religion in Secular Society*.
4. R. Robertson, *The Sociological Interpretation of Religion* (Oxford, 1970), 240.
5. D. Martin, *A Sociology of English Religion* (London, 1967), esp. 76; Martin, *General Theory*.
6. J. Cox, *The English Churches in a Secular Society: Lambeth 1870–1930* (Oxford, 1982), 15–16.
7. Ibid. 266.
8. E. R. Wickham, *Church and People in an Industrial City* (London, 1957); K. S. Inglis, *Churches and the Working Classes in Victorian England* (London, 1963); R. Currie, A. D. Gilbert, and L. Horsley, *Churches and Churchgoers: Patterns of Church Growth in the British Isles since 1700* (Oxford, 1977).
9. A. D. Gilbert, *The Making of Post-Christian Britain* (London, 1980), 74, 78–9.
10. Cox, *English Churches*, 265.
11. R. Gill, *Competing Convictions* (London, 1989), 55.

12. A review of this issue is to be found in R. Wallis, *The Elementary Forms of the New Religious Life* (London, 1984), 59–64.

13. See B. R. Wilson, *Religion in Secular Society*, 109–26, for a summary.

14. R. Wuthnow, *The Restructuring of American Religion: Society and Faith Since World War II* (Princeton, NJ, 1988).

15. Gill, *Competing Connections*, 56–60.

16. C. Y. Glock and R. Stark, *Religion and Society in Tension* (Chicago, 1965), 73–82.

17. B. R. Wilson, *Religion in Secular Society*, 122.

18. To sample the study of this important concept in very different approaches, see R. Q. Gray, *The Labour Aristocracy in Victorian Edinburgh* (London, 1976); H. McLeod, 'White Collar Values and the Role of Religion', in G. Crossick (ed.), *The Lower Middle Class in Britain 1870–1914* (London, 1977); M. Phayer, *Sexual Liberation and Religion in Nineteenth-Century Europe* (London, 1977), esp. Ch. 4; and E. Ross, 'Survival Networks: Women's Neighbourhood Sharing in London Before World War One', *History Workshop* 15 (1983).

19. Laslett, *World*, 71.

20. M. Spufford, 'Can We Count the "Godly" and the "Conformable" in the Seventeenth Century?', *Journal of Ecclesiastical History* 36 (1985); Callum G. Brown, *The Social History of Religion in Scotland Since 1730* (London, 1987), 101, 106–7; A. D. Gilbert, *Religion and Society in Industrial England: Church, Chapel and Social Change 1740–1914* (London, 1976), 98–103.

21. R. Finke and R. Stark, 'Religious Economies and Sacred Canopies: Religious Mobilization in American Cities, 1906', *American Sociological Review* 53 (1988), 41–9.

22. K. J. Christiano, *Religious Diversity and Social Change: American Cities, 1890–1906* (Cambridge, 1987).

23. C. G. Brown, 'Urbanization'.

24. Currie, *et al.*, *Churches and Churchgoers*.

25. C. G. Brown, 'Religion, Class and Church Growth', in W. H. Fraser and R. J. Morris (eds.), *People and Society in Scotland: ii, 1830–1914* (Edinburgh, 1990), 314–15; C. G. Brown, 'Religion and Secularization', in T. M. Dickson and J. Treble (eds.), *People and Society in Scotland: iii, 1914 to the Present* (Edinburgh, forthcoming).

26. S. Yeo, *Religion and Voluntary Organizations in Crisis* (London, 1976); P. Thompson, *Socialists, Liberals and Labour: The Struggle for London 1885–1914* (London, 1967); J. Cox, *English Churches*.

27. C. G. Brown, 'Religion and Secularization'.

28. See McLeod in Ch. 4, and L. Hölscher, 'Die Religion des Burgers: Bürgerliche Frömmigkeit und Protestantische Kirche im 19 Jahrhundert', *Historische Zeitschortr* 256 (1990), 595–630.

29. C. G. Brown, 'Religion and Social Change', in T. M. Devine and R. Mitchison (eds.), *People and Society in Scotland: i, 1760–1830* (Edinburgh, 1988); C. G. Brown, 'Urbanization'; C. G. Brown, 'The Costs of Pew Renting: Church Management, Church-Going and Social Class in Nineteenth-Century Glasgow', *Journal of Ecclesiastical History* 38 (1987).

30. One of the major empirical problems in establishing this conclusively is that the concept of church membership was itself emerging during this process in Britain between the 1740s and 1850s, and sufficient statistical evidence only becomes available after the suggested decline was reversed. The American evidence, however, does seem to offer some support for this interpretation. However unreliable the US data may be, there seems to be every reason to believe that the extant church adherence figures for the late nineteenth century faithfully reflect an historically low level of *per capita* church membership.

4

Secular Cities?
Berlin, London, and New York in the Later Nineteenth and Early Twentieth Centuries

HUGH MCLEOD

BETWEEN the later seventeenth century and the late twentieth, most western societies moved from being, at least on paper, monolithically Christian, to a situation in which a significant proportion of the population professes no religious belief and has little or no connection with any kind of church.[1] An essential precondition for this was the gradual development of religious toleration from the later seventeenth century onwards. The pioneers were England, the Netherlands, and some of the British colonies in North America. But gradually in the course of the eighteenth century effective toleration spread to most other parts of western Europe. The crucial significance of this development was that unorthodox religion, or irreligion, or simply religious non-practice, became legally permitted alternatives.

It is hardly surprising that in most countries there were at least some people who took advantage of these new opportunities, and that all three forms of religious dissent showed some growth in the eighteenth century. Most notably, deism, and later atheism, began to be fashionable in some intellectual circles from the later seventeenth century onwards, and from this time there was a regular flow of publications questioning various aspects of Christian orthodoxy. As a result, what would previously have been perforce private speculations became generally available to the educated public, at least in those countries which did not have rigorous censorship. In the eighteenth century, religious practice was declining at the upper and the lower ends of the social hierarchy: at the upper end, for the intellectual reasons just mentioned; at the lower end, for demographic reasons, notably the growth of poor suburbs with little religious provision in the larger towns, and of isolated weaving and mining communities, where such provision was equally poor. Unreformed established churches were ill-equipped to respond to changes of the latter kind, and at this stage the State tended to give a low priority to support for religion. Indeed 'enlightened' monarchs saw the Church and popular religiosity as obstacles to their modernizing programmes. On the other hand, the weaknesses of the established churches provided a stimulus, at least in Protestant countries, to evangelistic movements, often staffed predominantly by lay people, which tended to have their biggest impact on craftsmen and small farmers. So, the eighteenth century saw important revival movements, as well as strong secularizing tendencies.

In the political upheaval that followed the French Revolution of 1789 this tendency towards a polarization between the religious stance of different sections of the population became more marked. Between the revolutions of 1789 and 1848 there were both some of the biggest religious revivals and some of the most drastic secularization in the history of Europe and North America. Revived religious interest was seen both on the side of the State and of many élite groups, which came to believe that established churches were the only forces strong enough to hold back the tide of revolution. At the same time, religious sectarianism held a strong appeal to many middle- and lower-status groups who were in the process of establishing their own identity and cultural autonomy. However, it was also in this period that the revolutionary government in France conducted the first of the State-directed anti-religious campaigns that have been a major feature of modern European history; in the 1790s political radicals popularized deistic and atheistic ideas, which gained a mass following for the first time; and many people on the political left became strongly anti-clerical. The onset of rapid industrialization and urbanization in this period, beginning in Britain, was also two-edged in its religious implications. On the one hand, the massive shifts of population from rural areas to towns and industrial regions presented the churches with major logistical problems which, at least in the short term, most were unable to solve. On the other hand, in Britain and the USA, the new industrial communities were often strongholds of Protestant sectarianism. Furthermore, the great mixing of populations from different religious and ethnic backgrounds in many of the new industrial regions often led to a close intertwining of ethnic and religious identity, which enhanced people's religious awareness, and sometimes led to bitter sectarian conflict.

In the second half of the nineteenth century a number of quite separate factors all seemed to be working in the direction of church decline. In the cities and industrial regions intense social conflict between the working class on the one side and the middle and upper classes on the other made it increasingly difficult for those of different social classes to worship together in the same churches. The most frequent result was the alienation from their churches of a large section of the working class, and sometimes the adoption of socialism as a kind of substitute religion. At the same time, agnosticism was gaining ground in the middle and upper classes as a result of new intellectual developments, ranging from Darwinism to biblical criticism, and more generally because of the rising prestige of science, and the belief that the latter had superseded religion. A related development was the progress of agricultural and medical technology, reducing dependence on magic, which, especially in rural communities, was sometimes closely bound up with religion: this process was neatly summed up by the Dutch saying that 'Artificial fertilizers make atheists'. State power was also making rapid strides during this time as a result of increasing resources and improved communications, and the State was tending to take an ever larger role in areas, such as education and charity, previously dominated by the Church. Finally, in a less direct and almost imperceptible way, increasing affluence in the industrializing countries was reflected in growing leisure facilities, and a tendency for leisure to become the emotional centre for many people's lives, and as such a kind of alternative religion.

At first sight then, the picture in the later nineteenth century is one of headlong church decline. Yet, once again it

would appear that several of the factors making for decline
were two-edged in their implications. For instance, the
greatest disaster to hit the churches in this period was the
massive drop in working class participation in many areas.
On the other hand, fear of the working-class and a rediscovery
of the social benefits of religion contributed to a 'return to the
Church' by the bourgeoisie, most notably in France. The
growth in State power was even more ambiguous in its
religious consequences: at the institutional level, the expand-
ing State has been an important source of secularization; but
at the popular level resentment of the over-mighty State has
provided a major stimulus to religious revival in the nineteenth and twentieth centuries. In the later nineteenth century
the best example of this was Bismarck's *Kulturkampf*, designed
to cripple the Roman Catholic Church, which had the
ultimate effect of strengthening the ties between clergy and
people and their common sense of Catholic loyalty: when the
State has turned to direct attack on religion, the results have
usually been counter-productive. Even the rise of leisure may
in the short run have done as much to strengthen as to
undermine the churches, since religious and political organizations effectively exploited the growing popular obsession
with sport and entertainment by establishing their own
football teams and cycling clubs, staging concerts, and later
building parish cinemas. Meanwhile, the relationship between
the decline of magic and the decline of religion in the
nineteenth century has been greatly exaggerated by some
historians. In France and Spain in the nineteenth century
there were huge differences between the various backward
rural regions in the strength of the Church, yet magic was at
least as strong in the irreligious as in the religious areas;
indeed, the more religious areas may have modernized more
rapidly, as the Church often took the lead in setting up credit
banks, forming peasant co-operatives, and organizing the sale
of fertilizers. Once again, the more mechanistic versions of
secularization suffer both from an over-simplified conception
of religion, and a tendency to underestimate the adaptability
of religious organizations.

In the eighteenth century, church decline was most marked
in France; for most of the nineteenth century, the front-runner

was Germany. In the first half of the twentieth century the situation stabilized in France, and to some extent in Germany. Rapid church decline was now most evident in England and Scandinavia. The crucial group was now the middle class, and the *leitmotiv* was individual freedom and rejection of the dogmatism and puritanism of nineteenth-century religion and ethics. This phase reached its climax in the 1960s, when the revolt in the name of individual freedom against all restrictive moral codes swept across the whole western world, making its biggest impact in predominantly Catholic countries and communities, where changes in the first half of the century had come more slowly. In many west European countries the decline in church attendance and membership rates which had been spread over several decades in England and Scandinavia, was compressed into a few years. Yet, just as drastic church decline was taking place in many parts of western Europe, religious revival was taking place in the Communist-ruled east.

In this chapter I focus on the period in the later nineteenth and early twentieth centuries when church decline appeared to be particularly rapid. It was generally assumed that the religious crisis was most acute in the cities. By comparing the religious situation in three of the world's greatest cities, I shall assess the relative significance of the various factors that have been suggested as explanations for this crisis.

One of the many confusing aspects of the debate over secularization is the fact that the term has been used to mean so many different things. I will concentrate on secularization at the level of individual behaviour and attitudes rather than of public institutions, and I shall be asking why far fewer people were actively involved in religious organizations in Berlin than in London or New York, and why in Berlin a secularized view of the world was apparently more wide-spread. Using the term in this sense, I believe that there has been a long-term secularizing trend in the predominantly Christian nations of Europe and the Americas during the past three centuries, and that the analysis and interpretation of this trend is one of the most important problems facing historians of the modern period. Clearly the trend has been much stronger in some countries and at some times than others, and, as I have already indicated, it has always been to some degree modified by countervailing forces. I shall not speculate as to whether the secularizing trend has been equally characteristic of non-Christian cultures, or whether it is likely to continue in the future. The former question is well worth investigating, but no one has yet done the kind of detailed comparative research that would provide the basis for a meaningful answer. Any answer to the latter question is unlikely to be more than guesswork, informed by wishful thinking.

The sense of the term 'secularization' that I am using is somewhat different from that suggested by Wilson, and Wallis and Bruce, who define it as 'the process whereby religious thinking, practice and institutions lose social significance'.[2] By this they mean the change from the kind of society where religion permeates all areas of social relationships, providing legitimation for the political system, a basis for shared moral values, and so on, to one in which religion is no more than an option. In my view, secularization in this latter sense is primarily a consequence of the trend towards pluralism in modern societies. It may or may not be associated with a decline in the extent and intensity of individual belief. Nor does it preclude the possibility that some of the most important social and political movements will be religiously inspired. The USA, the first western nation to separate Church from State, provides a good example of a highly pluralistic society, in which religion is no more than an option, yet it is an option which a very considerable proportion of the population chooses. Moreover, their religion is not just a private hobby: two of the most important new social–political developments of the last forty years, the civil rights movement and the new right, were vitally influenced by different forms of Protestantism, in the one case liberal and in the other fundamentalist. Conversely, as I shall argue in this chapter, nineteenth-century Germany was a good example of a society where religion retained a great deal of 'social significance', yet levels of individual belief and practice were low.

THE THREE CITIES

At the end of the nineteenth century, London, New York, and Berlin were the metropolitan centres of the world's three most powerful nations. In population they ranked respectively first, second and fourth amongst the world's cities. London, with some 6 million inhabitants, was a city on a different scale from any seen before: capital of a world-wide empire, the biggest port and the most important financial centre in the world, and also the site of thousands of (mostly small) workshops and factories. Greater New York was growing at a stupendous pace, and had already reached 3.4 million. Whereas the other metropolitan giants were first and foremost capital cities, New York was above all a port, and on this foundation was built its greatness as a commercial, industrial, and cultural centre. As the point of entry for the majority of immigrants to the USA, New York was also the most cosmopolitan city on earth. Half its population had been born abroad, and they came from a bewildering variety of countries. Berlin had 2.7 million people if the suburbs are included. As capital first of Prussia, and then of the German Empire, it was primarily a political and military centre. This was the foundation for its position as focal point of the national communications network, and its growing pre-eminence in commerce and industry.

In religious terms these three giant cities had certain points in common, and also much that separated them. In all three Protestantism was historically dominant and most of the powerful and the wealthy were members of Protestant churches. All three cities had, however, substantial Roman Catholic and Jewish communities, and in New York Roman Catholics outnumbered Protestants by the end of the nineteenth century. In Berlin, very precise figures of religious affiliation are available. In 1900, 84 per cent of those living within the city limits were members of the official Protestant Church, 10 per cent were Roman Catholics, 5 per cent were Jews and less than 1 per cent belonged to other churches or to none. Surveys undertaken in New York around 1900 of the religious affiliations of heads of households permit me to estimate that 47 per cent of the population were Roman Catholics, 39 per cent were Protestants of one kind or another,

12 per cent were Jews, and 2 per cent of no religion. In
Greater London, no statistics of religious affiliation are
available, though we have a lot of information about church
attendance. On this basis, I would estimate that about 66 per
cent of the population were at least nominally Anglican, about
20 per cent were Protestant Nonconformists, and about 10 per
cent were Roman Catholics. Though London had the largest
Jewish community in Britain, it only accounted for 2 to 3 per
cent of the population.[3]

Berlin had the highest proportion of nominal church-
members in its population, but most contemporaries would
have regarded it as the most secularized of the three great
cities. Indeed a city guide published in 1905 twice compared
the religiosity of London with the secularity of Berlin.
Certainly church attendance was considerably lower in
Berlin. At a rough estimate, attendance on an average Sunday
around 1900 would have been about 5 per cent. In 1902–3 a
survey which included both churches and synagogues produced
an adult attendance level of 22 per cent in the county of
London. A survey in Manhattan borough in 1902 suggested
that 38 per cent of Gentile adults attended church on the day
of the census.[4] Evidence about people's beliefs is necessarily
less precise; but this too suggests that a secularized view of the
world was more widespread in Berlin than in the other two
cities. Most obviously, the powerful Social Democratic Party,
which in the early twentieth century attracted the support of
three-quarters of the Berlin electorate, preached a synthesis of
Marxism and Darwinism, in terms of which all forms of
supernatural religion had been superseded by the onward
march of science. Adolf Levenstein's surveys of the religious
beliefs of workers belonging to the socialist Free Trade Unions
showed a majority of professed non-believers amongst the
Berlin respondents—though surveys of working-class
women or of unorganized male workers might have shown
rather different figures. Scientific–materialist writers like
Haeckel, and in earlier years Büchner and Moleschott, were
eagerly read not only by militant Social Democrats, but also
by many of the city's middle class.[5] In London, atheism and
agnosticism were much less widespread in the middle class,
though by the 1880s and 1890s they were beginning to gain

ground. For most of the nineteenth century, irreligion had a somewhat disreputable air to it in London, and middle- and upper-class sceptics tended to keep their doubts to themselves, although the suburb of St John's Wood had by the 1840s established a reputation as a centre of 'advanced' thought, including religious heterodoxy. Secularism was thus a working-class movement, and at certain points, most notably the 1880s, it seemed to have quite a substantial working-class following. On the other hand, London socialism was much more religiously mixed than its Berlin counterpart. Whereas, in Berlin a hostile attitude to the Church was general amongst Social Democrats, and explicit atheism was widespread, London working-class politics was more pluralistic, with secularists, Christians of various kinds, and the religiously neutral working side by side.[6] It is also worth noting that secularism has left little trace in the various oral-history surveys that tapped the memories of elderly Londoners.[7] There is evidence both of religious indifference and of largely privatized kinds of religious belief, but not much sign of the explicit atheism or militant irreligion that was quite wide-spread in Berlin. New York resembled London in the fact that for most of the nineteenth century, religion and respectability were closely related, and most native-born middle-class people made some kind of religious profession. In the city's numerous immigrant communities the position was much more complicated. The Irish Catholics were akin to native-born Protestants in the respect they accorded to the clergy, their tendency to regard church-going as a normal part of being a good citizen, and their discouragement of overt irreligion. On the other hand, Germans of whatever class were much more tolerant of religious heterodoxy, and the east European Jews were deeply split over religion. Though many immigrants were strongly Orthodox, they probably included in their ranks larger numbers of professed atheists than in any other section of the New York population, with the possible exception of the Czechs. However, the concentration of the various forms of irreligion within particular ethnic com-munities limited its impact on the population as a whole.[8]

In terms, then, of the level of active participation in organized religion, Berlin was certainly the most secular of the cities. The same would probably apply if we were to ask what proportion of the population held to a secularized view of the world. However, if a different kind of criterion for secularity were to be used, the position might be reversed. In Berlin strong personal religious commitment was rare, but the public profile of religion was high. The relationship between Church and State was close and the head of State was also head of the Protestant Church. Nineteenth-century kings of Prussia frequently took a close interest in Church affairs, concerning themselves with the theological orientation, as well as the politics, of the clergy. The Church–State tie was tightest at times of national crisis, such as the uprising against the French in 1813 and the wars of 1870–1 and 1914–18, when Prussian patriotism tended to take on a distinctly Protestant colouring. The Conservative Party was almost as Protestant as the Centre Party was Catholic; and the aggressive secularism of the Social Democrats, and of some left Liberals, might be taken as a tribute to the prominence of religion in Prussian public life. Religious education had a prominent place in the school syllabus; teenage children generally received a year of confirmation instruction, and the subsequent ceremony was an important festive occasion.[9] By comparison, New York, where Church and State were separated, where most children attended non-sectarian public schools, with no religious instruction,[10] and where religion played little direct part in politics, might be taken as a prototype of the modern secular city. Judgements on the secularity of a city thus depend very much on the criterion that is being used, and it cannot be assumed that a city that scores high on one measure will score high on the others.

COMPARATIVE RELIGIOUS STATISTICS

To begin with the statistics of religious participation, it must be emphasized that city-wide averages conceal wide internal variations. In London and Berlin the crucial differentiating factor was social class. In London, adult church-going on a given Sunday averaged 37 per cent in wealthy suburbs and 12 per cent in poorer working-class districts, with middle-class districts a little above the city average, and upper-working-class districts a little below. The association between the social status of a district and the level of church-going was particularly clear-cut in the case of the Church of England: Nonconformists were weak at either extreme of the social hierarchy, but were relatively evenly spread between the intermediate social groups.[11] In Berlin, statistics are available which show the proportion of Protestants who took communion in the course of the year, and once again there is a clear hierarchy, with the richest group of parishes having the highest rate (23 per cent in 1890) and the poorest group of parishes having the lowest rate (10 per cent). In Berlin, there was also an important political dimension to the statistics of religious practice. The highest rates of practice were found in the Conservative Tiergarten, with its aristocrats, army officers, and higher civil servants; figures were somewhat lower in the more bourgeois, and thus Liberal, city centre, and probably also in *nouveau riche* Charlottenburg, which was then outside the city limits, and thus excluded from the statistics. Levels of weekly church attendance were much lower, but show the same class differentials. A survey in 1869 found that 2 per cent of the members of the Protestant *Landeskirche* attended the Sunday morning service, but that the average was only 1 per cent in working-class parishes. Another survey in 1913 suggested an average of 0.5 per cent attendance by Protestants in working-class parishes.[12]

In New York the crucial factor was ethnicity. Some indication of the wide differences between ethnic groups in their level of religious practice can be obtained from the Manhattan church census of 1902. Relating the church attendance statistics recorded in this census to the statistics of religious affiliation collected in various surveys by the Greater New York Federation of Protestant Churches, I have estimated that 50 per cent of adult Roman Catholics attended church on the day of the census, 51 per cent of Methodists, 33 per cent of Presbyterians, 28 per cent of Episcopalians, but only 5 per cent of Lutherans. As this might indicate, Irish New Yorkers, together with British immigrants and the native-born had relatively high levels of church-going, whereas Germans went much less frequently. Surveys of attendance by the Federation of Protestant Churches reached similar conclusions, though they sometimes placed the Irish a bit lower and the white Anglo-Saxon Protestants a bit higher than the above figures might suggest. These surveys showed that some other immigrant groups besides the Germans had low rates of church-going, and they demonstrated that the city's high average could not be explained simply by reference to the large numbers of immigrants in the population. The most detailed survey was undertaken on the Upper West Side of Manhattan, where 36 per cent out of a sample of married women living in tenements claimed to be church-goers, including 47 per cent of those born in Canada, 45 per cent from Britain, 40 per cent of the Irish, 37 per cent of those born in the USA, 32 per cent from France, 29 per cent from Germany, 29 per cent from Sweden, and 27 per cent from Italy. Not all areas surveyed show precisely the same pattern, and there may have been significant differences between sections of the city. However, these surveys generally show average or somewhat above average rates of religious practice for those born in the USA, and wide variations between different communities of immigrants.[13]

As in Britain and Germany, middle-class New Yorkers within each ethnic group attended church in greater numbers than their poorer compatriots. For instance, the Upper West Side survey found that 48 per cent of married women living in what were called 'private houses' claimed to be church-goers. There is also literary evidence to suggest that the poorest sections of the population had little involvement in their churches.[14] However, class differences in religious practice seem to have been narrower than in most parts of Europe, and they were certainly less significant than ethnic differences. Whereas working-class church-going was below average in all three cities, it was lower in Berlin than in London, and lower in London than in New York. Differences between the patterns of working-class practice in the three cities corresponded to the general pattern of differences.

There was also a general tendency for Roman Catholics to attend church in greater numbers than Protestants. In Manhattan I have estimated that 51 per cent of Roman Catholics and 25 per cent of Protestants attended church on the day of the census. In Berlin in the early twentieth century Roman Catholic attendance at mass may have been around 30 per cent,[15] whereas Protestant attendance was around 3–4 per cent if the Free Churches are included. In London the difference between Protestants and Catholics was relatively narrow: Catholic attendance was estimated at between 20 and 30 per cent,[16] as against a city-wide average of 22 per cent. However, the Catholic figure becomes more impressive when it is noted that most of their members were working class, including a large element who were very poor. Whereas the very high level of church-going in New York can be explained partly in terms of the larger proportion of Catholics in its population, it should also be noted that New York Catholics had higher rates of practice than their co-religionists in London or Berlin, and also that New York Protestants attended church in slightly greater numbers than those in London, and in much greater numbers than those in Berlin.

CLASS, ETHNICITY, AND POLITICS

The line of interpretation which sees urbanization and industrialization as being in themselves major causes of church decline would seem to offer little help in explaining why the process had gone much further in Berlin than in London or New York. It might help in explaining differences between these cities and other smaller towns or rural areas in the same country, though the evidence on this is inconclusive. The US religious censuses of 1890 and 1906 showed that average levels of church affiliation were slightly higher in urban than in rural areas, and that the figures for New York were around the urban average. In England the urban average was somewhat lower than that for rural areas, and London was below the urban average, though Callum Brown's work on the 1851 religious census suggests that the size of a city was not in itself a factor determining the level of church-going (Bruce, however, in Chapter 8, comes to a very different conclusion). In Germany, where Protestant communicant statistics are available for the 1890s, there is a high negative correlation between the level of urbanization in the

various states and provinces and the communion rate; though
separate figures for individual towns are not always available,
Berlin seems to be fairly typical of the larger towns.[17]

These urban and rural averages conceal a major qualitative
difference. In England (and this is probably typical) the
highest and the lowest levels of church attendance were found
in rural areas, and the range between the two extremes was
enormous. Large towns fell somewhere in the middle, and the
range was much narrower: the more pluralistic and loosely
knit urban culture did not lend itself to the extremes either of
religious practice or non-practice that were sometimes found
in villages and small towns. Similarly, the approach which
interprets church decline in cities simply in terms of the
generalized effects of urbanization and industrialization glosses
over the important internal differences within each city. A
more profitable approach, therefore, might be to compare
three distinct elements in the population of the cities: the
aristocracy, the middle class, and the working class.

Beginning with the aristocracy, the comparison here is
between London and Berlin, since, whatever might be said
about steel barons and railroad kings, the US had no
hereditary aristocracy or gentry in the European sense. The
religious situation in the West End of London had a good deal
in common with that in the West End of Berlin. In both cases,
church-going was normal, and the Royal Family set the
pattern. In London the upper class was strongly Anglican,
though with some admixture of Roman Catholics. In Berlin it
was strongly Protestant. Both cities had their fashionable
churches, which people in Society attended. If there was a
difference, it lay in the fact that the religious traditions of the
English gentry and aristocracy (and, indeed, of the Royal
Family) tended to be rather low-key—enthusiasm was vulgar,
and often associated with religious dissent. On the other hand,
there were important Pietist traditions in Prussia's East
Elbian aristocracy, which continued in certain circles of Berlin
High Society. In Berlin, enthusiastic religion was an aris-
tocratic more than a bourgeois phenomenon. Furthermore,
one nineteenth-century monarch, Frederick William IV
(1840–61), was an avowed Pietist, and his successor, William
I (1861–88), also showed a preference for Pietist clergy. In

return, the Pietist clergy in Berlin, as in other parts of north Germany (though less frequently in the south-west) showed a preference for Conservative politics and monarchical rule—which limited their ability to attract support in those sections of the population where liberalism and socialism were strong.[18]

This has an important bearing on what seems to me the crucial comparison—that between the business and professional classes in the three cities. Already in the 1830s and 1840s there is evidence of declining religious enthusiasm on the part of middle-class Berliners,[19] whereas middle-class Londoners and New Yorkers remained strongly involved in their churches through most of the century, and there is little evidence of decline before the 1880s. In New York, the revivals of 1828–9, 1835, and 1857–8 had their main impact on the middle class, and throughout the century most of the business élite belonged to one of the Protestant churches of British origin, most commonly the Episcopalians or Presbyterians. Prominent business magnates like the Presbyterian Tappan brothers, who were leading patrons of the revivalist Finney, or, later in the century the Baptist John D. Rockefeller or the Episcopalian J. Pierpoint Morgan, were generous benefactors of churches and themselves active in church affairs.[20] Irish doctors, lawyers, and politicians were equally strongly committed to their Catholic parishes, though the New York German élite tended to be less interested in the Church.[21] Meanwhile in London, wealthy suburbs like Hampstead, Highbury, and Blackheath were noted for their flourishing churches, both Anglican and Nonconformist, and perhaps especially for their huge Congregational chapels, with famous preachers. As in the industrial north, employers frequently had close links with particular places of worship, acting as patrons, and often holding leading offices.[22] No doubt London offered the less conventional members of the middle class opportunities to go their own way, with less neighbourly harassment than might be expected in smaller towns; there were also middle-class areas (including St John's Wood, Putney, and Brixton) which were reputed to be less church-going than others.[23] But until agnosticism achieved a degree of social acceptability in the 1880s and 1890s, some kind of religious profession was a normal part of London middle-class life. This requirement was facilitated by the existence of a very wide choice of denominations, and of types of liturgy and theology within many of the larger denominations. A French observer in the 1870s claimed that Londoners did not mind what kind of church a person attended, whether it were Anglican, Nonconformist, Catholic, or if indeed rationalist doctrines were preached (as, for instance, at South Place chapel), as long as they spent part of Sunday attending a service and being preached to by a minister.[24]

In looking at the differences between Berlin on the one hand and London and New York on the other, there are three major factors which help to explain the greater secularity of the middle class in Berlin. The first is political: the degree of subordination of the Protestant Church to the Prussian State, and its consequent identification with repressive State policies was a major cause of alienation from the Church. The second is the more pluralistic religious structure in London and New York, and the tolerance achieved by religious beliefs and institutions of many different kinds. The third is intellectual: the fact that new scientific and philosophical ideas of a kind that threatened orthodox religious belief won a hearing much more rapidly in Berlin than the other two cities. The first factor is the most fundamental, and indeed it probably provides part of the explanation for the receptivity of middle-class Berliners to heterodox ideas. The most prosperous period for the Protestant Church in Berlin during the nineteenth century came during and immediately after the War of Liberation of 1813–15. The patriotic enthusiasm of the war period took on a strong religious colouring, and the impetus for reform in the years immediately following victory was also frequently religious; Schleiermacher, the greatest preacher and theologian of this period, enjoyed a following that none of his successors quite equalled.[25] But in 1819 the Church suffered the first of many State-directed purges, designed to weaken the influence within it of liberals and democrats. Gradually politically and theologically conservative Pietists got the upper hand within the Church, and in the process fatally narrowed its constituency. By the 1830s and 1840s the intellectual avant-garde in Berlin were turning away from Christianity under the influence of Strauss and Feuerbach. The Friends of Light, the movement for reform in Church and State in the 1840s, won an important middle-class following in Berlin, as elsewhere, but they were forced out of the Protestant church. They, like the German Catholics, a radical breakaway from the Catholic Church, made an important contribution to the politics of the 1848 revolution. Conversely, the Protestant Church allied itself with the royal counter-revolution in Berlin, and gave powerful support to the policies of the reactionary 1850s, when measures to suppress political and religious dissent and to ban controversial newspapers went hand in hand with those to increase the time given to religious instruction in schools and to enforce stricter observance of Sunday. So, from the point of view of many of the liberal middle class the church was seriously compromised. In the 1860s, with the lifting of most of the restrictions on the press, and the rise of the Liberals to political leadership in the city, the Protestant Church found itself frequently under attack in the newspapers and by some Liberal politicians, and though the great majority of middle-class Berliners remained nominal members of the church, levels of active participation were low. Some sought salvation through science or politics, while more preferred a quiet Sunday at the zoo, in a beer garden, or beside one of the many lakes on the edge of the city.[26]

While London also had its conservative established Church, it was, by the second half of the nineteenth century, less reactionary than its Prussian counterpart, partly because the looser discipline of the Anglicans allowed a wide variety of politics to flourish amongst the clergy. Furthermore, middle-class liberalism found its principal religious expression in Nonconformity. There certainly were secular liberals in London too, but they were far outnumbered by Congregationalists, Baptists, Methodists, Unitarians, and Quakers. A crucial difference between Britain and Germany in the nineteenth century lay in the fact that the Free Churches were both far smaller in Germany and largely apolitical. Though split between Anglicans and Nonconformists, middle-class Londoners of all religious persuasions held fairly similar views on Christian morality, the desirability of regular church-going and observance of the Sabbath, and the social utility of the churches.

In New York, with no established Church, no monarchy or aristocracy, and no press censorship, most of the issues that concerned European liberals were irrelevant. On the other hand, the oligarchic structures of the Protestant churches lent themselves to leadership by business and professional men, and many businessmen were attracted by the moral crusades and the philanthropic efforts of the Protestant churches, which seemed to offer the basis for a prosperous, hard-working, well-educated and socially harmonious community. And these pious Protestant merchants and professional men established norms of Americanism which would be adopted by subsequent generations of immigrants and their descendants anxious to win acceptance. Indeed there is some evidence that for immigrants from such countries as Germany and Italy, who often brought traditions of non-church-going with them, becoming active in a church was a sign of Americanization.[27]

In both London and New York middle-class money and voluntary effort kept in operation a wide range of religious institutions which, in their various ways, were attractive to many working-class people.[28] Poor families often willingly used the charitable facilities provided by the churches, without themselves wishing to become actively involved in the religious community. But for many of the more prosperous and self-improving members of the working class, the educational facilities offered by the churches were of vital importance in their intellectual development. It is instructive here to compare the intellectual biographies of pioneer German Social Democrats with those of pioneering members of the British Independent Labour Party or Social Democratic Federation. In both cases, educational classes provided on Sundays or on weekday evenings by middle-class liberals played a significant role in their progress towards adulthood. But there were differences in the religious content of the knowledge imparted. In Germany, the Workers Educational Associations were an important means for the propagation of scientifically based religious scepticism, and we find such a notable figure as the later Social Democratic leader August

Bebel becoming an atheist in the early 1860s as a result of the ideas learnt in evening classes. On the other hand in many parts of Britain, including London, Sunday schools and adult schools sponsored by Nonconformist chapels enabled many subsequent political activists to take the first steps towards independent thinking and critical reflection on the world about them. Perhaps for this reason, the first generation of British socialists frequently justified their criticisms of contemporary society by reference to the Bible, whereas in many parts of Germany the political use of the Bible was monopolized by conservatives.[29]

This brings us to the subject of differences between working-class religiosity in the three cities. Put very crudely, the difference is between a relatively high level of militant irreligion in Berlin; low levels both of militant secularism and of active church-involvement in London; and relatively high levels of active church-involvement in New York.

The most important difference between New York and the other cities was that working-class consciousness was much less fully developed in the American metropolis. This was partly because of the crucial role of ethnicity in the city's life, in providing the basis for ties between rich and poor within each ethnic group, and for antagonisms between workers of different origins. Also important were the relatively high levels of upward social mobility in New York. In Berlin working-class traditions of political radicalism, and frequently of antagonism to the Church, were passed on over several generations. London too had a large, hereditary, working class, even if its political and religious traditions were less sharply defined. In New York the children of immigrant workers frequently moved into white-collar jobs and out to the suburbs, as low status jobs passed to newer immigrant groups, and new opportunities were continually opening up one step higher up the status ladder. This seems to have been one of the biggest problems faced by the Socialist Party as it sought to prolong its brief period of success in early twentieth-century New York.[30] It attracted immigrants in considerable numbers, but failed to hold their upwardly mobile children. The churches often did well with immigrant workers and often did even better with their lower-middle-class children. On the other hand, there is some evidence that they did less well with those second-generation immigrants who stayed in the working class. So the distinctive social structure of later nineteenth- and early twentieth-century New York seems to have inhibited the development of the sharply defined class boundaries that in Berlin and London made it difficult for those of different social classes to worship in the same church.

The Roman Catholic Church, in its Irish parishes, was particularly successful in bringing together a wide spectrum of social groups, ranging from politicians and contractors to labourers and servants. Here the important role of the Democratic Party, and its local headquarters Tammany Hall, should be mentioned. Tammany Hall enjoyed friendly relations with the Roman Catholic Church in the later nineteenth and early twentieth centuries, and both bodies were dominated by the Irish. Tammany hegemony depended on an alliance of Irish businessmen, workers, politicians, and priests, and in spite of some major hiccups in the relationship, especially during the 1880s, the majority of the Irish community continued to believe that this alliance was in their best interests. The United Labor Party, formed in 1886 with considerable Irish support, proved a flash in the pan, and the subsequent rise of the Socialist Party of America in the early twentieth century made very little impact on the Irish. New York's Irish community thus escaped the political fragmentation on class lines which proved so disastrous to the Roman Catholic Church in many European cities at that time.[31]

Certainly later nineteenth-century America had its own version of the 'Church and Labour' problem so familiar in Europe.[32] Clergy were criticized by trade unionists for being too closely identified with employers, and for enjoying a comfortable middle-class lifestyle; wealthy laymen often held key positions in their churches, and were said to hold a veto over what was said in the pulpit; working men claimed to be made unwelcome in affluent congregations. Such criticisms were more often directed at the Protestant churches than at the Catholic Church, which was less conspicuously middle-class in atmosphere, but whose priests were often more politically conservative. Nonetheless, the crisis in relations between churches and workers was much less acute than in most European countries. There was, of course, no established Church in the USA, so one of the major sources of religious discontent in many parts of Europe simply did not exist. The leading Protestant denominations of British origin, notably the Episcopalians, Presbyterians, Congregationalists, and Methodists, were often seen as constituting an informal establishment, and certainly a high proportion of the wealthiest men in New York, as elsewhere in the USA, belonged to one of these churches. However, New York, like other American cities, contained a multiplicity of Protestant denominations, catering for the needs of a wide range of constituencies. And even these most prestigious bodies were sometimes quite effective and resourceful in attracting working-class recruits. In New York the most notable were the Episcopalians, second to the Roman Catholics in the number of worshippers. The Episcopalians were best known for the numbers of millionaires amongst their members, and Trinity downtown or St Thomas's on Fifth Avenue ranked amongst the wealthiest congregations in the USA. On the other hand, they had flourishing churches on the East Side, some of them directed especially at German immigrants, and also several black congregations. By the early twentieth century, the Episcopalians, like a number of other Protestant denominations, were influenced by the Social Gospel, and part of their appeal lay in the broad programme of social facilities of all kinds associated with many of their churches. This certainly seems to have been one reason for their ability to draw some German immigrants away from the more austere atmosphere of Lutheranism.[33]

In all three cities, the Roman Catholic Church did better than the Protestants at retaining the loyalty of its working-class members. This cannot be entirely explained in terms of factors inherent to Catholicism, as many parts of Catholic France and Spain saw a working-class alienation from the Church as acute as that in Protestant Berlin.[34] However, there were various reasons why the Catholic minorities in Britain, the USA, and Germany were able to maintain a certain degree of religious solidarity which was lacking in countries where Catholics were the great majority of the population. In Germany the various attacks on the Catholic community,

culminating in the Kulturkampf of the 1870s, strengthened
the sense of common identity, and provided a great stimulus
to Catholic organization.[35] (Admittedly, this process went less
far in Berlin than in the Rhine/Ruhr industrial region, which
was the stronghold of Catholic organization, and the Catholic
sub-culture in Berlin reached its fullest development only in
the 1920s.) For the Polish element amongst Berlin's Catholics,
religion and national identity were closely intertwined, and
this was equally true for the Irish Catholics of London and
New York. Furthermore, anti-Irish and anti-Catholic prejudice
in Britain and the US (the 'No Irish need apply' syndrome)
was highly effective in keeping alive a strong Irish Catholic
identity in the land of emigration. However, in the absence of
the political disincentives to working-class Catholicism which
were so potent in countries like France and Spain, it may be
that Roman Catholicism, at least in its nineteenth-century
ultramontane form, had certain advantages over the Protestants in appealing to the working class. Nineteenth-century
Catholicism was a religion of miracles, which offered imme-
diate help to those suffering illness or living under the threat of
imminent dangers. It was also a highly visual religion, with
statues and banners, processions and saints' day celebrations,
which tended to outdo the more cerebral attractions of
Protestantism.[36]

In London levels of religious involvement by the working
class were fairly low, and certainly lower than in many other
parts of Britain. Attendance at church on a single Sunday in
1902–3 averaged 12 per cent in poor areas, 13 per cent in more
typical working-class areas, and 16 per cent in upper working-
class areas. (Of course not all church-goers attended every
week; an oral-history survey which questioned elderly
Londoners about the church-going habits of their parents in
the Edwardian period found that 20 per cent of fathers and 24
per cent of mothers had been frequent church-goers.)[37]
However, this level would have seemed quite high by Berlin
standards. One should beware of exaggerating the contrast
between the two cities. For instance, the Secularist leader
Bradlaugh was an important figure in working-class London
from the 1860s to the 1880s, and at its peak in the 1880s,

during Bradlaugh's campaign to take his seat in Parliament, the movement enjoyed quite widespread support, especially amongst certain groups of skilled artisans in London. One should also note evidence of anti-clericalism in London, and of religious men sometimes being subjected to mockery by their workmates.[38] Conversely, in Berlin, most working-class teen-agers continued to be confirmed even at the height of Communist strength in the 1920s, and in spite of a good deal of generalized criticism of the clergy, some individual cler-gymen seem to have had good relations with their parish-ioners; the great majority of working-class adults continued to be church members, and most criticism of the Church, rather than being from an atheistic viewpoint, focused on the alleged failure of the clergy to live up to Christian ideals.[39] None the less there was a real difference between the religious atmos-phere of the two cities. In particular, I would argue that, in spite of the weaknesses of the churches in working-class districts of London, there was a greater degree of integration of the churches into the life of these areas in London than in Berlin; conversely, I would argue that militant secularism was a relatively minor aspect of working-class communities in London, but was of major importance in Berlin.

Leaving on one side the Catholic minorities, I would suggest that there were important differences between Protes-tantism in the two cities. The first obvious difference is the much greater role of the Free Churches in London. In spite of their irreligious reputation, the working-class districts of south and east London were full of Nonconformist places of worship of all kinds. These ranged from huge centres of evangelistic and temperance preaching like the Great Assembly Hall, to back street 'Little Bethels', maintained by small groups of Brethren, and from Methodist Central Halls, with their keen interest in marketing religion in forms that would attract the maximum number of working-class customers, to more traditional Baptist and Congregational churches, which made few concessions to popular taste. The latter had appealed mainly to the business and shopkeeping classes, and were in serious decline, as more and more of the middle class moved out to the suburbs. But in the early twentieth century the Methodist Central Halls, combining popular preaching, simple services with plenty of music, and a huge programme of social facilities and recreational activities, were attracting large, mainly working-class congregations.[40] The Church of England was also doing a bit better than the Evangelical Church in Berlin in attracting working-class congregations. One reason for this was the greater political flexibility of the Anglicans. In working-class areas of London by the 1890s the clergy were no longer conspicuously identified with the Conservative Party, and there was a small but vocal group of radicals and socialists amongst them.[41] Radical clergy did not necessarily pull people in; but the emphatic conservatism of the Prussian Church drove them away. The main reason for the difference lay in the tighter State control over the Prussian than over the English Church, and the deliberate harnessing of the clergy by the Prussian State for its own purposes. The most notable example in the later nineteenth century was the combined assault by Church and State on the Evangelical–Social movement amongst the clergy in the 1890s.[42]

In speaking of the Church of England in later nineteenth- and early twentieth-century London, one should also make some mention of the Anglo-Catholic and ritualist movement, which was prominent in working-class areas of the city at the time.[43] It was in certain respects a reaction against those aspects of contemporary Anglicanism which set up barriers between Church and workers. First, the Anglo-Catholic clergyman gave priority to his status as a priest, rather than as a gentleman (though authoritarian styles of priestly leader-ship could of course create new problems). Secondly, the celibacy of many Anglo-Catholic priests was an advantage in terms of their commitment to their parishes: there was less likelihood of them adopting a conspicuously middle-class lifestyle, and some of them made a special point of always being available or, in the case of the famous Father Wainright, of never sleeping outside his parish. Third, they were often reacting against the puritanism and the strict separation of sacred and secular practised by many evangelicals. They attempted to identify themselves with the whole life of the community in which they lived, which meant that living and working conditions, education, recreation, and entertainment, were all the legitimate concern of the Church, as well as more strictly spiritual matters in the narrower sense of the term. Fourth, this led some, though by no means all, Anglo-Catholic clergy into acting as spokesmen for their people, and sometimes getting involved in local politics as a result. London clergy could not expect a deference due to their office: they had to earn respect. But the evidence of oral history suggests that a fair number of them achieved respect and popularity in the working-class areas of early twentieth-century London, and that amongst these, Anglo-Catholics were particularly numerous.[44]

Finally, in explaining the greater strength of militant secularism in Berlin, two elements would seem to be of paramount importance. The primary factor was a political one. In Germany the Protestant churches were emphatically anti-socialist in the period up to the First World War, and the few clergymen who declared support for the Social Democrats were disciplined.[45] Though some clergy were liberals, the majority were conservatives, and loyalty to king and father-land were preached as Christian virtues which were above questioning. The Roman Catholic Church was equally anti-socialist and was identified with the Centre Party. For working-class Berliners who sympathized with Social Democracy—and in the later nineteenth and early twentieth centuries that meant the great majority—the churches were seen as a major obstacle to their aspirations. While German working-class secularism had primarily political motives, its precise form was influenced by the more general intellectual and cultural atmosphere of later nineteenth-century Germany. Social-Democratic workers saw themselves as part of a broader movement of progressive thinking, which also included some members of the intelligentsia, and they were influenced by the contemporary scientific and philosophical avant-garde. In later nineteenth-century Germany, this meant Darwinism, materialism, and a faith in science as the provider of ultimate solutions to all human problems. Many of them were also influenced by a characteristically German phenomenon, which has no British counterpart, namely the tendency for the classics of German literature (particularly Goethe and Schiller) to become the basis for a secular faith, built round such values as freedom, the endless pursuit of knowledge, and reverence for nature. This faith was believed by its adherents to answer fully to humanity's spiritual needs and to obviate any need for supernatural religion. By comparison, nineteenth-century British secularism was narrower in scope and appeal. It was limited mainly to criticism of inconsistencies and absurdities in the Bible and, as Christianity remained a stronger influence on intellectual and cultural life in Britain, and alternative traditions were much less fully developed, it received little nourishment from wider cultural and scientific concerns.[46]

CONCLUSIONS

What conclusions can be drawn from these comparisons? First, I would suggest that the search for some master factor, which might provide a key to the whole process of secularization, is misguided. Reference to 'modernization' or to 'the disenchantment of the world', to the effects of industrialization, or of the rise of science, does not get us very far towards explaining the differences between these three cities, or, indeed, the religious divisions within them. In particular, generalized explanations of this kind usually imply that the most 'modern' sectors of the population, those most conversant with modern science, technology, and business methods, and those enjoying the benefits offered by an industrial economy, are those most likely to reject religion, whereas most of the evidence for nineteenth-century Europe suggests that such rejection was most common in the working class, and particularly the poorer working class. It makes more sense to think in terms of the religious situation in the nineteenth century being influenced by the interaction of a complex mix of factors, which were present in varying proportions in different countries and regions. For instance, political factors seem to me to have been of decisive importance in explaining the exceptional degree of secularization in Berlin. However, these political factors had such a great effect because of the intellectual and ecclesiastical context within which they operated. On the one hand, the Protestant *Landeskirche* and the Roman Catholic Church dominated organized religious life in

Prussia, and religious dissent had been so effectively restricted that there were no significant Free Churches, of the kind that flourished in most other Protestant countries in the nineteenth century, to offer an alternative. On the other hand, the foundations for a vigorous, secular, intellectual culture had already been laid in the later stages of the German Enlightenment: in the 1830s and 1840s, at a time of widespread dissatisfaction with the existing order in Church and State, radical intellectuals, many of them located in Germany's thriving universities, built on these foundations, combining political liberalism, religious heterodoxy, and cultural romanticism in a mixture that would be characteristic of Germany for several decades.

Comparison between the cities also suggests that in the short run at least, historical factors—events and experiences specific to particular countries, regions, ethnic groups—were of considerable importance, and should not be neglected in the search for more general explanations of secularization. A striking example of this is provided by the very different religious cultures of the various immigrant communities in New York.

I would like to make one other concluding point. Comparisons of the kind I have been making carry with them, in particularly acute form, dangers that are inherent in the whole exercise of tracing the causes of church decline. Focusing on the question of whether at any given time or place religion is rising or declining can lead to undue emphasis on quantitative measures of religious commitment, rather than qualitative changes, which are less easily analysed in such terms. It can also lead to stereotyping—a danger that I have deliberately tried to avoid here, but which is always lurking in the background. Most of all, in seeking to identify the direction of change, or to define the broad pattern of differences between three cities, it is easy to lose sight of the nuances and the ambiguities, which are of the essence of any real historical situation. Here the statistical evidence is little help, and we need to turn to such sources as autobiographies and novels. These ambiguities may indeed offer vital clues to the causes of change. For, even the most powerful religious revival is likely to cause resentments and frustrations that will prepare the way for its ultimate decay; and even the most decisive secularization may cause dissatisfactions that prepare the way for ultimate revival. As a dramatic example of the latter, who would have predicted in 1889 that the Protestant Church, said by friends and enemies alike to be on its last legs in Berlin, would a century later play a vital role in a revolution in that city?

NOTES

1. This chapter is mainly based on H. McLeod, *Religion and the People of Western Europe 1789–1970* (Oxford, 1981).
2. B. R. Wilson, *Religion in Secular Society*, 14; Wallis and Bruce, in Ch. 2.
3. For Berlin, H. Matzerath, 'Wachstum und Mobilität der Berliner Bevölkerung im 19. und frühen 20. Jahrhundert', in K. Elm and H-D. Loock (eds.), *Seelsorge und Diakonie in Berlin* (Berlin, 1990), 214; for London, see H. McLeod, *Class and Religion in the Late Victorian City* (London, 1974), xii, 34, 314. For New York I have used the surveys published from 1897 onwards in the Protestant journal *Federation*. I. Rosenwaike, *Population History of New York City* (Syracuse, NY, 1972), 85–8, 122–30, also provides useful data, but underestimates the number of Catholics.
4. *Berlin und die Berliner: Dinge, Sitten, Winken* (Karlsruhe, 1905), 374–5. For church attendance in London, McLeod, *Class and Religion*, 314. For New York, see figures published in *New York Times*, 24 Nov. 1902: I have estimated the Jewish population of Manhattan as 15% on the basis of the surveys of religious affiliation in *Federation*. Evidence on attendance by members of the official Protestant church in Berlin is fairly plentiful and consistently points to a weekly rate of around 2%. See W. Ribbe, 'Zur Entwicklung und Funktion der Pfarrgemeinden in der evangelischen Kirche Berlins', in Elm and Loock (eds.), *Seelsorge*, 252. Material on Roman Catholics and sectarians is more fragmentary, but see ref. in n. 15, and W. Wendland, *Siebenhundert Jahre Kirchengeschichte Berlins* (Berlin, 1930), 344.
5. A. Levenstein, *Die Arbeiterfrage* (Munich, 1912), 326–34; O. von Leixner, *Soziale Briefe aus Berlin* (Berlin, 1891), 347–66; Wendland, *Siebenhundert*, 330; more generally: Hölscher, 'Religion des Burgers', 595–630.
6. McLeod, *Class and Religion*, 66–8, 153–4, 200; H. McLeod, 'Religion in the British and German Labour Movements',

Bulletin of the Society for the Study of Labour History, 51 (1986), 25–35; P. Thompson, *Socialists*; A. Bartlett, 'The Churches in Bermondsey 1880–1939', Ph.D. thesis (Birmingham, 1987), 360–9.

7. H. McLeod, 'New Perspectives on Victorian Working-Class Religion: The Oral Evidence', *Oral History Journal* 14 (1986), 31–49.

8. *Federation*, 2 (1902) published statistics of church membership in each district of New York City: the percentage was highest in middle-class Protestant districts such as Brooklyn Heights, and in tenement districts with a large Irish Catholic population, such as the West Side of Manhattan; the lowest ratio was in the strongly German Upper East Side of Manhattan. For discussion of specific ethnic or religious groups, see H. McLeod, 'Catholicism and the New York Irish 1880–1920', in J. Obelkevich, L. Roper, and R. Samuel (eds.), *Disciplines of Faith* (London, 1987), 337–51; D. D. Moore, *At Home in America: Second-Generation New York Jews* (New York, 1981); R. Orsi, *The Madonna of 115th Street* (New Haven, Conn., 1985). A stimulating interpretative essay is J. J. Bukowczyk, 'The Transforming Power of the Machine: Popular Religion, Ideology and Secularization amongst Polish Immigrant Workers in the United States 1880–1940', *International Labor and Working Class History* 34 (1988), 22–38.

9. K. R. Pollmann, *Landesherrliches Kirchenregiment und Soziale Frage* (Berlin, 1973); W. Ribbe (ed.), *Geschichte Berlins*, 2 vols. (Munich, 1987), i, 670–4; P. Bloth, 'Zum Verhältnis von Religionsunterricht und Konfirmandenunterricht unter seelsorgerisch-diakonischem Aspekt', in Elm and Loock (eds.), *Seelsorge*, 329–39; H. Ermel, *Die Kirchenaustrittsbewegung im Deutschen Reich 1906–14* (Cologne, 1971), 63–72; J. Kniffka, *Das kirchliche Leben in Berlin-Ost in der Mitte der zwanziger Jahre* (Münster, 1971), 119–23.

10. N. Glazer and D. P. Moynihan, *Beyond the Melting Pot* (2nd edn., Cambridge, Mass., 1970), 237; D. Ravitch, *The Great School Wars: New York City 1805–1973* (New York, 1974), 405.

11. McLeod, *Class and Religion*, 304–7.

12. L. Hölscher, *Weltgericht oder Revolution?* (Stuttgart, 1989), 156–63; Wendland, *Siebenhundert*, 309–16, 344.

13. *Federation*, 3 (1903). For the church census, see refs. in n. 4.

14. McLeod, 'Catholicism and the New York Irish', 343–4.

15. W. Simon, 'Katholische Schulen, Religionsunterricht und Katechese in Berlin', in Elm and Loock (eds.), *Seelsorge*, 369, 384.

16. McLeod, *Class and Religion*, 34; Bartlett, 'Churches', 303.

17. Christiano, *Religious Diversity*, 19–21, 160–3; C. G. Brown, 'Urbanization', 1–14; H. McLeod, 'Protestantism and the Working Class in Imperial Germany', *European Studies Review* 12 (1982), 324–6.

18. McLeod, *Class and Religion*, 189–213; K. Kupisch, 'Christlich-kirchliches Leben in den letzten hundert Jahren', in H. Herzfeld (ed.), *Berlin und die Provinz Brandenburg im 19. und 20. Jahrhundert* (Berlin, 1968), 481–513.

19. Wendland, *Siebenhundert*, 287–8.

20. C. S. Rosenberg, *Religion and the Rise of the American City* (Ithaca, 1971), 44–69; R. Carwardine, 'The Religious Revival of 1857–8 in the United States', in D. Baker (ed.), *Religious Motivation* (Oxford, 1978), 393–406; C. Griffen, 'An Urban Church in Ferment: The Episcopal Church in New York City, 1880–1900', Ph.D. thesis (Columbia, 1960), 7–10.

21. Thus only 21% out of a sample of the notables listed in O. Spengler, *Das deutsche Element von New York* (New York, 1913) mentioned a religious affiliation, whereas in a sample of persons living or working in New York City who appeared in *Who's Who in New York City and State*, 1914, 52% did so. For comments on New York's Irish Catholic élite, see J. T. Smith, *The Catholic Church in the Archdiocese of New York*, 2 vols. (New York, 1905), i, 312–15, 323–5.

22. McLeod, *Class and Religion*, 147–53; Cox, *English Churches*, 110–19.

23. McLeod, *Class and Religion*, 132–3, 200, 304; McLeod, 'White Collar Values', 65.

24. McLeod, *Class and Religion*, 36.

25. F. Schnabel, *Deutsche Geschichte im 19. Jahrhundert*, 4 vols. (Freiburg im Breisgau, 1937), iv, 309–20; F. G. Lisco, *Zur Kirchengeschichte Berlins* (Berlin, 1857), 309–15.

26. R. M. Bigler, *The Politics of German Protestantism* (Los Angeles, 1972); Kupisch, 'Christlich-Kirchliches Leben'; Wendland, *Siebenhundert*, 300–43.

27. Glazer and Moynihan, *Beyond the Melting Pot*, 203–5.

28. For extensive information on the social facilities provided by London churches, see Cox, *English Churches*, and Bartlett, 'Churches'.

29. McLeod, 'Religion in the British and German Labour Movements'; V. L. Lidtke, 'August Bebel and German Social Democracy's Relationship to the Christian Churches', *Journal of the History of Ideas* 27 (1966), 249.

30. C. Leinenweber, 'The Class and Ethnic Bases of New York City Socialism, 1904–1915', *Labor History* 22 (1981), 29–56. My

comments on the churches are based on analysis of membership records of Catholic and Lutheran parishes in New York.

31. T. N. Brown, *Irish-American Nationalism 1870–1890* (Philadelphia, 1966), 133–78.

32. F. Perry, 'The Working Man's Alienation from the Church', *American Journal of Sociology* 4 (1898–9), 621–9; H. F. May, *The Protestant Churches in Industrial America* (New York, 1949).

33. Griffen, 'Urban Church'; W. Welty, 'Black Shepherds: A Study of Leading Negro Clergymen in New York City 1900–1940', Ph.D. thesis (New York University, 1969).

34. R. Gibson, *A Social History of French Catholicism 1789–1914* (London, 1989), 212–26; F. Lannon, *Privilege, Persecution and Prophecy: The Catholic Church in Spain 1875–1975* (Oxford, 1987), 16–20.

35. J. Sperber, *Popular Catholicism in Nineteenth-Century Germany* (Princeton, NJ, 1984).

36. S. Gilley, 'Vulgar Piety and the Brompton Oratory', in R. Swift and S. Gilley (eds.), *The Irish in the Victorian City* (Beckenham, 1985), 255–66; H. McLeod, 'The Culture of Popular Catholicism in New York City in the Later Nineteenth and Early Twentieth Centuries', in L. H. van Voss and F. van Holthoon (eds.), *Working Class and Popular Culture* (Amsterdam, 1988), 71–82.

37. McLeod, *Class and Religion*, 304; McLeod, 'New Perspectives', 33.

38. McLeod, *Class and Religion*, 66–8, 71.

39. Kniffka, *Kirchliche Leben*, 120–3, 149–53, 164–5.

40. Bartlett, 'Churches', 261–94.

41. Ibid. 360–9; McLeod, *Class and Religion*, 118–20.

42. Pollmann, *Landesherrliches Kirchenregiment*, 232–73.

43. See, for instance, D. B. McIlhiney, 'A Gentleman in Every Slum: Church of England Missions in East London 1837–1914', Ph.D. thesis (Princeton, NJ, 1977), Chs. 2–3.

44. G. Richman, *Fly a Flag for Poplar* (London, 1976), 92–102.

45. McLeod, 'Religion in the British and German Labour Movements', 26–7.

46. For Germany, see T. Nipperdey, *Religion im Umbruch: Deutschland 1870–1918* (Munich, 1988), 124–53. The most comprehensive study of British secularism is S. Budd, *Varieties of Unbelief* (London, 1977).

5

Secularization and Census Data

ROBIN GILL

ONE of the many paradoxes of the sociology of religion as it has developed over the last twenty years is that it has given more attention to sects and to new religious movements than it has to long-established denominations or churches. With a few important exceptions,[1] mainstream churches have not received the sort of detailed attention that one might expect given their prevalence and greater size. In part this may be due to lingering suspicions of 'Religious Sociology' and to the ecclesiastical control often thought to lurk behind it in France. It may also be due to the sheer difficulty of analysing amorphous religious institutions. Small-scale religious bodies are often exotic and deviant and hence more interesting and, because they usually have a very clear notion of who is a member, they are easier to study.[2] Whatever the reason, long-established churches remain surprisingly unresearched. Even when sociologists have shown an interest in churches they have typically relied upon generalized data. Currie, Gilbert, and Horsley are a major exception.[3] Yet even they are notoriously lacking in information about Sunday-by-Sunday church-going and tend to put forward factors deemed responsible for church decline in a highly impressionistic manner. The now vast literature on secularization frequently avoids statistics altogether or uses *both* statistics indicating church decline in Europe *and* statistics showing persisting (but supposedly epiphenomenal) church-going in the USA as indications of secularization.[4]

In contrast, a number of younger social historians have shown a developing interest in churches as social phenomena. The detailed study of Reading in the nineteenth and early twentieth centuries by Yeo was a pioneer work and is well known to sociologists of religion,[5] as are the influential statistical studies of Victorian churches by McLeod.[6] Rather less well known is Cox's impressive study of churches in

Lambeth,[7] Obelkevich's study of nineteenth-century South Lindsey,[8] and Brown's important social history of religion in Scotland.[9] Together they suggest that there is considerably more data available on churches as social phenomena than is often imagined and that these data are directly relevant to understanding the decline of most British churches throughout the twentieth century. Far from being generalized studies, they each show that an intense analysis of churches in specific areas yields insights that cannot be deduced from national church 'membership' statistics. The cumulative effect of these studies has been to undermine the approach championed by Currie, Gilbert, and Horsley and underpinning the second half of Wallis and Bruce's analysis of secularization. Currie, Gilbert, and Horsley argued that church-going statistics collected through various local censuses 'have contributed little to the formation of time series' and insisted that national church membership statistics are the most valuable resource:

> But religious statistics of [local attendance] are, however useful, of secondary importance compared with those collected by the churches themselves. Just as, for example, it would be impossible to study the growth of trade unions or political parties without reference to their own membership series, it is impossible to study church growth unless the churches' own membership returns are used; and these returns are probably unique amongst those available for organizations in Britain, both in quantity and in variety.[10]

Although this claim might seem plausible, it faces formidable difficulties. Not the least of these is that the very concept of 'church membership' is a Free Church concept. Comparison of, say, varieties of Methodist membership at a single point of time might have real value. In all probability they shared an understanding of 'church membership' and even had similar procedures for measuring it. But the Church of England has never had a comparable concept of membership and nor has the Catholic Church.

To remedy this obvious deficiency Currie, Gilbert, and Horsley and, more recently, MARC Europe[11] treat Easter Communicants as indicators of Church of England membership, presuming that Easter Communion is a requirement of belonging. In reality, despite many attempts by bishops and clergy to make it a requirement, Easter Communion has not been a serious indicator of Anglican belonging or 'conformity' since the seventeenth century. And even then seasonal conformity was compatible with regular attendance at Dissenting chapels. An abundance of evidence shows that Anglican Easter communicants were a very small proportion of regular attendances in both rural and urban areas in the mid-nineteenth century.[12] Further, the ratio between regular attendances and Easter communicants shows considerable local variations today. In rural areas of England, Easter communicants represent as much as three times average Sunday congregations: in urban areas they are seldom more than half as much again. Thus, Easter communicants vary as an indicator of Anglican belonging both over time and within time; variations are diachronic as well as synchronic.

Confusions about how the notion of membership applies to Catholics are even more obvious. Currie, Gilbert, and Horsley rely primarily upon 'estimated Catholic populations': guesses by local Catholic priests of the number of Catholics in their parishes, regardless of whether or not they are practising. Often estimated from baptisms, they are, in most Free Church understandings, affiliation rather than membership statistics. Aware of this difficulty, MARC Europe rely instead upon regular mass attendances (measured on the last Sunday every October) to produce statistics which can be compared with 'membership' in other denominations. Unfortunately in the process they wholly confuse membership and church-going.

It is clear that 'church membership' is a very odd concept for the two largest denominations in England and Wales. Because a number of Free Churches (especially Methodists) have kept national membership figures for such a long period of time, it is understandably tempting to squeeze Anglicans and Catholics into the same mould, but in the process a minority criterion is transformed into a yardstick for measuring all, and some very curious statistics emerge to be used in scholarly analyses. They cannot be considered as a serious means of assessing relative interdenominational strengths and weaknesses.

Membership may not even be a very consistent measure of Free Church belonging because the ratio of members to quarterly communion attenders in a number of Free Churches changed significantly over time.[13] This century has seen a widening gap between official communicant membership-rolls and numbers of people actually registered as attending seasonal communion services. Further, the urban church-going statistics that will be reviewed later suggest that national Methodist membership statistics at the Union of 1932 considerably exaggerated the strength of Methodism at the time.[14] Many chapels already had a higher proportion of largely dormant 'members' than they would have had in the mid-nineteenth century.

What emerges from this is the realization that an intense study of churches at a local level and over a sufficient period of time—using records of local attendances rather than national membership figures—is a prerequisite for investigating the social factors underlying church decline or, more broadly, secularization.

This would be a standard premise in the sociological study of sects or new religious movements. Ever since the 1950s, and in particular the pioneering study of Birmingham sects by Wilson,[15] the detailed local study of religious bodies has been preferred to generalized discussions of them as national or international institutions. Presumably this is based upon the realization that national information is often partisan and may not accurately represent the way a religious body functions in practice. But this applies *a fortiori* to churches. The claims that a church makes at a national level may or may not be based upon local realities. Indeed, part of the skill of the social scientist involves comparing claims with actual behaviour. To make such comparisons there is no substitute for detailed empirical research and it has, perhaps, been the signal failing of the literature on secularization that it has seldom been based upon such research.

LONGITUDINAL DATA

In this chapter I will examine some of these detailed local data, much of them from local censuses and most previously uncorrelated. With additional and considerably more detailed

material, they will form part of a longer study.[16] It is odd that
so many generalizations about church decline have been made
without anyone surveying these data before. Too many
sociologists have assumed that little longitudinal data on
regular church-going are available outside the three nation-
wide censuses—namely the 1851 religious census and the
1979 and 1989 MARC Europe censuses.[17]

In fact there are a wealth of data from at least six major
sources. There is the 1851 religious census, which covered the
whole of England and Wales and (with more gaps and no
surviving original returns) Scotland. There are independent
newspaper censuses for the 1880s, and occasionally for the
1890s and 1900s. There are occasional censuses conducted by
statistical societies and by such individuals as Rowntree[18] for
the 1830s, and for several points in the twentieth century.
There are numerous local clergy returns to bishops, Catholic
records and sometimes Free Church records, with information
about average Sunday attendances. These often start in the
1850s or the 1860s and, in some cases, continue without any
substantial breaks right up to the present day. Further,
several denominations now go to considerable lengths to
collect average Sunday attendances on a systematic basis.
Finally, there are the church-going statistics for the whole of
Britain compiled from clergy returns to the censuses carried
out for the Bible Society by MARC Europe. There are some
gaps in the information supplied from local churches to
MARC Europe, but with an overall return rate of 70 per cent
for 1989 this is an invaluable resource. That said, the MARC
Europe data are more useful than the largely ahistorical
commentaries about 'church growth' that accompany them.

Altogether there are a great deal of long-term data on
regular church-going in England and Wales covering some
150 years that have not been properly correlated or used in the
debate about secularization. In so far as those discussing
secularization in Britain refer to statistics at all, they
characteristically use the weakest data. Baptism, membership, and (worst of all) affiliation statistics of religious
institutions tend to be cited. Few have made serious use of a
much more obvious and more reliable indicator, namely
diachronic regular church or chapel attendance.

There are several possible reasons for this curious situation. It may be that sociologists and social historians have been unaware of the extensive urban census data that exist— sometimes well hidden in local newspaper reports or ecclesiastical archives. There may be unease about how these data can be satisfactorily compared. It may be thought that clergy returns cannot be reliably compared with independent enumerations of church attendances. The second and third of these reasons require a response but first it is useful to be clear about the consequences of such data for the secularization debate. Church- or chapel-attendance statistics will never provide evidence about the non-institutional forms of religion usually contrasted with regular attendance[19] nor about the cognitive worlds of those attending. But they do provide evidence about one of the most socially visible aspects of institutional religion (others being church buildings and the presence or absence of clergy). Membership or affiliation numbers would perhaps be known to office-bearers in churches and might occasionally (very occasionally in my experience of reading nineteenth-century newspapers) be reported more widely, but they would hardly impinge on the consciousness of most people. Seasonal conformity would clearly be more socially visible, at least at Christmas and Easter, but because its social significance changes within denominations and varies between them, records of ordinary church attendance remain preferable. They offer an important means of controlling variables and they offer the most consistent social manifestation of churches and chapels. Doubtless individuals attend churches and chapels Sunday by Sunday for a variety of reasons which may change between denominations, within denominations, and even within the life cycle or just the moods of the people. Very little of this is now accessible for the past, and even in the present it would take a remarkably subtle questionnaire or interview to fathom the different layers of motivation that encourage individuals to sustain regular church-going. However, there is also an obvious physicality to church-going and it is this which *can* be measured over time and across denominations.

What is more, unlike church membership, regular church-going as a social phenomenon is not primarily a Free Church, an Anglican, or a Catholic construct but is encouraged (even if not practised) by all denominations. In addition, all denominations provide buildings and functionaries at considerable expense to maintain regular church-going. And finally, it is possible to establish diachronic patterns in church-going as a social phenomenon which do not seem to be dependent upon the whims of individuals.

In everything that follows it is vital to insist that other non-measurable variables may have been instrumental in general church decline. It would indeed be surprising if such a diffuse subject as church decline, or (broader still) secularization, could be easily resolved by statistical arguments. Yet it is clearly a prerequisite of the debate that that which is measurable is measured before the statistically uncontrollable is used in any form of explanation. When so many and varied explanations have been offered—both by scholars and by the general public—it is imperative that church-going statistics are examined carefully. So far in the secularization debate this simply has not been done.

PROBLEMS OF COMPARING DATA

How can census data on church/chapel attendances be satisfactorily compared? There are several problems which all those engaging seriously in this area soon encounter. Mann's Report on the 1851 religious census[20] amalgamated church-going and Sunday-school statistics, whereas subsequent censuses seldom included, or even gave separately, Sunday school figures.[21] But it is easy, although arduous, to go back to the (for England[22] and Wales[23]) almost complete original returns and count the Sunday-school statistics separately, removing them from the published results or computing them afresh. In all the 1851 statistics given later, unless stated otherwise, this has already been done. And it is important that it is done, since it will be seen that for some decades urban churchgoing was declining whilst Sunday-schools were still growing. Sunday school enrolments in England and Wales (between two-thirds and three-quarters of whom generally attended on a Sunday) grew from some 12 per cent of the population aged under fifteen in 1818, to 38 per cent in 1851, to 52 per cent in 1891. After a further slight rise in 1901 to 53 per cent, it fell to 51 per cent in 1911, 46 per cent twenty years later and by 1961 was down to 20 per cent. By 1989, only 14 per cent of the under-15s attended church or Sunday school. Urban church-going, in England at least, started to decline much earlier.[24]

Much more problematic is the long-standing issue of relating attendances to attenders. The 1851 census gave attendances for morning, afternoon and evening, whilst most subsequent censuses gave those only for morning and evening, despite the fact that in 1951 in a few areas (for example Suffolk) more people went to church in the afternoon. And only the occasional census attempted to estimate the proportion of attenders who were present at two or even three services. Further there are many indications that double or treble church-going (itself largely a nineteenth-century innovation) faded significantly as the twentieth century developed. Thus total attendances in 1851 might not have represented the same number of attenders as the total attendances in 1881, and they would certainly have been different from those in 1989.

Whilst recognizing them, these difficulties may not be quite so serious in the context of the secularization debate. If regular church-going is taken as an important indicator of the social visibility of religious institutions, then the number of attenders as distinct from attendances is not so crucial. Whether churches and chapels were seen to be predominantly full or empty on a Sunday is far more apposite. Viewed from the perspective of the consumer, most people would have had little idea of what proportion of a given congregation attended more than once, or about how great the church-going rate was in relation to the total population of the area; what they would have known was how many church buildings there were and how full they appeared. Manifestly most churches and chapels in Britain, with the exception of Catholic and a few evangelical churches, are today more empty than full. It is popularly supposed that before 1914 most were more full than empty. I will show presently that this supposition is not confirmed by the census data on church-going.

Even when our concern is the social visibility of religious institutions, problems remain. The absence of Sunday-afternoon attendances from most censuses after 1851 is certainly less than desirable. Yet there are several reports that by 1881 it was no longer so significant a church-going time of day,[25] although it remained an important time for Sunday schools. Instead, throughout urban England and Wales the evening seems to have overtaken the morning as the time of highest church-going.[26] Doubtless this change had something to do with the development of urban street-lighting.[27] Today this pattern is fully reversed again, with evening services becoming increasingly infrequent, except amongst Catholics.

In the context of the secularization debate, the emphasis should be upon longitudinal data. Census data only become interesting when they can be measured in the same geographical area over at least two points of time. The 'index' used by ecclesiastical historians to compare synchronic data in the 1851 census is less appropriate.[28] It simply amalgamated all attendances—church-going and Sunday school, morning, afternoon, and evening—expressing them as percentages of local populations in order to provide comparators from one area to another. Diachronic comparisons certainly should not amalgamate church-going and Sunday-school attendances (even where this is possible) and can usually amalgamate only morning and evening attendances, since it is these alone which are generally available. Alternatively one can compare the busiest service in one census with the busiest in a later census of the same area. These are likely to be morning in the first census and evening in the second. Yet in both censuses attendances should represent separate attenders. Whichever system is used (the second is useful in Wales where evening attendances in 1881 were often the only ones given)[29] particular attention should also be given in such diachronic comparisons to changes in average levels of attendance per congregation.

There is also the difficulty of the comparability of censuses based upon clergy returns and those based upon independent enumerations (usually by newspaper 'tellers' standing outside churches and chapels). Clergy reports of parish populations in the twentieth century are notoriously exaggerated.[30] We may suppose a general clerical habit of inflation and assume that the 1851 census can be compared reliably with few subsequent censuses. Some social historians have even written disparagingly about the 'round numbers' that are characteristic of clergy estimate of attendances.[31] Fortunately this assumption can be tested. Anglican clergy returns to their bishops from the 1850s (and sometimes the 1840s) frequently contain statistical information about 'average attendances' which can be compared directly with returns from the 1851 census, congregation by congregation, and with independent enumerations carried out usually by local newspapers. The urban-clergy returns do supply additional corroboration of successive decline, as well as synchronic comparisons of these two forms of census-data collection. In Chelsea, for example, Church of England morning/evening attendances measured 19 per cent of the total population in the clergy-returned 1851 census, and in the subsequent clergy returns to the Bishop of London, 15 per cent in 1858, 13 per cent in 1862, 9 per cent in 1883, and 11 per cent in 1900.[32] Independent enumerations produced figures of 14 per cent in 1887 and 12 per cent in 1903.[33] In York, too, independent enumerations, although not as specific as those for London, do broadly match the patterns established by long-term clergy enumerations.[34]

Rather surprisingly, then, independent enumerations can be higher than the nearest clergy returns, and, where I have been able to test them, the two have always been found to be consonant with each other. Scholars may have been rather too quick to assume that clergy would tend to exaggerate their attendances and have thus ignored the independent verification these statistics provide, both of declining attendances and of the comparability of these two systems of census-data collection.

Church-going data tell us more about the origins of empty churches than membership or affiliation statistics but on their own they give an incomplete picture. Empty churches consist of physical space as well as a lack of attenders. And, since it is a central aim of this study to take religious physicality seriously, information about the relative size of church buildings is obviously crucial. Fortunately the Victorians were obsessed with the size of their churches and chapels and left behind them a wealth of detail about their various seating capacities. Few scholars have given these data any attention; Wickham was an important exception.[35] Yet he was often regarded as rather quaint for doing so. It has perhaps been generally assumed that all those figures that the Victorians recorded about seating were basically a product of their failing church policies and have very little relevance to the twentieth century. In contrast, I shall argue that these seating figures provide a vital clue about church decline. Once set alongside church-going statistics, they provide crucial, and curiously counter-intuitive, information about the origins of empty churches: they frequently show that *empty churches preceded church decline*.

By comparing church seating, church attendances, and population statistics in Sheffield, Wickham argued that initially an important reason for urban church decline was that churches failed to keep pace with the rapid growth of the late nineteenth-century cities. Church failure was thus a physical one: denominations failed to accommodate the burgeoning industrial working classes. Then, of course, secularization took over. Working classes in Sheffield, who could not be fitted into the churches of the nineteenth century, did not want to be accommodated in those of the twentieth. Finally the urban middle classes followed them in abandoning the churches.

The census data suggest that Wickham was mistaken at every point. Free Churches, especially, *over-provided* in urban and rural nineteenth-century Britain. Unfortunately Wickham based his thesis upon a comparison of the censuses for Sheffield for 1851 and 1881. Had he examined a wealth of data for other urban areas, he would have realized that the Sheffield data were thoroughly atypical and might have noticed some of the contemporary warnings that this was so. The data for 1881 in Sheffield,[36] showing how full churches were there, did not give reliable average Sunday attendances. Stronger than usual local rivalries between churches and pre-publicity for the census ensured that it represented a high point of church-going there.[37] Elsewhere I will show in detail how these data compare with those for other comparable towns and cities at the time.[38]

Whilst the secularization model reigned, Wickham's analysis of Sheffield could be regarded as a perhaps interesting, but essentially marginal, contribution to understanding church decline. By adopting the language of secularization himself he may even have contributed unwittingly to this assessment. The working classes were physically excluded from the urban churches in the nineteenth century, but it was secularization that was the main cause of church decline in the twentieth. So Wickham's task of relating attendances and seating to local populations was not widely seen as a priority for understanding church decline.

DATA AND THE SECULARIZATION THESIS

Once the secularization model is demythologized, the extensive body of data that Wickham touched upon become distinctly more interesting. Perhaps they offer clues to understanding the origins of church-going decline which were largely unsuspected at the time. Elsewhere I have argued that in rural areas, at least, an excess, over local populations, of seating accommodation in churches and chapels occurred by 1901 in many areas of England, and that this excess fostered decline.[39] Elsewhere I will show in much greater statistical detail this same process happening in rural Wales as well.[40] Even when it is grudgingly admitted that over-building caused problems in many parts of rural Britain by the turn of the century, it is commonly supposed that it was under-building that characterized urban areas in the second half of the nineteenth century. As a result, a somewhat modified version of the secularization thesis as it relates to church-going might run as follows. Several denominations throughout Britain built vigorously against declining rural populations in the nineteenth century. This happened extensively in rural England and Wales. But it also happened in Scotland. Here whole counties had a very considerable excess of seating accommodation by 1901. If the seating capacity for counties, excluding the major towns within them, is taken from the 1851 religious census (together with proportional estimates for missing returns) and compared with 1901 populations, this becomes evident. Without any additional building, by 1901 Kinross would have had seating for 102 per cent of its rural population, Dumfries and Bute for 95 per cent, Orkney and Shetland for 94 per cent, Argyll for 87 per cent, and Berwickshire for 82 per cent. The creation of the Free Church in the Disruption of 1843 was within a decade producing excessive capacity for a declining rural population. Since building continued vigorously over the next few decades, rural Scotland, like rural England and Wales, manifestly had a major problem by 1901. It is a difficulty that the Church of Scotland, like the Church of England and the English Methodists, has been struggling with ever since the union of the Kirk and the Free Church in 1929.[41]

Once this problem is observed across rural Britain, the impact of various factors associated with a decline in church-going becomes obvious. Many rural churches and chapels have been closed; chronic debt typically preceded these closures; ordained ministers of any denomination progressively have had charge of an increasing number of churches and chapels; decreasing rural congregations find it difficult to integrate marginal churchgoers and become increasingly elderly; and finally, largely empty churches and chapels become social signs of secularization. On this understanding, 'secularization' is not the cause of a decline in rural church-going; more physical factors seem to be responsible. Secularization is rather an end product.

However, in this modified version of the secularization thesis, in urban contexts it was secularization which appeared, at least in the long term, to be the cause of church-going decline. If anything, denominations under-provided for burgeoning urban, industrial populations. Significant sections of urban working-classes could not have gone to church because there were not enough places. There was both a shortage of buildings and a lack of 'free' accommodation because many churches and chapels financed themselves through pew rents which were beyond the resources of working people. Thus, the five factors identified in rural contexts apparently did not apply in urban contexts. Here it was progressive secularization—a product, as Wallis and Bruce argue, of modernization in the form of social differentiation, societalization, and rationalization—which was responsible for the church-going decline evident since the First World War.

AN ALTERNATIVE TO SECULARIZATION

There are some serious flaws in the urban part of this analysis. Anyone who walks around central Aberystwyth, York, or Edinburgh today may soon notice a proliferation of churches and chapels, many still holding services but also quite a number now used for more secular purposes. One former church in Edinburgh today displays a sign reading 'Sweet Services'—not, as it happens, an invitation to mellifluous acts of worship. Another, more notoriously, is a betting shop. And all are in central urban areas which once supported far larger populations. Central urban depopulation (with consequent suburban growth), it will be observed, began, like rural depopulation, in the late nineteenth century. In the City of London it goes back to the early eighteenth.

Another flaw lies in the assumption that excesses of seating over local populations occurred only in rural, and never in urban, areas. Llanelly provides a startling counter-example. In 1851 it had seating in its various churches and chapels for 85 per cent of its population of 8,415. By 1881 this population had more than doubled to 19,655. However a local newspaper census estimated that it now had seating for 103 per cent of its much enlarged population.[42] This claim, and the newspaper commentary that accompanied it, caused considerable local controversy. The editorial of a rival newspaper denounced it in the following revealing manner:

The writer says that no more chapels will be required 'for at least 15 or 20 years. For the present attendances the edifices are too numerous, and this is one reason why the debts are so heavy.' We presume if this writer had his own way every chapel and church would be closed at once. Noble philanthropist, to advise the churches 'to forget past little differences' when all his aim has been to bring religion into scorn and disrepute! It is a blessing that Nonconformity is not dependent on this miserable caviller. This is not an attack upon Church or Dissent, upon this sect or that, but upon 'religious Llanelly' as a whole, and we denounce the 'Census' and expose it as a deliberate and malicious attempt to sneer down the morality and religion of Llanelly as one of the foremost communities in Bible-loving God-fearing Wales.[43]

In the same edition, a letter from the Vicar of Llanelly disputed the seating estimates in ten of the churches and chapels in the town, on the basis of a census that he conducted himself eight years earlier. His estimates for these buildings showed a seating capacity some 30 per cent less than that given in the 1881 census. But, even on his estimates, eight years out of date, there was still a remarkable amount of seating accommodation available in Llanelly.[44]

This example already provides indications of some of the factors identified in rural areas. Of course the population of Llanelly was growing, and growing very considerably. But so were churches and chapels, and seemingly they were growing faster than the population. Evidently there were considerable religious rivalries in the town and there was already mention of debt. And, if the 1881 census is to be trusted, Anglican churches, on average 96 per cent full in 1851, were down to 40 per cent thirty years later. Free Church chapels, which in 1851 were 75 per cent full, in 1881 were 42 per cent full. Even allowing for possible exaggeration of capacity in 1881, there were evidently a great number of churches and chapels in Llanelly by then and they would have appeared distinctly emptier than they had been in the previous generation.

It has been so widely assumed that the Victorians barely kept pace with the rapid growth of cities in their provision of churches and chapels, that widespread evidence to the contrary has been persistently ignored by most social historians and by the Victorians themselves. However my empirical research on church decline indicates that this assumption is mistaken. Fine details will be given in later publications; here I will set out only the broad outlines revealed by these comparative census data.

Specifically, I will argue that a careful analysis of London and Liverpool census data suggests a continuous decline in Sunday attendances in the Church of England since the 1851 religious census. There has also been decline in the Free

Churches since the 1800s. In both cases, new churches and chapels were built even when existing ones were only one third full on a typical Sunday. By 1902 all major denominations except the Catholics had empty churches. I will also argue that the census data show a major difference between the Free Churches and the Church of England which may throw light on their mutual decline since the 1880s.

Even the five broad factors identified in rural areas are relevant to the urban data examined in this way. In Inner Greater London, for example, the Free Churches had 1,512 chapels in 1903, but had reduced them to 1,443 by 1914. By the turn of the century there was widespread discussion about the debts and plight of many chapels.[45] The Church of England, in contrast, increased its churches in London from 1,014 in 1903 to 1,155 in 1914—despite thin attendances. There is even evidence, especially in the Church of England, of some city-centre churches today sharing priests. And, as already observed,[46] it is precisely these factors—chapel closures, chapel debt, and pluralist ministries—which have been shown by other scholars to be strongly associated with church decline.

Too many churches inevitably means emptier churches—in urban as well as rural Britain. Empty churches themselves may act as agents of overall decline in church-going in two ways. First, they provide an obvious perceptual signal of secularization. Despite the real sophistications of many more properly sociological understandings of secularization, it is the very social visibility of empty churches and churches sold and used for secular purposes which may strongly shape and reinforce public perceptions of secularization in cities. Empty or redundant churches in rural areas may also reinforce this perception but the decline of most rural public facilities is known to be widespread. Little-used or redundant urban churches contrast sharply and unfavourably with urban pubs, discos, theme parks, and shopping centres. Further, when other urban voluntary associations cease to function—as undoubtedly they have during the twentieth century—they generally leave behind few physical traces. Redundant urban churches—preserved for ever as listed buildings—stubbornly remain as visible reminders of a once-religious past.

Secondly, empty urban churches, like their rural counter-parts, may also deter 'marginal' church-goers. To attend occasionally a full church or chapel may not be too difficult: to attend a large urban building (they are characteristically far larger than those in the countryside) containing a small, predominantly female, and probably elderly, congregation might be much more daunting.

There has been a persistent tendency for sociologists to ignore these physical factors when analysing church-going decline. Secularization as a theory attracts to it a whole cluster of variables, both cultural and socio-structural, few of which are concerned with the internal structures of churches themselves. Thus, it is attenuations of faith, liberalization and perhaps ecumenism that are isolated as factors causing church-going decline, or it is the effects of two world wars, urban anomie, or even television. The census data on urban attendances suggest otherwise. From this, church-going decline in Britain seems to be much more long-standing than most scholars have previously thought. It also appears to owe much to the physical factors already contained within this census data.

It is interesting that even those involved in collecting data around the turn of the century tended to explain declining attendances in very similar terms to present-day sociologists. The otherwise excellent report of the London census of 1902–3 (which unlike other contemporary censuses provides rich data on the age and sex of church-goers) wrongly saw decline as a feature just of the Church of England and attributed it to a lack of its commitment to evangelism.[47] Black too, in one of his reports to the *British Weekly* of the unique 1927–8 sample surveys of London church-going, suggested a variety of factors responsible for church decline.[48] All three of his samples (two working- and one middle-class) showed a decline in average attendances at churches and chapels of at least 50 per cent from 1902–3. Yet it was the middle-class decline in what he described as 'a suburban area', in both the Church of England and the Free Churches, that he found particularly surprising. The identity of the suburban area has long puzzled scholars.[49] It was Putney/Roehampton and is particularly interesting because attendances there in 1886–7 and 1902–3 corresponded closely to the mean for Inner Greater London for those dates and provide rare inter-war census evidence. To explain decline in this area, Black suggested that it was 'partly due to causes beyond the control of the churches', namely the First World War, distractions provided by 'the gramophone, cinema, wireless' etc, improved social and travel conditions, 'and, last, the intellectual unsettlement, within the Church and outside, consequent upon modern Biblical scholarship and the new scientific explanations of man's place in the universe'.[50]. Yet, having offered such largely unmeasurable factors, elsewhere he noticed something quite different. Almost in passing he noted that Catholic churches, even in one of his working-class samples (which may have been Battersea), had not declined to the same extent as other denominations. In the latter, 'no church or chapel, in view of its seating capacity, has an adequate attendance. The big chapel without exception is a burdensome problem.' But of the Catholics he remarked: 'How wise has been this Church in limiting the number of its centres, using them more fully, and concentrating strength in a few rather than dividing limited energies over many.'[51] In his final report Black did not return to his unmeasurable factors. Instead, he saw co-operation between churches as a key factor, since 'to continue without change, with diminishing numbers and power is not business—is not Christianity. The resources of the churches in men, money and buildings are not used to full advantage.'[52]

This crucial difference between urban Catholics and others has been largely ignored by subsequent commentators. Unfortunately Catholic attendance figures were frequently underestimated in religious censuses—including the 1851 census[53]—due to the tendency to count a single morning mass when there were several. Yet such figures as were given show that at every stage urban Catholics had more attendances than they had church accommodation. Today Catholics in Tyne and Wear have twice as many church-goers on an average Sunday as the Church of England but only a quarter of the number of churches. And in the whole of England, Catholics slightly exceed Anglicans in church attendances, yet they have less than a fifth of their churches.[54] Even in

Catholic Liverpool non-Catholics had proportionately more churches in relation to church-goers than Catholics.[55] In 1851 there were sixteen Catholic churches (out of a total of 165 churches and chapels): by 1912 there were forty Catholic churches (out of a total of 415): by 1931 there were fifty Catholic churches (out of a total of 440). Yet at each date Catholics represented between a third and two-fifths of all church-goers. And, of course, Catholic church-going decline is far more recent. Irish immigration—and thus 'cultural transition' in the Wallis and Bruce argument—may not be the only factor in this situation.

TWO PATTERNS

What emerges very clearly from the urban census-data is that the Church of England expanded more slowly but for longer than the Free Churches. Yet it continued (often to the present) with churches which had tiny congregations and in some cases little surrounding population. The Free Churches expanded very vigorously, competing between themselves and spreading attendances more and more thinly. They then collapsed dramatically. In some rural areas the Free Churches have all but disappeared and in many central urban areas their presence is much reduced. The interaction of these two patterns—subsidized persistence and free market expansion and collapse—seems to have been mutually destructive. And this, of course, is the same economic pattern that has already been observed in rural churches and chapels.[56]

These claims will be supported with data drawn from various surveys of church attendance in the following three cases: Inner Greater London in 1851, 1886–7 and 1902–3, Liverpool in 1851, 1881, 1891, 1902 and 1912, and a group of eleven large towns (Bolton, Bradford, Coventry, Derby, Hull, Ipswich, Leicester, Nottingham, Portsmouth, Sheffield, and Warrington) in 1851 and 1881.[57] Reference will be made to more intense data from places such as Newcastle upon Tyne.[58] In each of the three major sources—with a combined population in 1851 of 3.4 million representing just over a fifth of the population of England and more than a third of the urban population—the same broad pattern has emerged for the Free Churches:

1. Free-Church attendances expanded or held steady between 1851 and the 1880s. In Liverpool and London they increased from 11 to 13 per cent of the population and in the large towns they held steady at about 12 per cent.

2. In all cases church seating in the Free Churches increased between 1851 and 1881: in Liverpool from seating sufficient for 13 to 16 per cent of the population, in London from 11 to 16 per cent, and in the large towns from a striking 22 per cent to 26 per cent. In Birmingham, too, the proportion of the population which could be accommodated increased from 15 per cent in 1851 to 16 per cent in 1872.

3. In all three cases chapels were less full on average in the 1880s than they were in 1851.[59] In London in 1851 chapels on average were 54 per cent full. For 1887 the figure was 43 per cent and and by 1903 it had fallen to 35 per cent. The figures for Liverpool chapels show a steady decline: 45 per cent in 1851, 44 per cent in 1881, 38 per cent in 1891, 37 per cent in 1902, and 32 per cent in 1912. The chapels in the eleven large towns were 46 per cent full in 1851 and 41 per cent full thirty years later. In other words, *whether church-going was increasing or decreasing, chapels everywhere looked and indeed were emptier.*

4. In every new survey more denominations entered the picture. If the original larger denominations—Methodists, Congregationalists, Baptists, and Presbyterians—are isolated then the pattern of progressively empty churches becomes clearer. Some, like the Church of England, declined in real terms immediately after the 1851 census; Congregationalists and non-Welseyan Methodists in London and Liverpool, and Congregationalists, Wesleyan and non-Wesleyan Methodists, and Baptists in the large towns. By 1902–3 in London and Liverpool all of these denominations had declined. In contrast new denominations, such as the Salvation Army, flourished briefly but declined in the following census.

5. In all cases where it can be measured, Free-Church attendances overall have declined since the 1880s. In Greater London they declined from 13 per cent in 1887, to 11 per cent in 1903, and to 4 per cent in 1979.[60] In Putney/Roehampton

they declined from 12 per cent in 1887, to 11 per cent in 1903, and to 5 per cent in 1927. Attendances at Liverpool Free Churches declined from 13 per cent in 1881, to 12 per cent in 1891, to 11 per cent in 1902, and to 9 per cent in 1912. A sample for 1931 suggests attendance of little more than 7 per cent.[61] By 1979 adult Free Church attendances in the whole of Merseyside amounted to only 2.4 per cent.

The pattern for the Church of England is rather different:

1. In Liverpool and London, Church of England attendances declined between 1851 and the 1880s and, with only one exception, continued to decline thereafter. In Liverpool they fell from 15 per cent in 1851, to just 10 per cent thirty years later, rose slightly to 10.5 per cent in 1891, but then declined to 9.6 per cent in 1902, to 8 per cent by 1912, to no more than 5 per cent in the 1931 sample. In the Diocesan one-third sample for 1962, the figure was again 5 per cent.[62] In 1979, only 3 per cent of adults in the whole of Merseyside attended an Anglican church and the 1985 Diocesan returns showed a figure of 2.2 per cent.[63]

Anglican attendances in London fell from 16 per cent in 1851 to 14 per cent in 1881 and 10 per cent in 1903. In 1928 in Roehampton it was 5 per cent. In the dioceses of London and Southwark sample for 1962 it was 4 per cent. The figure for London in 1979 was 2.5 per cent and in the London and Southwark diocesan returns for 1985 it was 1.7 per cent. Only in the eleven large towns did it rise slightly between 1851 and 1881: from 11.5 to 12.4 per cent. Oddly Sheffield largely accounted for this rise: as suggested earlier, it was more unusual than Wickham realized.

2. Church of England seating did not immediately keep pace with the rapid rise of most urban populations. In Liverpool it was sufficient for 16 per cent of the population in 1851 and for 14 per cent in 1881. In London, Anglican churches could have sat 17 per cent in 1851 and 16.5 per cent in 1887.[64] In the large towns it was sufficient for 16 per cent in 1851 and 13 per cent in 1881. Only in Birmingham did it rise slightly from seating sufficient for 13.2 per cent of the population in 1851 to 13.8 per cent in 1872; still a distinctly smaller rise than that in the Free Churches. However, in

London and Liverpool (data for the towns are lacking) the next census shows a significant increase in church building: London in 1902–3 could accommodate 17.3 per cent of the population while Liverpool Anglican churches could hold 14.3 per cent by 1891.

3. Putting these two sets of figures together shows that for Liverpool and London in all but one census after 1851 Church of England churches were ever more empty. In London they were 50 per cent full in 1851, 44 per cent full in 1887, and less than 33 per cent full in 1903. The comparable figures for Liverpool churches are 54 per cent in 1851, 36 per cent in 1881, 37 per cent in 1891, 36 per cent in 1902, and 32 per cent in 1912. It was only in the large towns that Church of England churches *appeared* fuller; 37 per cent in 1851 but 47 per cent in 1881 (again Sheffield had some effect).

4. On more detailed investigation this slightly surprising finding for the large towns is skewed. If the original churches in a large town are looked at separately they typically declined radically. It is the new churches which were full. So in Newcastle church-going rose from 12,703 attendances in 1851 to 18,973 in 1887 (a slight drop from 14.2 per cent of the population to 13.1 per cent).[65] However church-going in the original ten churches dropped from 12,703 to 9,950. Many of these original churches in the centre of Newcastle are still in use as churches—albeit for the most part without effective congregations or surrounding populations. Unlike the Free Churches, the heavily subsidized Church of England typically persisted, closing churches very reluctantly.

CITY CHURCHES

These contrasting patterns seem to have been mutually damaging. Purely free market churches (as in the USA) or, less frequently, largely uncontested established churches (as in Eire) can flourish even in an urbanized, and supposedly secular, environment. But can they flourish together? Up to the 1880s it would seem that the Free Churches expanded faster and generally more successfully in urban areas than the Church of England, but then they ran into serious problems.

The slow-moving Church of England expanded for longer and persisted with churches (in city centres as well as in the countryside) which had lost most of their populations. Together they presented by the turn of the century a picture of widespread and visible church decline.

By studying the churches in the City of London between 1700 and 1900 these twin processes can be observed more accurately. Elsewhere I shall show these processes working in the context of quite different urban population changes.[66] Unusually, in the City of London it is possible to measure churches and populations during this period. If in 1700 the population (within the walls) was about 139,000,[67] by 1801 it was down to 64,615, and then to just 10,640 by 1901. How did the various denominations respond to this drastic urban depopulation?

In 1700 the Church of England had seating in its churches for some 30,000 people but the Free Churches (mostly Independents) could hold 3,000 more; these were sufficient together for 45.3 per cent of the population.[68] By 1801 the Church of England still had some 29,500 seats (sufficient for 45.7 per cent of the population) but the Free Churches had reduced to some 21,000 (32.5 per cent). A century later the Free Churches had just three chapels, with capacity for 2,100 (sufficient for 19.7 per cent) but the Church of England still had seats for 22,087 people: provision for over 200 per cent of the resident population. From contemporary records, it appears that people were commuting back to the City on a Sunday.[69] In theory, the church-going rate in relation to the local population was going up. In practice, Church of England churches, which were on average almost 33 per cent full in 1851, were only 13 per cent full in 1902. And, perhaps not surprisingly, these City of London churches were seen by otherwise intelligent contemporary commentators as providing clear evidence that 'religion' was on the wane.[70]

Most dramatically, a church like St Andrew by the Wardrobe had seating for 1,020 and had a morning congregation in 1851 of 470 and an evening congregation of 691: by 1902 it had just 57 in the morning and 56 in the evening. St Swithin, Cannon Street, with seating for 400 had a morning congregation in 1851 of 130 and an evening congregation of

189: by 1902 its congregation numbered 32 and 44: and by 1929 it was 'attended by seven or eight people'.[71] Ironically a Bill to dispose of nineteen City churches in 1926 was passed by the House of Lords but then thrown out by the House of Commons. The Bishop of London, speaking for the Bill in the Lords, regarded it as a 'scandal' that '£50,000 to £60,000 annually' was spent on the City churches when 'a dozen churches would suffice, and £23,000 a year would be saved'.[72] It was only after the Second World War that this century-old issue was partially resolved. With the formation of City churches as guild churches they were no longer required by law to hold Sunday services. Thus, rather than being parish churches, they became and continue to be churches in search of alternative functions. Twenty-four of the fifty-nine churches in existence in 1851 were still functioning as churches in 1988 (only nine with regular Sunday services), employing twenty-five clergy.[73]

Of course the City of London, with all those Wren churches, was unusual. However the general pattern is to be found up and down the country. In response to population increases—urban or rural—the Free Churches expanded vigorously. When populations slowed down or contracted they collapsed. The Church of England in contrast responded lethargically to population changes and continued to subsidize churches (again, urban as well as rural) whether or not they had active congregations or were serving viable populations. And both continued to build new churches when existing churches were more empty than full.

The results of these differing patterns would have been obvious to all: empty churches and chapels throughout the countryside; chapels with mounting debts; central urban churches in search of a function; rural chapels closing everywhere; rural and sometimes urban clergy having multiple charges. However, the physical factors behind them seem to have been more invisible. By concentrating more carefully upon these physical, and indeed measurable, factors scholars might avoid some of the less controllable speculations about secularization.

NOTES

1. E.g., M. P. Hornsby-Smith, *Roman Catholics in England: Studies in Social Structure Since the Second World War* (Cambridge, 1987).
2. B. R. Wilson, *The Social Dimensions of Sectarianism: Sects and New Religious Movements in Contemporary Society* (Oxford, 1990).
3. Currie *et. al., Churches and Churchgoers*.
4. E.g., B. R. Wilson, *Religion in Secular Society* and *Contemporary Transformations of Religion* (Oxford, 1976).
5. S. Yeo, *Religion and Voluntary Organizations*.
6. See refs. in McLeod, Ch. 4.
7. Cox, *English Churches*.
8. J. Obelkevich, *Religion and Rural Society: South Lindsey 1825–1875* (Oxford, 1976).
9. C. G. Brown, *Social History of Religion*.
10. Currie *et al., Churches and Churchgoers*, 12.
11. P. W. Brierley (ed.), *Prospects for the Eighties* (London, 1980) and *UK Christian Handbook (1989/90 Edition)* (London, 1988).
12. Gill, *Competing Convictions*.
13. Ibid.
14. R. Currie, *Methodism Divided* (London, 1968).
15. B. R. Wilson, *Sects and Society* (London, 1955).
16. R. Gill, *The Myth of the Empty Church* (London, forthcoming).
17. N. Yates, 'Urban Church Attendance and the Use of Statistical Evidence, 1850–1900', in D. Baker (ed.), *The Church in Town and Countryside* (Oxford, 1979).
18. B. S. Rowntree, *Poverty: A Study of Town Life* (London, 1901); B. S. Rowntree, *Poverty and Progress: A Second Social Survey of York* (London, 1941); B. S. Rowntree and G. R. Lavers, *English Life and Leisure: A Social Study* (London, 1951).
19. P. H. Vrijof and J. Waardenburg, *Official and Popular Religion: Analysis of a Theme in Religious Studies* (Hague, 1979).
20. British Parliamentary Papers, *1851 Census, Great Britain, Report and Tables on Religious Worship, England and Wales*, 1852–3 (reprinted Irish University Press 1970).
21. *Keene's Bath Journal*, 12 Nov. 1881, is an exception.
22. Held in Public Records Office, Kew Gardens, London.
23. See I. G. Jones and D. Williams (eds.), *The Religious Census of 1851: A Calendar of the Returns Relating to Wales*, 2 vols. (Cardiff, 1976 and 1981).
24. 1818 and 1851 figures calculated from British Parliamentary Papers, *Religious Worship and Education, Scotland, Report and Tables*, 1891–1961 from Currie *et al., Churches and Churchgoers*, which

does not include Catholics or sects; 1989 from Brierley, *UK Christian Handbook*.

25. E.g., *Hampshire Telegraph and Sussex Chronicle*, 24 Dec. 1881 reporting on Portsmouth and Gosport. See also the Mission Hall returns for London in the *British Weekly*'s *The Religious Census of London* (London, 1888) and the afternoon attendances for Chelsea in R. Mudie-Smith (ed.), *The Religious Life of London* (London, 1904).

26. See *Ipswich Free Press*, 19 Nov. 1881.

27. E.g., *Yorkshire Gazette*, 29 Sep. 1838.

28. See K. S. Inglis, 'Patterns of Religious Worship in 1851', *Journal of Ecclesiastical History* 11 (1960), 74–86; R. B. Walker, 'Religious Changes in Cheshire, 1750–1850', *Journal of Ecclesiastical History* 17 (1966), 77–93 and 'Religious Changes in Liverpool in the Nineteenth Century', *Journal of Ecclesiastical History* 19 (1968), 195–211; D. M. Thompson, 'The 1851 Religious Census: Problems and Possibilities', *Victorian Studies* 11 (1967), 87–97.

29. For Llanelly, see *Western Mail*, 25 Nov. 1881; for Corwen, see *Wrexham Advertiser*, 19 Nov. 1881.

30. See the Appendix to L. Paul, *The Deployment and Payment of the Clergy* (London, 1964).

31. H. McLeod, 'Class, Community and Religion: The Religious Geography of Nineteenth-Century England', in M. Hill (ed.), *Sociological Yearbook of Religion in Britain*, vol. vi (London, 1973).

32. Kept in the Library at Lambeth Palace.

33. See the *British Weekly*'s *The Religious Census of London* (London, 1888), and Mudie-Smith, *Religious Life*.

34. From the Rowntree studies, see n. 18.

35. Wickham, *Church and People*.

36. *Sheffield Telegraph*, 24 November 1881.

37. See *Supplement* to the *Nonconformist and Independent*, 2 Feb. 1882, 112: 'The day was fine, and owing to local rivalry the fact that the enumeration was about to be taken was known. The attendance was, therefore, something of a maximum.'

38. Gill, *Myth*.

39. Gill, *Competing Convictions*.

40. Gill, *Myth*.

41. J. N. Wolfe and M. Pickford, *The Church of Scotland: An Economic Survey* (London, 1980).

42. Reported in *Western Mail*, 25 Nov. 1881 and *Llanelly Guardian*, c.17 Nov. 1881.

43. *South Wales Press*, 1 Dec. 1881.

44. The parish church seating he gave as 570 whereas in 1851 it was given as 650: Capel Newydd he gave as 663 whereas then it was 828.

45. For a full list of the churches and chapels in London in 1914, as well as an account of contemporary chapel debts there, see H. W. Harris and M. Bryant, *The Churches and London* (London, 1914). London chapel debts also feature in C. Booth, *Life and Labour of the People in London: Third Series: Religious Influences* (London, 1902). Welsh chapel debts were much discussed in the 1880s: see A. G. Edwards's letters written to *The Times* on 10 and 31 Oct. 1887 and 3 Jan. 1888; and later in British Parliamentary Papers, *The Royal Commission on the Church of England and other Religious Bodies in Wales and Monmouthshire 1905-6* (London, 1911).

46. Gill, *Competing Convictions*.

47. J. T. Stoddart, 'The *Daily News* census of 1902-3 compared with the *British Weekly* census of 1886', in Mudie-Smith, *Religious Life*.

48. A. Black, 'London Church and Mission attendances', *British Weekly*, 23 Feb., 1 Mar. and 8 Mar. 1928.

49. C. E. M. Joad, *The Present and Future of Religion* (London, 1930); M. Argyle, *Religious Behaviour* (London, 1958); Cox, *English Churches*.

50. Black, *British Weekly*, 1 Mar. 1928.

51. Ibid., 23 Feb. 1928.

52. Ibid., 8 Mar. 1928.

53. For example, in the original 1851 returns for Chelsea (held at the Public Record Office, Kew Gardens) the Catholic morning attendances of 2,300 (which must represent several masses since the church seating was only 600) have been reduced subsequently in pencil to 700 and it is this second figure which appears in the Census Report; in Marylebone similarly morning return figures have been reduced from 7,300 to 5,400, afternoon from 1,950 to 900, and evening from 2,750 to 1,500. The problem of underestimating Catholic morning attendances is acknowledged in the London 1886-7 census and Liverpool censuses.

54. Calculations based on data in Brierley, *Prospects*.

55. Liverpool newspaper censuses were all published by *Liverpool Daily Post*: 15 Nov. 1881, 24 Nov. 1891, 11 Nov. 1902 and 13 Dec. 1912. For the 1930s, see C. C. Jones, *The Social Survey of Merseyside*, vol. iii (London, 1934).

56. Gill, *Competing Convictions*.

57. *Bolton Weekly Journal*, 10 Dec. 1881; *Bradford Observer*, 22 Dec. 1881; *Coventry Herald*, 9 Dec. 1881; *Derby Gazette*, 23 Dec. 1881;

Hull News, 10 Dec. 1881; *Ipswich Free Press*, 19 Nov. 1881; *Leicester Mercury*, 23 Nov. 1881; *Nottingham Express*, 8 Dec. 1881; Portsmouth in *Hampshire Telegraph*, 24 Dec. 1881; *Sheffield Telegraph*, 24 Nov. 1881; *Warrington Examiner*, 12 Nov. 1881.

58. *Birmingham Daily Times*, 31 May 1887 (morning only) and *Birmingham News*, 3 Dec. 1892 (and the three Saturdays following).

59. Average attendance figures for churches and chapels were calculated by dividing amalgamated morning and evening attendances by the seating of the churches and chapels actually open for each service and multiplying by 100.

60. All 1979 figures are calculated from Brierley, *Prospects*.

61. Calculated from C. C. Jones, *Social Survey of Merseyside*.

62. Calculated from Paul, *Deployment and Payment* but using the 1961 Census statistics for population given in the Appendix rather than the clergy information used in the body of the Report.

63. See *Church Statistics: Some Facts and Figures about the Church of England* (London, 1987).

64. Calculated from the 1886–7 census with allowances for the extra churches mentioned in the 1902–3 census which does not estimate seating.

65. *Clergy Visitation Returns, Diocese of Newcastle* for 1887 are held in Northumberland County Record Office, Gosforth.

66. Gill, *Myth*, forthcoming.

67. The estimate made in the 1811 *Census of Population*.

68. Estimates based on the information given in J. G. White, *The Churches and Chapels of Old London* (London private circulation, 1901) and A. E. Daniell, *London City Churches* (London, 1895).

69. See White, *Churches and Chapels* and Daniell, *London City Churches*.

70. Joad, *Present and Future*.

71. Ibid., 14.

72. Ibid.

73. Calculated from H. Willows (ed.), *A Guide to Worship in Central London* (London, 1988).

6

Recent Transformations in English Catholicism: Evidence of Secularization?

MICHAEL P. HORNSBY-SMITH

THIS chapter addresses the secularization thesis by considering the transformations which can be discerned in English Catholicism over the past three or four decades.[1] First, it will examine a wide range of empirical evidence relating to contemporary English Catholicism which indicates a move out of a defensive, 'fortress' model of the Church, whose walls have steadily been dissolved, and a shift from what Hammond has called a 'collective-expressive' to an 'individual-expressive' view of the Church.[2] Secondly, it will report evidence for 'customary' religion and transformations of religious authority. Thirdly, it will offer an overview of post-war social and post-Vatican II religious changes in English Catholicism in terms of Dobbelaere's three dimensions of secularization[3] and levels of analysis.[4] It concludes that there is evidence of both decline and new life, growth or revival at each of these levels.

Leading exponents of the secularization thesis have admitted that its progress does not follow a steady path[5] and that there occurs 'the spasmodic countervailing occurrence of resacralization in certain areas and instances of cultural revitalization exemplified by the emergence of charismatic leaders and prophets'.[6] In this essay I wish to explore the extent to which one can find in the post-war transformations that have taken place in English Catholicism evidence not only of secularization but also of counter-tendencies.

In addressing this thesis, two main types of data, collected between the mid-1970s and the mid-1980s, will be considered.[7] In the second part of the essay I will report the quantitative results of surveys of representative samples of different groups of English Catholics, and in the third part I will review the more qualitative data derived from tape-recorded focused interviews. Reference will also be made to some of the early findings from a study of the RENEW process (an American revitalization movement) which commenced in 1988 in every parish in one English diocese.[8] Finally, the transformations which have taken place in English Catholicism in the post-war years will be summarized in terms of Dobbelaere's analytical framework.

Let me start by recognizing the danger of confusing 'the evaluative and the analytic',[9] and with a biographical confession. I was substantially convinced by David Martin's critique of the concept of secularization when I first read it a quarter of a century ago.[10] In spite of the fact that he has subsequently modified his position, it still seems to me to raise questions and objections to the secularization thesis which have not been satisfactorily answered or resolved.[11] Nearly a decade before I commenced a programme of research into the changes taking place in English Catholicism, Martin's robust attack on the ideological usages of the concept fell on receptive ears and elicited an immediately sympathetic response in my defensive Catholic heart! All the same, I have attempted here to recognize clearly the distinction between the process of social and religious change and the espousal of the ideology of secularism.[12] But it was three other points which I found particularly telling and of more lasting consequence in Martin's critique.

First, the existence or not of a process of secularization is largely a definitional matter. In its simplest formulation, Bryan Wilson defined it as 'the process whereby religious thinking, practice and institutions lose social significance'.[13] Given an exclusive, substantive definition of church-oriented religion, evidence of institutional decline appears to be a clear indication of secularization. In his early work Wilson seems largely to have taken this view, and he commences with a comprehensive review of statistical trends of religious indicators.[14] On the other hand, when an inclusive, functionalist definition of religion is employed, secularization almost seems to be ruled out *tout court*. Thomas Luckmann's 'invisible' religion seems to fall into this category.[15] As an Australian writer has observed: 'at the heart of many disputes about the definition of secularization . . . lie differences about the very notions of religion and the sacred'.[16]

Secondly, secularization refers to a *process* so that historical data across two points in time are necessary for any empirical testing of the secularization hypothesis. In a recent analysis of religious trends in post-war America, Greeley has taken this quite literally and confined himself to an investigation of survey findings only where the same question wording has been employed at two points in time.[17] But what earlier point in time? I was impressed with Martin's argument as to the arbitrariness of the starting point usually selected by proponents of the thesis.

I still find these two points to be major stumbling-blocks to any conversion to the secularization thesis. What historical data I have come across in the course of my own research into English Catholicism—and I readily acknowledge a great debt to the historical studies of Victorian religion by Hugh McLeod[18]—have persuaded me that as far as English Catholicism in the post-Reformation period is concerned, there never was a 'golden age' of consistently high levels of religious belief, practice, and commitment, and have thus reinforced my scepticism. I wish to take seriously Dobbelaere's requirement that 'we should be ready to falsify our theories on the basis of new empirical material'.[19] In the case of English Catholicism in the post-war period there is strong evidence of persistence and some vitality, albeit of a transformed version of Catholicism, which does not support the secularization thesis.

Thirdly, it is necessary that the indicators of religion selected meet the methodological canons of reliability, validity, and clarity so that the same or similar phenomena are not ambiguously susceptible to interpretation as 'religious' in some circumstances and 'secular' in others. Thus care must be taken to avoid putting different interpretations on religious attendance frequencies so that a decline can be interpreted as evidence of secularization in the case of Britain[20] but high rates of attendance in the USA and Poland can be discounted because of the different significance of attendance for nation-building or legitimated dissent. In my view, this objection cannot be dismissed simply on the grounds that it fails adequately to take due note of differences of cultural meanings and historical contexts. The concept 'secularization' is ambiguous and inconsistently applied. Thus many American sociologists refer to indicators of individual religious beliefs, attitudes, and practices to reject secularization theories[21] while some European sociologists have restricted the term to the macro level of the social system.[22]

One further autobiographical reflection is, perhaps, not out of place. When I first graduated in the 1950s I was a fairly active member of the Newman Association of Catholic graduates, the local arm of Pax Romana, a semi-autonomous branch of international Catholic Action. Its task, as I recall it, was the 'intellectual apostolate' and, in the words of Pope Pius XII, 'the service of the Church and the permeation of contemporary thought'. Two interesting points arise out of this. First, we can see changing (but not declining) notions about the vocation of lay people. The theologies and corresponding authority structures which saw the Newman Association and similar Catholic organizations as part of the official lay apostolate and under the more or less direct authority of the hierarchy, have been transformed in the past three decades. It is not manifestly obvious to me that the legitimation of the ministry of lay people and the articulation of their vocation of Christian witness in the world, independently of official hierarchical control and direction, which one can find in post-Vatican II theology, is evidence of secularization rather than a developed and transformed understanding of the Christian vocation in the world.

Secondly, I concede that the 'permeation of contemporary thought' as a goal was undoubtedly articulated more explicitly by activist Catholic intellectuals in the 1950s than it is now. In the heady post-war days of Catholic Action, such a task was envisaged as being directed from the top down. While some organizations, such as Opus Dei, may continue to take this line, in general there is little doubt that in the 1990s the chances of 'permeating contemporary thought' are regarded more cautiously, perhaps more realistically, and certainly less arrogantly. In so far as it remains a goal, albeit a latent one, it is seen much more in terms of a bottom-up, grassroots process, not so much a product of the mobilization of Catholic power, especially at the societal level, as of patient cultivation by committed individuals starting at the local level. But the issue is important in drawing attention to the different levels relevant for the analysis of religious transformations or secularization. The 'permeation of contemporary thought' is clearly a goal at a societal level of analysis. It is at this level, that of national politics, the role of religion in legitimating the state, the symbolic importance of major institutions such as the monarchy or parliamentary democracy, especially in a society which has become much more obviously multi-cultural, with significant proportions identifying with non-Christian faiths, that it seems most likely to find evidence of secularizing tendencies.

I remain unconvinced that it is helpful to interpret the evidence of institutional decline on some measures (but not on others) as indicative of inevitable secularization processes. It is more appropriate, in my submission, to acknowledge the multi-dimensional nature of religion and seek to understand and interpret the transformations which have undoubtedly taken place. It is clearly the case that on some dimensions, such as church attendance or priestly vocations and possibly the political significance of religion as a legitimating ideology, there is evidence of decline. But measures on other dimensions, such as lay participation or group prayer or the significance of religion as an ideology of political protest, have increased. Emergent forms of spirituality are replacing older forms of devotionalism. At first sight, then, there are sufficient grounds for a healthy scepticism about secularization and a plea for the careful mapping of differential religious trends on different dimensions.

It will be argued that the structural and attitudinal changes which have undoubtedly taken place in English Catholicism in the post-war years, and especially since the Second Vatican Council, cannot be regarded as unambiguous evidence of a process of secularization. It is claimed that the evidence points to a need to map the empirical transformations which have taken place (decline in some areas and new growth in others), and to recognize the multidimensionality and partial independence of different religious phenomena. Church-oriented religion shows signs of considerable resilience, at least in the case of contemporary English Catholicism.

Karel Dobbelaere has distinguished three dimensions of secularization: *laicization* at the macro or societal level, the process of structural differentiation whereby 'institutions are developed that perform different functions and are structurally different'; *religious involvement* at the micro or individual level, which 'refers to individual behaviour and measures the degree of normative integration in religious bodies'; and *religious change* at the sub-systems' or organizational level, which 'expresses change occurring in the posture of religious organization . . . in matters of beliefs, morals, and rituals, and implies also a study of the decline and emergence of religious groups'.[23] Dobbelaere postulates 'an underlying modernization process—i.e. differentiation, rationalization, societalization, industrialization, urbanization, bureaucratization, mobility, etc.—on the disengagement of modern man from religious bodies'.[24] On the other hand he allows for contrary processes of 'delaicization' and 'desecularization'[25] and that 'secularization is not a mechanical process, and it allows for religious groups to react'.[26] Dobbelaere's framework is useful and will be used in the last section of this essay to summarize post-war changes in English Catholicism.

THE DISSOLUTION OF A DISTINCTIVE RELIGIO-ETHNIC SUBCULTURE

Up to the 1950s, English Catholicism could be said to have been characterized by policies of 'cultural defence' of its distinctive subculture, as Wallis and Bruce (See Chapter 2) suggested would be the case. By the 1980s, however, the protective walls around this subculture had all but dissolved away.

It is first necessary to note the strongly immigrant background of English Catholics. The best estimates available, based on the country-of-birth data from the 1971 and

1981 censuses, suggest that very nearly one English Catholic in four was born outside Great Britain. This is over four times the proportion of first-generation immigrants amongst the rest of the population.[27] Roughly half of these immigrants were from Ireland. Apart from those born outside Great Britain, a similar proportion were the children of immigrants. In sum, approximately one in eight Catholics are in each of the following categories: 'recusants' (that is those who could trace their Catholicism from pre-Reformation England), first-generation Irish, other immigrants, and second-generation Irish. There are around 8 or 9 per cent converts (allowing for children) and a similar number of second-generation immigrants with origins outside the British Isles. The balance of around one-third of English Catholics has a variety of other and mixed backgrounds but it is likely that the bulk of them will have an Irish ancestry which originated three or more generations ago. The strong immigrant background of many English Catholics is reflected in their lower age and social-class profiles.

Contrary to the myths, the Catholic Church during the nineteenth century and up to the 1950s was not a cohesive, tightly knit body, sharing the same values and beliefs, nor was it substantially united under a clerical leadership, and without divisive conflicts. Rather, the weak structural position of the Church in Ireland before the famine of 1845–9 had resulted in 'a low level of participation in the cycle of parish rituals and general ignorance of orthodox Catholic doctrine'.[28] There was concern about the massive 'leakage' of Irish Catholics from the faith well before the end of the nineteenth century and low levels of mass attendance were reported in the urban slums.[29] There were national and social class differences between English and Irish Catholics and evidence of clerical authoritarianism and lay resistance.[30] What historical evidence there is provides sufficient grounds to caution against an over-romanticization of the past. This is crucial to the interpretation of religious transformations which seem to indicate stronger elements of continuity than of decline.

Having warned against a 'golden age' view of English Catholicism and any exaggeration of its social and religious homogeneity, it is nevertheless useful to identify a number of features which led to its characterization as a distinctive religio-ethnic subculture at least up to the 1950s. Thus, it has been suggested that in the pre-Vatican II years it had an 'ultramontane' leadership with a special allegiance to the Pope and a stress on obedience in all religious matters (often widely defined) to the Roman See. It was said that it displayed distinctive norms and values of marital, sexual, and familial morality; that it had a unique sense of identity and separateness fostered by peculiarly Roman Catholic practices such as the retention of Latin in the liturgy and Friday abstinence.[31] It was particularly visible in supportive inner-city parishes[32] where there was a strong sense of boundary-maintenance and a fear of the erosion of Catholic values, which resulted in a tendency to defensiveness and 'keeping themselves to themselves',[33] and an emphasis on all-Roman Catholic marriages and on the segregated Catholic schools' system. Finally, it claimed to have distinctive views on social issues, with a special emphasis on the family, property ownership, and the principle of subsidiarity.[34]

This distinctive pre-Vatican II subculture, however, was largely dissolved in the post-war years as a result of both social and religious changes. First, the heterogeneity of religious beliefs and practices of English Catholics was demonstrated by the 1978 national survey. Surveys in four parishes showed that there was a considerable overlap in the beliefs and patterns of church attendance between Catholics and non-Catholics in England and Wales. There was strong evidence of considerable disaffection with the institutional church on the part of the youngest age-groups, similar to that common to other mainline churches which rely for member-ship recruitment primarily on the socialization of the children of existing members. There was also evidence of working-class alienation[35] and a growing gap between educated middle-class activists and ordinary Catholics, which is also a phenomenon familiar to other Christian churches.

Secondly, in the post-war period of relative affluence and expanded opportunities for educational and occupational advancement, the overall mean upward social mobility movement of Catholics was no greater than, and may even have been less than, that experienced in the population generally. However, when account was taken of the country of birth of the respondent, it appeared that Catholic men born in Great Britain had indeed a slight upward 'mobility momentum' relative to men in England and Wales generally but first-generation immigrants, especially the non-Irish Catholics, experienced either lower mobility movement or even downward mobility. In sum the evidence suggested that structural assimilation on the part of immigrant Catholics might take several generations but that for Catholics born in Great Britain the process had very largely been achieved. When considering patterns of religious practice and belief, there appeared to be some differences between Irish Catholics, who came to Britain from a tradition of high levels of religious practice, and other Catholic immigrants who appeared to bring with them a norm of non-practice. The relatively high rates of church attendance of first-generation Irish immigrants are consistent with the thesis of cultural defence on the part of a religio-ethnic group challenged by its early experiences in an alien secular culture, as Wallis and Bruce suggested would be the case. However, by the second generation evidence of cultural assimilation is indicated by a process of convergence to the religious norms of English Catholics. In the case of other immigrants it seemed that there might be a growing alienation from the institutional Church over two generations.

TABLE 6.1. *Distribution of Catholics by marriage type and year of marriage (%)*

Marriage type	Year of marriage					All R.C.s
	Up to 1939	– 1940–9	– 1950–9	– 1960–9	– 1970–7	
Valid non-mixed	68.5	64.6	68.5	51.6	30.2	52.8
Valid mixed	22.2	19.5	20.8	28.3	33.5	25.7
Invalid non-mixed	3.7	3.7	1.5	1.2	3.2	3.0
Invalid mixed	5.6	12.2	9.2	18.9	33.0	18.6
Weighted N = 100%	55	84	134	254	185	813

Source: Hornsby-Smith and Lee, *Roman Catholic Opinion*, 232.

TABLE 6.2. *Estimates of communal involvement over time*

Indicator of involvement	Late 1930s	Late 1950s	Late 1970s
Proportion of Roman Catholics in England and Wales (p%)	7	10	11
Proportion of Roman Catholics marrying Roman Catholics (m%)	72	60	31
Proportion of valid marriages (v%)	85	80	68
Proportion of Roman Catholics with half or more friends Roman Catholics (f_1%)	59	48	39
Proportion of Roman Catholics with half or more friends Roman Catholic at 17 (f_2%)	68	37	35
Index of marital endogamy (m/p)	10	6	3
Index of current in-group friendship (f_1/p)	8	5	4
Index of early in-group friendship (f_2/p)	10	4	3

Notes:
1. Estimates of the proportion of Roman Catholics in England and Wales have been based on Currie, *et al.*, *Churches and Churchgoers*, 153–5.
2. Estimates of communal involvement have been made from the analysis of age differences reported in Hornby-Smith and Lee, *Roman Catholic Opinion*. For Catholics marrying in the late 1930s the 65 and over cohort has been considered; for those marrying in the late 1950s the 35–49 year old cohort has bee taken; for those marrying in the late 1970s the 15–29 year old cohort has been taken.

Source: Hornsby-Smith, *Roman Catholics in England*, 183.

Thirdly, the full extent of the dissolution of the distinctive subculture is most apparent when the changing marital norms of Catholics are considered. Whereas before 1960 under one-third of Catholics were in religiously mixed marriages and around one in eight in canonically invalid (in the sense that they had not been solemnized by a priest) marriages, by the 1970s these proportions had increased dramatically to two-thirds in exogamous unions and well over one-third in invalid marriages (Table 6.1). These figures are eloquent testimony to the fact that, even if English Catholics were still more than three times as likely to marry other Catholics as their proportion in the general population would warrant (Table 6.2), by the 1980s there had been a major dissolution of the boundaries which for decades had safeguarded the religious identity of Catholics and ensured the distinctiveness of their separate subculture by the enforcement of religious and social sanctions against out-marriage. The evidence also showed that mixed marriages and, to a very much greater extent, invalid marriages were associated with deviation from the official norms of belief and practice. Apart from the evidence from marriage patterns, changes in the degrees to which Catholics selected their friends primarily from amongst other Catholics also indicated clearly the extent to which the boundaries separating the Catholic community from the rest of the population have steadily been dissolved since the end of the Second World War.

Fourthly, there has been substantial assimilation of Irish Catholics in England.[36] Some have stressed that where there is cultural defence in areas of strong and enduring community support, the process can be resisted.[37] All the same, analysis of the General Household Surveys indicates that well over half the first generation and nearly all the second-generation Irish immigrants marry non-Irish born (mainly British-born) spouses; such intermarriage greatly facilitates structural assimilation. There has also been convergence towards the indigenous English Catholic norms of religious intermarriage and canonically invalid marriage by the second generation. The Irish Catholics who contracted religiously endogamous marriages seemed to be able to retain distinctive patterns of religious beliefs and practices through to the second generation, while for those with non-Catholic spouses, assimilation to the norms of British Catholics in exogamous unions was complete by the second generation. It can be inferred, therefore, that the dissolution of the distinctiveness of the Catholic subculture can be retarded by the experience of migration but only where religious endogamy is preserved.

Fifthly, the dissolution of the boundaries defending a distinctive Catholic subculture can also be discerned through an examination of the political weight of English Catholicism. The argument here is more interpretive and points, for example, to the 'end of "passionate intensity" '[38] over the whole question of the Catholic schools' system and its financing, and the political impotence of Catholics substantially to ameliorate the legislation relating to abortion since the 1967 Act and to mobilize opposition to embryo experimentation. Although numerous, Roman Catholics are by no means united in their social, moral, and political beliefs and attitudes, even on such issues as abortion and the dual system of schooling in Britain. Furthermore, they have become widely dispersed throughout British society. The potential, therefore, for mobilizing them behind any particular campaign is strictly limited. This is particularly so as the tightly knit Catholic subculture of the early post-war years breaks down. Indeed Catholics in England prefer a 'domesticated Gospel' to a 'political Christianity'. It seems as if the long historical drive of English Catholics for respectability has ended in the demonstration that in political and social matters, their religion makes little discernible difference.

On the other hand one should be cautious about assuming that there was once a time when English Catholics had greater political clout. Thus in the review of English Catholicism to celebrate the centenary of the restoration of the hierarchy, Beck argued that:

the influence of the Catholic community in England on public life is by no means commensurate with its size, and there seems to be a good case for arguing that, at least until very recent years, this influence has been throughout the greater part of this century declining . . . Politically, since the withdrawal of the Irish Members [from the House of Commons], the Catholic influence has, on the whole, been negligible.[39]

The findings relating to the contemporary political weaknesses of English Catholicism do not, therefore, provide unambiguous support for a secularization thesis.

In sum, the changes in English Catholicism over the past three or four decades can best be interpreted as a process of increasing relaxation of the boundaries which once defended a distinctively Catholic subculture from contamination in a basically secular society. It is too simplistic, however, to regard such a process as one of decline. Rather it indicates that far-reaching changes have taken place in the relationships between the Church and British society since the Second World War. These have necessarily entailed radical changes in the nature of the Catholic identity in England and Wales today. English Catholicism has become more respectable and acceptable; it is subject to lower levels of hostility and increasing tolerance. These are the consequences of the post-war economic recovery and the attendant processes of social and geographical mobility. The result is the structural and cultural assimilation of a substantially immigrant ethnic community. There is no need to presume that these changes have an exclusively religious significance and hence are indicative of a process of secularization. Philip Hammond's thoughtful discussion of the persistence of (changed forms of) religious identity in a time of rapid social change seems to capture well the reality of the transformations which have taken place in English Catholicism.[40] In spite of the protestations of its proponents that 'countervailing factors may sometimes operate', as Wallis and Bruce have conceded, secularization is seen as a normal concomitant of moderniza-tion. This appears to prejudge the issue and inhibit the process of discerning elements of new life as well as evidence of decline.

CUSTOMARY RELIGION AND CHANGES IN RELIGIOUS AUTHORITY

Apart from the quantitative data obtained from representative samples of English Catholics, a large number of tape-recorded, focused interviews were carried out with various samples of Catholics ranging, on the one hand, from 'core' Catholics, such as members of the bishops' national advisory commissions, to, on the other hand, random samples of Catholic electors in four parishes, and people who attended one of the public events during the visit of the Pope to Britain in 1982, that is 'ordinary' Catholics.[41]

In a recent study I have described and interpreted the wide range of religious accounts given by both 'core' and 'ordinary' Catholics. In the first instance, the religion of core Catholics demonstrated a considerable measure of heterogeneity of belief and practice. For ordinary Catholics, however, the most striking phenomenon was the pervasiveness of 'customary'

Catholicism, which consists of those beliefs and practices that are derived from official Catholicism but are not subject to continued control by the Church. When considering questions of religious authority, there was evidence of a surprising amount of contestation on the part of the national activists and the paradox of overwhelmingly favourable responses of ordinary Catholics to the Pope as a person, but also a quite definite willingness to disregard his teaching and to 'make up one's own mind' on a wide range of issues, but particularly those of personal morality, such as contraception.[42]

What the data indicated was that there was a pluralism of Catholic beliefs and practices which pointed to a distinct 'hierarchy of truths' in the minds of most Catholics. In the absence of directly comparable data over a significant time span, it is perhaps hazardous to comment on probable changes over time. But it does seem likely that up to the 1950s Catholics differentiated relatively little between creedal beliefs, non-creedal beliefs such as papal infallibility, teachings on moral issues (especially those dealing with personal sexuality, such as contraception), and disciplinary rules (such as the mass attendance obligation, the prohibition of intercommunion or the frequency of confession). In a strongly rule-bound and guilt-ridden Church, where notions of mortal sin and eternal damnation were strongly emphasized, it seems that Catholics were just as likely to feel coerced to conform on matters of abstinence (or what was generally referred to as 'fish on Fridays'!) as they were to avoid contraception or to believe in the Trinity. It also seems likely that with the 'loss of the fear of hell'[43] from the 1960s, this is much less true today.

It is, therefore, a reasonable inference from the interview data that beliefs have become more differentiated in recent decades and that from a relative uniformity of beliefs in a fortress Church there has emerged a more pluralistic set of beliefs in the more voluntaristic, post-Vatican II Church. Such a pluralism of beliefs has been reflected in the plurality of responses to clerical, and especially papal authority in the Church. The evidence is that very few English Catholics confer an unqualified legitimacy on the teaching of the Pope, but it is not at all clear that they, as opposed to their clerical leaders, ever did. The data indicated a considerable degree of pluralism and a clear propensity to differentiate between 'religious' matters (where the clerical leaders still have legitimate authority, though even here, in a participatory, 'people of God' model of the Church, some committed lay people feel perfectly entitled to a share in that authority), and 'moral' and 'regulatory' or 'disciplinary' issues (where the individual in a human context familiar only to him or her has the legitimate authority in the last analysis to make up his or her own mind).

How are we to evaluate the qualitative data obtained from a wide range of English Catholics in the decade between the mid-1970s and the mid-1980s? Directly comparable data from earlier periods, say the 1950s, are not available. Claims that there have been significant transformations in the nature of the beliefs and ways of legitimating religious authority in recent decades have therefore been made on the basis of reasonable inferences about what the situation was at some earlier point in time. Some independent validation of these inferences was provided by our interviewees (1) when they referred to changes which they had themselves experienced in the course of their lives, and (2) when they contrasted their own religious socialization and beliefs with those of their own adult children.

Can the transformations which we have reasonably inferred to have taken place be regarded as evidence of secularization? First, on the point of selecting an appropriate earlier starting point, it has been argued that, at least since the rapid growth of the Roman Catholic community in England from the time of massive Irish immigration in the nineteenth century, there never was a 'golden age'. Secondly, I have previously concluded that theories of secularization are difficult to substantiate because of the problematic nature of the relevant criteria for the measurement of the 'religious' and because there have been changes in the meaning and significance of traditional practices over the past two decades.

The detailed analysis of the focused-interview data does not shake that judgment. My suspicion is that a more detailed comparison of the transcripts with the accounts of Catholic belief and practice in the early years of this century, such as are to be found in Hugh McLeod's analyses of the Booth researches of religion in working-class London, would indeed show substantial similarities in the categories of belief.[44] When due allowance is taken of the special leadership role of the priest for Irish working class immigrants in the impoverished working-class ghettos of the time, similar categories for the legitimation of religious authority are also likely. Certainly there is evidence of a less than total compliance to the priests and of some bitter struggles with the clerical leadership in this historical material.

In his Riddell Memorial Lectures, Wilson suggested that secularization 'is the major contemporary transformation of religion'[45] which follows an inevitable 'gradual, uneven, at times an oscillating, trend, the general direction of which is none the less unmistakable, in the nature of human consciousness, towards what might be called a "matter-of-fact" orientation to the world'.[46] There is well-documented evidence of decline, in terms of many traditional indicators of involvement in institutional religion (for example, mass attendance, priestly vocations, adult conversions, endogamous marriages, confessions, etc.). The interview data have also provided evidence for the existence of a rational–pragmatic worldview and its concomitant emphasis on 'making up your own mind'. Some changes reflect the fact that as Catholics have moved, both socially and religiously, out of the static, defensive, fortress Church, their identity has shifted from the involuntary 'collective–expressive' form to the voluntary 'individual–expressive' form as Hammond has suggested.[47] On the other hand it is necessary to allow for the emergence of new manifestations of religious vitality, such as weekly communions, participation in new forms of communal prayer, emergent forms of spirituality and of social concern, or participation in programmes of renewal such as that in one diocese where nearly one-third of adult mass attenders met in small groups during the five, six-weekly 'seasons' of RENEW. In sum, in spite of Wilson's confident assertions, the empirical evidence provides good grounds for being wary of the concept of secularization.

The evidence summarized in this section has been mainly concerned with Dobbelaere's individual level of analysis and only secondarily with the organizational level. There are indications of an emergent pluralism, especially of religious beliefs and ways of legitimizing religious authority. According to Dobbelaere, 'religious and cultural pluralism . . . stimulates the privatization or individuation of religion'.[48] Such a process seems to have been particularly evident in the challenges to clerical authority over contraception, in the criticisms which I have categorized as inadequate reasoning, and 'incoherent' or 'resented' authority, and 'confined', 'appropriated' and 'redefined' legitimacy.[49] Berger has pointed out, however, that a danger of 'subjectivization', where 'subjective emotionality takes the place of objective dogma as a criterion of religious legitimacy', is that there is a relativization of the religious content.[50]

There is, therefore, first an increasing differentiation of religious belief and moral decision-making where previously it might be inferred that the priest was the sole focus of legitimate teaching and arbiter of morality. Secondly, there has been a decline of some traditional forms of religious involvement, but against this it is necessary to take due account of new, emergent forms of religious vitality, what Hervieu-Léger has called the 'paradox of modernity'.[51] Thirdly, there is clear evidence of religious change from the pre- to post-Vatican II models of the Church and theological legitimations.[52] According to Koopmanschap, for the individual Catholic it is precisely at the crossroads between tradition and modernity, between old symbols of old authoritarian social structures and new social experience, that the contemporary Roman Catholic is called to perform his *bricolage*.[53] In sum, in the rich plurality of religious thinking and practice reported by our respondents we can discern evidence of both secularizing and counter-secularizing tendencies.

ENGLISH CATHOLICISM AND DIMENSIONS OF SECULARIZATION

In this final section a brief and tentative sketch is offered of transformations in English Catholicism in the post-war period in terms of Dobbelaere's three dimensions of secularization.

Figure 6.1 offers a summary of both secularizing tendencies and counter-secularizing tendencies or indications of religious revitalization at each level.

	LEVEL		
	Societal	Organizational	Individual
TENDENCY			
Secularizing	Welfare State Public Policy	Bishops' Commissions (+) Teaching Religious (−) Catholic Organizations (−) Catholic Action (−)	Privatization (+) Trad. Indicators (−) Trad. Devotions (−) Confession (−) Trad. Morality (−)
Counter-Secularizing	Church Lobby for 'Guildford Four' Hospice Movement Development Lobby	Dual School System Child Welfare work (+) CIIR/CHAS Lay Participation (+) Ecumenism (+) Married Deacons (+) Brusselmann Catechesis Multiple Groups (+) Pastoral Centres (+) Renewal Programmes (+)	Anti-dualism (+) Social Justice (+) Lay Spirituality (+) Lay Participation (+) General Absolution Holy Communion Lay Catechism (+)

Note: (+) and (−) indicate 'more' and 'less'.

FIG. 6.1. *Summary of examples of secularizing and counter-secularizing tendencies in post-1945 English Catholicism*

The first three cells indicate that there clearly are some secularizing tendencies at all three levels. In the first cell, which refers to the process of 'laicization', there does seem to be evidence of the societal processes of structural differentiation. There seems to be little doubt that over time the churches have gradually lost control over many areas, such as medicine and welfare, which have increasingly become dominated by differentiated occupational groups controlled by the State. This long-term process has continued in the post-war years and Catholic welfare agencies have had to become increasingly professionalized since the initial strong opposition of the Catholic bishops, who feared the concentration of State power in the Welfare-State proposals of the early post-war years.[54]

In general the influence of English Catholicism on public policy issues has been slight. I have argued elsewhere that there has been a significant decline in the political clout of English Catholicism since the early post-war years and the battles over the operation of the 1944 Education Act.[55] This is also apparent in the continuing failures substantially to influence public policy in the matter of abortion and embryo research. Such a decline is perhaps the inevitable consequence of the social and cultural transition of the largely immigrant community and the dissolution of the distinctive English Catholic subculture. On the other hand one can, perhaps, point to Cardinal Hume's influence in the case of the release of the Guildford Four, and the emergence of the hospice movement and the strength of a reputable development lobby as indications of counter-secularizing tendencies at the societal level.

At the organizational level there has been the emergence of bureaucratically administered advisory structures both at the national and at the diocesan levels. Secularizing trends are perhaps most obvious in the massive reductions in the numbers of priests and members of religious orders teaching in Catholic schools in recent years. While there were 202 secular clergy in Catholic schools in 1964, the number in 1988 had declined to only 26. Over the same period the number of men teachers from religious orders fell by three-quarters and female members of religious orders by nine-tenths. On the other hand one can point to the development of a very extensive Catholic schools' system and the continuation of Catholic welfare agencies as indications of counter-secularizing tendencies.

There has also been a steady decline and a noticeable ageing of the memberships of many traditional Catholic lay organizations. They are less obviously regarded as being under direct hierarchy control and as an arm of Catholic Action. But against this, there has been the emergence of powerful new, lay-run and substantially autonomous organizations such as the Catholic Institute for International Relations (CIIR), Pax Christi and the Catholic Housing Aid Society (CHAS). I would suggest that these represent new forms of commitment, with an explicitly religious legitimation, to a leaven-like mission to a variety of 'oppressed' groups.

There are a number of other indicators of religious vitality at the organizational level. I do not find Wilson's interpretation of ecumenical developments as signs of institutional weakness convincing.[56] I am more impressed by Towler's insistence that the theological rationale for renewed endeavours to seek Christian unity put forward by ecumenists must be given due weight.[57] Other signs of a renewed Catholicism at the organizational level include the shift from a mechanistic to a participative, organic organizational model of the Church at a time of massive social change and economic reconstruction.

There is also evidence of a plurality of small groups: prayer groups and neighbourhood, family, justice and peace and other special-interest groups, which provide some measure of social support, religious legitimation, and encouragement. The proliferation of pastoral centres and programmes of renewal, such as the RENEW 'process' mentioned above, testify to a vigorous religious life at the organizational level.

At the level of individual involvement, aggregate ecclesiastical statistics testify to significant declines on most of the traditional indicators in recent decades. Since 1960 the numbers of Catholics attending mass regularly is down by almost one-third. Growth is to be found only amongst the number of deaths recorded by parish priests! All other religious services, adult receptions or 'conversions', baptisms, first communions, confirmations, and marriages, are down by between one-third and two-fifths and the proportion of religiously 'mixed' marriages has increased from one-half in 1960 to two-thirds by the end of the 1980s. Traditional devotions such as benediction have also substantially disappeared. The number of priests has also declined, by about one-tenth in the same period. All these statistics of decline support a secularization hypothesis.

At the individual level, perhaps the most striking example of decline is in the frequency of personal confession, which may be interpreted as indicative of secularization. But against this it might be argued that there have been major shifts in the meaning and interpretation of confession and a shift of emphasis from the private confession of sins to a priest to the notion of reconciliation with both God and neighbour. Thus opportunities for general absolution are always hugely popular and well-supported by nominal Catholics. There has also been a major increase in the numbers attending holy communion regularly; again this seems best interpreted as reflecting a shift in the understanding of the sacraments in recent years.

Many parishes run schemes for the preparation of children for their first communion that involve parents, relatives and the wider parochial community in quite new ways. There seems to be little doubt that the reading of scripture, frequently in the context of small group participation, is very much more common amongst Catholics than it was a generation ago. All these trends are indicative of strong elements of religious revival and hence of counter-secularization. Other indications include the steady increases in the numbers of parish churches, permanent deacons, and lay catechists. There has also been a vigorous emergence of new forms of spirituality, notably influenced by the charismatic movement.

The increasing participation of lay people in the planning and practice of liturgical worship can only be regarded as evidence of secularization with very restricted definitions of the 'proper' place of lay people *vis-à-vis* the clergy. Mary Douglas has bemoaned the fact that 'Now the English Catholics are like everyone else' over such matters as fasting regulations.[58] As the evidence I have reviewed above indicates, there is also a considerable measure of privatization in their religion. On the other hand, it can be argued that counter-indications are to be found in the strong opposition to a dualism between religion and politics amongst justice and peace activists. There is also an increasing awareness of social justice concerns as being scripturally rooted and an essential component of a Christian commitment.

In sum, an analysis based on the Dobbelaere levels of analysis and dimensions of secularization indicates clearly that while there are certainly indications of decline on a large number of variables related to an older, pre-Vatican II style of Catholicism, there is also evidence, not only of the salience of a revived Catholicism, but of the emergence of new forms of being a committed Catholic. In an organic, participative, 'people of God', post-Vatican II model of the Church, new forms of interpreting the vocation of the lay person are emerging which cannot adequately be described as secularization.

CONCLUSIONS

I have shown that the major changes in English Catholicism in the post-war years of social change and the post-Vatican II years of religious change cannot unequivocally be regarded as convincing evidence for a secularization thesis. In the first place there are good conceptual, historical, and methodological reasons to be wary of such a 'catch-all' term. Rather, it is more helpful to sociological analysis to recognize the multidimensional character of contemporary Catholicism and hence the complexity of the empirical reality of both decline in some areas and new growth and vitality in others.

Secondly, I have summarized recent empirical studies of English Catholicism to argue that the high, defensive walls which protected the 'fortress' model of the Church (in an environment until the 1950s perceived as intrinsically hostile) have been dissolved in the solvent of social and religious change, declining hostility and increasing indifference, and more friendly ecumenical relationships. There has, therefore, inevitably been a decline of the politics of cultural defence. Such changes in the social context have inevitably changed English Catholicism but there is no reason to regard those changes as decline. As Catholics move from a tightly organized religio-ethnic community with its high premium on communal solidarity, marital endogamy, and 'pillarized' schools' system into the mainstream, it is only to be expected that there will be a fundamental change in the nature of being a Catholic.

With the emergence from the distinctive subculture, English Catholics have increasingly seemed like everyone else. But it is at least arguable that the evidence of a plurality of religious beliefs and practices, and especially of ways of regarding matters of religious authority, including the significant evidence of 'making up your own mind', are largely making manifest what was previously suppressed in an oppressive pre-Vatican II Church. With the loss of the fear of hell and of priests, 'paradoxical' Catholics can now happily delight in the character of the Pope while at the same time reserving substantial areas of moral judgment to themselves. There is no reason to suppose that the signs of customary Catholicism, which the qualitative interviews unmasked, would not also have been found, albeit in somewhat different forms, if similar styles of research had been undertaken in the pre-Vatican II period.

Thirdly, apart from my own research data, I have also offered a tentative sketch in terms of Dobbelaere's framework to demonstrate that, at each of his three levels, there is evidence of revival and new forms of religious growth to balance evidence of decline and secularizing tendencies. Such evidence supports the chief claim of this essay that, rather than interpret religious changes in Catholicism in terms of the relentless imperatives of the process of secularization, it is empirically more appropriate to distinguish between growth and decline along different dimensions of the contemporary expressions of religion. Behind the external evidence of a sleepy, domesticated, respectable, self-satisfied denomination, lurk numerous indications of growth and challenge, new forms of spirituality and ways of interpreting this-worldly concerns in the light of scriptural imperatives, new ways of being members of a more participative Church, and a greater recognition of the 'pilgrim' nature of being a Catholic than was ever the case in the mechanistic Church up to the 1950s. To call these transformations secularization is to fail to recognize the evidence of institutional revival.

NOTES

1. I am most grateful to Bryan Wilson and Karel Dobbelaere for their very generous and critically constructive reading of an

earlier version of this paper given at All Souls College, Oxford, on 8 Mar. 1990. As a result of their suggestions I have substantially revised the paper. Even so, they may not agree with much of it and I should stress that the weaknesses which remain are entirely my own responsibility. My thanks are also due to Steve Bruce for valuable editorial advice.

2. P. E. Hammond, 'Religion and the Persistence of Identity', *Journal for the Scientific Study of Religion* 27 (1988), 1–11.

3. K. Dobbelaere, 'Secularization: A Multi-Dimensional Concept', *Current Sociology* 29 (1981), 11–12.

4. K. Dobbelaere, 'Secularization Theories and Sociological Paradigms: A Reformulation of the Private–Public Dichotomy and the Problem of Societal Integration', *Sociological Analysis* 46 (1985), 377–87.

5. B. R. Wilson, *Contemporary Transformations*; Dobbelaere, 'Secularization: A Multi-Dimensional Concept'; K. Dobbelaere, 'Some Trends in European Sociology of Religion: The Secularization Debate', *Sociological Analysis* 48 (1987), 107–37.

6. B. R. Wilson, 'Secularization: The Inherited Model', in P. E. Hammond, (ed.), *The Sacred in a Secular Age: Toward Revision in the Scientific Study of Religion* (Los Angeles, 1985), 12.

7. Details of the main data sources, including the 1978 national survey of Roman Catholics in England, have been given in Hornsby-Smith, *Roman Catholics in England*, 9–13. The substantive findings have been presented chiefly there and in M. P. Hornsby-Smith, *Roman Catholic Beliefs in England: Customary Religion and Transformations of Religious Authority* (Cambridge, 1991) and in Hornsby-Smith and R. M. Lee, *Roman Catholic Opinion: A Study of Roman Catholics in England and Wales in the 1970s* (Guildford, 1979); Hornsby-Smith, Lee, and K. A. Turcan, 'A Typology of English Catholics', *Sociological Review* 30 (1982), 433–59 (1978: 9–13); Hornsby-Smith, Lee, and P. A. Reilly, 'Social and Religious Change in Four English Roman Catholic Parishes', *Sociology* 18 (1984), 353–65; Hornsby-Smith, Lee, and Reilly, 'Common Religion and Customary Religion: A Critique and a Proposal', *Review of Religious Research* 26 (1985), 244–52; Hornsby-Smith, Turcan, and L. T. Rajan, 'Patterns of Religious Commitment, Intermarriage and Marital Breakdown Among English Catholics', *Archives de Sciences Sociales Des Religions* 64 (1987), 137–55. Methodological problems in the interpretation of interview data were considered in Hornsby-Smith, 'Catholic Accounts: Problems of Institutional Involvement', in G. N. Gilbert and P. Abell (eds.), *Accounts and Action* (Aldershot, 1983), 132–52. An earlier attempt to

address the secularization debate in terms of Martin's *General Theory* (Oxford, 1978) was given in Hornsby-Smith, 'Into the Mainstream: Recent Transformations in British Catholicism', in T. M. Gannon (ed.), *World Catholicism in Transition* (London, 1988), 219–31.

8. M. P. Hornsby-Smith, J. Fulton, and M. Norris, 'Assessing RENEW: A Study of a Renewal Movement in a Roman Catholic Diocese in England', in J. Fulton and P. Gee (eds.), *Power in Religion: Decline and Growth?* (London, 1991), 101–14.

9. B. R. Wilson, 'Secularization: The Inherited Model', 11.

10. Martin, 'Towards Eliminating', 169–82.

11. Martin, *The Religious and the Secular*, and *General Theory*.

12. B. R. Wilson, 'Secularization: The Inherited Model', 11.

13. B. R. Wilson, *Religion in Secular Society*, xiv. A slightly modified wording is given in B. R. Wilson, *Religion in Sociological Perspective*, 149.

14. B. R. Wilson, *Religion in Secular Society*, 1–18.

15. T. Luckmann, *The Invisible Religion: The Problem of Religion in Modern Society* (London, 1970).

16. R. Ireland, *The Challenge of Secularization* (Melbourne, 1988).

17. A. M. Greeley, *Religious Change in America* (Cambridge, 1989), 5.

18. McLeod, *Class and Religion*; *Religion and the People*; and 'New Perspectives'.

19. K. Dobbelaere, 'The Secularization of Society? Some Methodological Suggestions', in J. K. Hadden and A. Shupe (eds.), *Secularization and Fundamentalism Reconsidered* (New York, 1989), 28.

20. B. R. Wilson, *Religion in Secular Society*.

21. E.g., Greeley, *Religious Change*.

22. E.g., B. R. Wilson, *Religion in Sociological Perspective* and 'Secularization: The Inherited Model'; Dobbelaere, 'The Secularization of Society?'.

23. Dobbelaere, 'Secularization: A Multi-Dimensional Concept', 11–12, and 'Secularization Theories'.

24. Dobbelaere, 'Secularization: A Multi-Dimensional Concept', 136–7.

25. Ibid., 67–70.

26. Dobbelaere, 'The Secularization of Society?', 37.

27. M. P. Hornsby-Smith, 'The Immigrant Background of Roman Catholics in England and Wales: A Research Note', *New Community* 13 (1986), 79–85.

28. L. H. Lees, *Exiles of Erin: Irish Migrants in Victorian London* (Manchester, 1979).

29. J. Hickey, *Urban Catholics: Urban Catholicism in England and Wales from 1829 to the Present Day* (London, 1967), 90–4; McLeod, *Class and Religion*, 34–5.

30. McLeod, *Class and Religion*, 74, and *Religion and the People*, 128–31.

31. M. Douglas, *Natural Symbols: Explorations in Cosmology* (Harmondsworth, 1973).

32. Hickey, *Urban Catholics*; J. Rex and R. Moore, *Race, Community and Conflict: A Study of Sparkbrook* (Oxford, 1967); C. Ward, *Priests and People: A Study in the Sociology of Religion* (Liverpool, 1965).

33. G. Scott, *The RCs: Report on Roman Catholics in Britain Today* (London, 1967).

34. P. Coman, *Catholics and the Welfare State* (London, 1977).

35. A. Archer, *The Two Catholic Churches: A Study in Oppression* (London, 1986).

36. Hornsby-Smith, *Roman Catholics in England*, 116–32, 212–13; Hornsby-Smith and A. Dale, 'The Assimilation of Irish Immigrants in England', *British Journal of Sociology* 39 (1988), 519–44; W. Ryan, 'Assimilation of Irish Immigrants in Britain', Ph.D. thesis (St Louis, 1973).

37. M. J. Hickman, 'A Study of the Incorporation of the Irish in Britain with Special Reference to Catholic State Education: Involving a Comparison of the Attitudes of Pupils and Teachers in Selected Catholic Schools in London and Liverpool', Ph.D. thesis (London, 1990).

38. J. Murphy, *Church, State and Schools in Britain: 1800–1970* (London, 1971), 121–9.

39. G. A. Beck, 'Today and Tomorrow', in G. A. Beck (ed.), *The English Catholics 1850–1950* (London, 1950), 585–614. Quotation is on 602–3.

40. Hammond, 'Religion'.

41. R. K. Merton and P. L. Kendall, *The Focused Interview* (Glencoe, 1956).

42. F. Houtart, 'Conflicts of Authority in the Roman Catholic Church', *Social Compass* 16 (1969), 309–25.

43. D. Lodge, *How Far Can You Go?* (London, 1980).

44. McLeod, *Class and Religion*, 72–80.

45. B. R. Wilson, *Contemporary Transformations*, 112.

46. Ibid. 11.

47. Hammond, 'Religion'.

48. Dobbelaere, 'Secularization: A Multi-Dimensional Concept'.

49. Hornsby-Smith, *Roman Catholic Beliefs*.

50. Berger, *Social Reality of Religion*, 156–9; Dobbelaere, 'Secularization: A Multi-Dimensional Concept', 117.

51. D. Hervieu-Lâger, *Vers un nouveau christianisme? Introduction à la sociologie du christianisme occidental* (Paris, 1986), 224–7; quoted in Davie, G., ' "An Ordinary God": The Paradox of Religion in Contemporary Britain', *British Journal of Sociology* 41 (1990), 395–421.

52. M. P. Hornsby-Smith, *The Changing Parish: A Study of Parishes, Priests, and Parishioners After Vatican II* (London, 1989).

53. T. Koopmanschap, 'Transformations in Contemporary Roman Catholicism: A Case Study', Ph.D. thesis (Liverpool, 1978), 49.

54. Coman, *Catholics*.

55. Hornsby-Smith, *Roman Catholics in England*, 157–81.

56. B. R. Wilson, *Religion in Secular Society*, 126.

57. R. Towler, *Homo Religiosus*, 165.

58. Douglas, *Natural Symbols*, 67.

7

An Unsecular America

ROGER FINKE

SINCE the founding of the discipline, sociologists have used the secularization model to explain the inevitable decay of religion. Harboured within the broad theoretical framework of modernization, the traditional model has long proposed that as industrialization, urbanization, and rationalization come to dominate a society, religion will recede. Yet support for this model is far from uniform and, in recent years, debate over the secularization model has come to the fore.

The debate, however, has often strayed from a systematic evaluation or testing of the traditional model of secularization. Indeed, Hadden has argued that support and opposition for the secularization model are driven by ideology as well as science. Hadden states that 'secularization theory has not been subjected to systematic scrutiny because it is a *doctrine* more than it is a theory'.[1] He suggests that the notion of secularization was quickly adopted because it fitted well with the evolutionary model of modernization and with the beliefs of sociologists.[2] Likewise, Martin has noted that the 'whole concept' of secularization 'appears as a tool of counter-religious ideologies'.[3] But those who offer revision or opposition to the secularization model have not been free of ideological baggage either. Johnson has proposed that 'divisions of opinion on the issues of secularization reflect religious and to some extent political predilections'.[4] Perhaps more than any other topic, debate over the secularization model has fallen prey to subjective beliefs, personal experiences, and historic nostalgia.

In this essay I propose to test the secularization model against the empirical evidence on religion in the USA. Does the evidence reveal a decay of religion since the advent of modernization? And what is the relationship between religious change and the major social changes of the past two

centuries? Since the secularization model describes an historical process that occurs in conjunction with modernization, I
will first use historical data to follow the long-term trends in
religion. Then I will select several time periods to test the
relationship between religion and the various measures of
modernization. Here I will attempt to test the specific
predictions the model offers on the relationship between
religion and the various aspects of modernization. For
example, is religion inversely related with urbanization,
industrialization, and rationalization? Finally, I will suggest
that the deregulation of religion in America helps to explain
why the religious changes there have not paralleled those of
western Europe.

But, first, let me clarify how the concept of secularization
will be defined and measured.

THE TRADITIONAL MODEL

When Hadden summarized the model of secularization
proposed by early sociologists, he offered the following three-
sentence translation of secularization theory:

Once the world was filled with the sacred—in thought, practice, and
institutional form. After the Reformation and the Renaissance, the
forces of modernization swept across the globe and secularization, a
corollary historical process, loosened the dominance of the sacred.
In due course, the sacred shall disappear altogether except, possibly,
in the private realm.[5]

Although this model has undergone revisions and challenges,
the core continues to guide the research and theory of
sociologists. The dominance of the sacred is in decline.

In contemporary work, Bryan Wilson is probably the most
widely cited and well-respected proponent of the traditional
model. He has written extensively on how the traditional
model applies to contemporary societies and has helped to
clarify both the definitions and the relationships between the
concepts used in the traditional model of secularization. He
explains that secularization relates to the decrease in the
'social significance of religion' and goes on to outline how this
can be applied to contemporary societies:

Its application covers such things as the sequestration by political powers of the property and facilities of religious agencies; the shift from religious to secular control of various of the erstwhile activities and functions of religion; the decline in the proportion of their time, energy, and resources which men devote to super-empirical concerns; the decay of religious institutions; the supplanting, in matters of behaviour, of religious precepts by demands that accord with strictly technical criteria; and the gradual replacement of a specifically religious consciousness . . . by an empirical, rational, instrumental orientation; the abandonment of mythical, poetic, and artistic interpretations of nature and society in favour of matter-of-fact description and, with it, the rigorous separation of evaluative and emotive dispositions from cognitive and positivistic orientations.[6]

The applications, or indicators, proposed by Wilson fall into three broad areas. The first area addresses Church–State relations and the functions performed by each, the second touches on the vitality of religious institutions, and the third covers the behaviours, thoughts, and beliefs of individuals.

I will *not* attempt to test the first area since the principles for separating Church and State are given in the First Amendment, and are supported by numerous court cases.[7] Indeed, if the separation of Church and State is used as an indicator of secularization in the USA, the process of secularization preceded the advent of modernization and the USA is currently far more secularized than western Europe.[8] I would agree that the separation of Church and State plays an important role in explaining religious change in the USA, but I would question whether the changes are well explained by the traditional model of secularization.[9]

The next two areas—institutional vitality and individual behaviour, thoughts, and beliefs—will receive extensive attention in this essay. Have religious institutions followed a trend of 'decay'? Did the 'time, energy, and resources which men [and women] devote to super-empirical concerns' decline? For each of these areas there are historical data to document the long-term trends of institutional resources and individual commitment. Using a variety of indicators, I will look at the vitality of religious institutions and the willingness of individuals to commit time, energy, and resources to super-empirical concerns.

The most difficult challenge will be to measure historical trends in individual thoughts and beliefs. Documenting long-term trends in 'religious consciousness' or 'artistic interpretations of nature' would be nearly impossible even if we had the benefit of eighteenth and nineteenth-century surveys. None the less, I will report evidence that indirectly addresses these issues. Which churches continue to retain a popular appeal to the people? In order to attract members have they been forced to make their teachings more rational, more positivistic and less mythical? I begin by looking at American religion over the past two hundred years. Do the trends support the traditional model of secularization?

FROM COLONIAL TO CONTEMPORARY RELIGION

The vibrancy and growth of American religious institutions presents the most open defiance of the secularization model. Historians have long noted the low level of religious involvement in colonial America, as compared to modern levels of involvement;[10] but in recent work Rodney Stark and I have provided more accurate estimates on church membership during the late-eighteenth and mid-nineteenth century.[11] Figure 7.1 charts the church adherence rate from 1776 to 1980. The rate more than doubles from 1776 to 1860 (17 per cent to 37 per cent), declines slightly following the immense dislocations of the Civil War, and continues on a steady increase from 1870 to 1926. Since 1926 the rate has hovered around 60 per cent. If we were able to conduct a closer year-by-year inspection, the trend line would probably show a slight decline in the 1930s,[12] a small increase in the 1950s, another slight decline in the late 1960s and early 1970s, and a small increase in the 1980s; but the dominant trend since 1926 is that of stability. Rather than declining, the proportion churched showed rapid growth from 1776 to 1890 and has shown exceptional stability from 1926 to the present. Rather than decaying, religious institutions have shown a remarkable capacity for mobilizing people into the pew.

However, critics might rightfully suggest that church membership requires little individual commitment and provides no guarantee of institutional health. What happens after

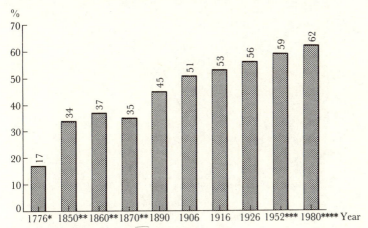

* Stark and Finke, 'American Religion in 1776'.
** Finke and Stark, 'Turning Pews into People'.
*** Zelinsky, 'Approach to Religious Geography'.
**** Stark, 'Correcting Church Membership Rates'.

FIG. 7.1. *Rates of religious adherence 1776–1980*

people join churches? Are they willing to sacrifice valuable personal resources for the survival of their church? In other words, will they give of their money and time?

Figure 7.2 shows the increase in contributions per member during the last century, even when standardized to 1967 dollars. The total contribution per member more than doubled between 1950 and 1986.[13] Moreover, Figure 7.3 illustrates a similar trend in the nineteenth century. The value of church property per adherent, as reported by the census, more than doubled between 1850 and 1906 (when controlling for inflation). And, since the rate of church adherence was increasing rapidly at the end of the nineteenth century, the value of church property per person in the population more than tripled (again, controlling for inflation). Whether it is the nineteenth or twentieth century, people are not simply joining churches, they are making large financial sacrifices to support their church, and the sacrifice per member is increasing rather than declining.

Unfortunately, other indicators of religious commitment and consciousness are restricted to recent survey data and are not able to show long-term trends. None the less, when we look

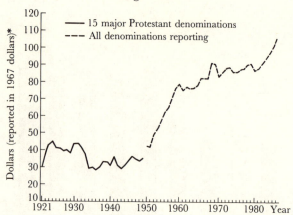

* The Bureau of Labour Statistics' Consumer Price Index was used to control for changes in the cost of living (US Bureau of Census 1975).

Note: The first part of the graph was compiled by Harry S. Myers and reported in the *Yearbook of American Churches* 1949 and 1952; the second part was drawn from data in the *Yearbook of American and Canadian Churches* (and the *Yearbook of American Churches*).

Fig. 7.2. *Church contributions per member 1921–86*

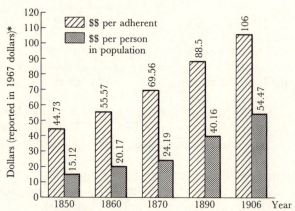

* The Bureau of Labour Statistics' Consumer Price Index was used to control for changes in the cost of living (US Bureau of the Census 1975).

Fig. 7.3. *Value of church property per church adherent and per person in US population 1850–1906*

at survey data beginning in 1939, as shown in Figure 7.4, we can see that there has been little variation in the percentage of

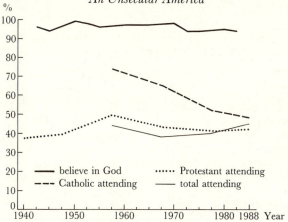

%
100
90
80
70
60
50
40
30
20 —— believe in God ····· Protestant attending
10 --- Catholic attending —— total attending
0
1940   1950   1960   1970   1980 1988 Year

Sources: Gallup Jr., and Castelli, *The People's Religion*; Gallup Organization, *Religion in America* (Princeton, NJ, 1987).

FIG. 7.4. *Percent attending church and who believe in God 1940–88*

the population stating a belief in God. And while the percentage regularly attending church has declined slightly, this seems to be largely a change in the attendance of Catholics and not Protestants.[14] Neither trend line shows a dramatic change in religious belief or behaviour.

But perhaps the most convincing evidence of the people's willingness to still give time, energy, and resources to religion is the rapid growth of the most demanding religions. In 1972 Dean Kelley's book, entitled *Why Conservative Churches are Growing*, documented the growth of strict and demanding churches. The trend has not changed since 1972. Table 7.1 shows the remarkably close correspondence between a denomination's membership growth and the commitment of their membership from 1972 to 1984. In fact, the Pearson r between membership growth and denominational commitment is a huge ·79, and the correlation between membership growth and percent attending church regularly is an identical ·79. The growing churches are making strong demands on their members' time, energy and resources.[15]

Moreover, this trend is not confined to recent decades.[16] In the early nineteenth century, Methodist members were expected to attend class meetings, Sunday services, and camp meetings, as well as conform to the strict demands of the *Discipline*. The demands were no less stringent for the clergy,

TABLE 7.1. *Membership growth, denominational commitment, and regular church attendance by denomination, 1972–84*

	1972–1984 % Change in Members	% High Denominational Commitment	% Attend Church Regularly
Assemblies of God	85.2	70	73
Mormons	64.8	59	64
Jehovah's Witnesses	61.8	58	77
Church of God	52.6	59	57
Adventists	42.2	59	63
Nazarenes	27.5	59	63
Southern Baptists	18.9	48	52
Catholics	7.9	42	55
Lutherans	−4.6	41	45
Reformed	−8.3	59	64
Presbyterians	−9.3	32	40
Episcopalians	−9.4	32	33
United Church of Christ	−10.5	39	44
Methodists	−10.6	32	38
Disciples of Christ	−16.3	50	51

Note:
The first column is based on denominational membership reports given in the *Yearbook of American and Canadian Churches* and the final two columns are based on General Social Surveys given between 1972–84 (taken from Roof and McKinney, *American Mainline Religion*). Since the GSS data are based on the respondent's self-reported denominational affiliation and refer to general denominational families, the measure on membership change is based on the largest denominations (over 200,000 members) within the denominational family. A few of the categories reported by Roof and McKinney were omitted since they did not correspond closely to specific denominations, or data on membership were not available.

indeed, the local clergy received little or no pay, and of the first 700 Methodist circuit-riders, nearly half of them died before age 30 due to the extreme hardships of travelling the circuits: 199 of them within the first five years of service.[17] Yet the Methodists went from 3 per cent of all adherents in 1776 to more than 33 per cent of all adherents in 1850. Once again, the demanding organizations showed the most rapid increase in membership.

Besides making greater demands of their members' resources, these growing churches also place greater demands on what their members believe. Rather than accommodating to the accepted beliefs of the dominant culture or de-emphasizing the mythical beliefs of religion, these churches have rigid beliefs on what God demands of the faithful, and members offer frequent testimonial on how God intervenes in their lives. One of the most consistent demands of sectarian churches in this century is that their members should hold a firm belief in the words of their sacred text. As shown in Table 7.2, members of the growing denominations are much more likely to believe that 'the Bible is the actual word of God and is to be taken literally, word for word'. Indeed, the correlation between denominational growth and the proportion of members believing the Bible is the literal word of God is .76. The denominations accommodating to modern thought are the very churches that are rapidly losing their membership, while the denominations that have resisted this process are showing rapid growth curves.

TABLE 7.2. *Membership growth and literal interpretation of the Bible**

	Members per 1,000 US Population			% Literal Interpretation
	1960	1983	% Change	
Church of God in Christ	2.2	15.9	623	90
Assemblies of God	2.8	8.5	204	76
United Pentecostals	1.0	2.0	100	81
Jehovah's Witnesses	1.4	2.8	100	61
Seventh-Day Adventists	1.8	2.7	50	62
Church of the Nazarene	1.7	2.2	29	47
Southern Baptists	54.3	60.7	12	60
Roman Catholics	234.7	223.4	−4	23
Ev. Lutheran Ch. in Am.	29.2	22.6	−23	34
United Methodists	55.1	40.3	−27	33
Episcopal Church	19.2	12.0	−38	15
United Presbyterians	23.2	14.0	−40	28
United Church of Christ	12.5	7.3	−42	15

Note: * Adapted from Stark, *Sociology*.

A final point should be noted from Table 7.2. The growing churches are not merely small denominations. The Assemblies of God is now larger than the United Church of Christ; the Church of God in Christ is larger than the United Presbyterians and the Episcopal Church; and the Southern Baptists are far ahead of the United Methodists. The growing churches, which are placing strict demands on the behaviour and beliefs of members, are rapidly outnumbering the so-called mainline denominations.

Regardless of the indicators used, the long-term trends do not show religion in a state of decay. On the contrary, the *long-term* trends have shown patterns of increasing vitality for religious organizations and increased commitment on the individual level. And the *short-term* trends, which I consider to be those of the last 50 years or so, show remarkable stability. The secularization model's prediction of religious decay is simply not supported by the historical trends in the USA. Modernization was not accompanied by the long-forecasted process of secularization.

But why not? Why did the process of modernization not lead to the anticipated decline of religion in the USA? Here we need to look at the measures of modernization and understand their relationship to religion.

URBANIZATION AND INDUSTRIALIZATION

Too often empirical tests of the traditional model of secularization have focused only on the rise or fall of religion. If religious activity is up and religious institutions are strong, then the model is questioned (or at least revised); if religion is down then the model must be right. Yet the model goes beyond this simple prediction. The model also explains the source of this anticipated change.

At the heart of the secularization model are the widely accepted propositions that urbanization and industrialization lead to secularization. Indeed, in the beginning pages of *A General Theory of Secularization*, Martin comments that 'certain broad tendencies towards secularization in industrial society have already been fairly well established'.[18] The first three tendencies he listed are as follows:

that religious institutions are adversely affected to the extent that an area is dominated by heavy industry;

that they are the more adversely affected if the area concerned is homogeneously proletarian; and

that religious practice declines proportionately with the size of an urban concentration.[19]

Based on existing research of industrialization and urbanization in Europe, especially in England, these 'tendencies' would seem be supported. But are these trends supported in the USA?

Once again, the evidence fails to support the predictions of the traditional model. As shown in Table 7.3, the results are quite the opposite of what it predicts. For each of the time periods tested, the rate of adherence for urban areas never falls below that of rural areas; and in three of the four time periods the rate of adherence is five to seven percentage points higher in urban areas than in the surrounding hinterland.[20] Moreover, the correlation between size of city and rate of adherence is never significant in either direction for any of the time periods tested.[21] Whether you were in the city or the countryside made a difference, the size of city did not. Contrary to the prediction of the traditional model, the process of urbanization did not undermine the individual's involvement in religion or the vitality of the religious institution.

TABLE 7.3. *Church adherence rates for urban areas, rural areas, and the nation: 1890, 1906, 1926, and 1980**

	Urban Areas	Rural Areas	Nation
1890	.49	.44	.45
1906	.56	.50	.51
1926	.63	.56	.58
1980*	.55	.55	.55

Notes: In 1890, 1906, and 1926, urban areas are defined as cities with a population of greater than 25,000. For 1980 all counties with a population of over 100,000 are defined as urban. Rural areas included all areas not defined as urban.

* The 1980 data are not corrected for the numerous small religious bodies omitted from data set used in Quinn *et al.*, *Churches*.

Indeed, the only time period where urban adherence rates do not exceed those of rural areas is in 1980. I would suggest that this change is the result of two factors. The first is the major improvement in transportation between 1926 and 1980. Whereas the urban resident has always had a church within a relatively short walking-distance, rural residents are often miles from the nearest church. This does not present a problem with modern roads and cars, but it was a major obstacle at the turn of the century. This improvement in transportation has also given the rural resident a greater number of choices. Rather than being confined to a nearby country church, rural residents now have the option of attending a variety of churches in the nearest community. For the rural residents of 1980, attending church is much easier and their choice of churches is much greater than the ruralites at the turn of the century.[22]

A second factor involves the data used to compute the rates.[23] Since the 1980 data do not include numerous denominations and small sectarian groups, the rates reported are lower than the true rates; the national rate is 0.55, instead of the more accurate 0.62.[24] Even though I have made corrections for the missing black denominations and Orthodox Jews, I could not make the necessary corrections for the other missing religious groups. Omitting these denominations would not be of major concern if they resided in equal proportions in the rural and urban areas; however, as Fischer has shown, small religious groups, like ethnic groups, tend to congregate in cities where they can attain a critical mass.[25]

I would suggest that with improved data, urban areas would still have slightly higher adherence rates than the countryside. The difference is not as great due to improved transportation, but a small difference probably still remains.

If urban areas have higher rates of adherence than the countryside, this also raises questions about the effects of industrialization. Why do cities have higher church adherence rates when they are the home of industries?

To test this proposition I looked at the relationship between the percentage of the labour force in manufacturing and the rate of adherence. The correlations are reported in Table 7.4. Regardless of whether states or urban areas are used as the unit of analysis, or whether it is the turn of the century or the last decade, the adherence rate increases in areas where a higher percentage of the labour force is employed in manufacturing. Based on these zero-order correlations it would be premature to suggest that manufacturing increases religious involvement. Yet it is clear that the results fail to support the traditional model. Churches were effectively mobilizing members even in areas with industry.

TABLE 7.4. *Correlations between percent of labour force in manufacturing and church adherence rates, 1906 and 1980 (using urban areas and states)*

States	Correlation
1906	.39**
(N = 48)	
1980	.31*
(N = 50)	
Urban Areas	
1906	.17*
(N = 150)	
1980	.27**
(N = 393)	

* $p < 0.05$
** $p < 0.01$

Why? One explanation concerns the presence of sectarian movements. Whether the sectarian movements were Baptist, Assembly of God, Church of the Nazarene, or Roman Catholic, they made an effective appeal to the industrial working class. Even in the late eighteenth century the established churches recognized that the sectarian groups had a unique appeal to the less privileged. In a tract entitled *Impartial Inquiries Concerning the Progress of the Baptist Denomination*, the Congregational minister Noah Worcester acknowledged the rapid growth of the Baptists, but noted that 'they reached only the most shallow, ignorant, and uneducated classes'.[26] This appeal to the 'uneducated' continued into the nineteenth century and it soon became clear that the sectarian groups, and their revivalistic style of religion, could appeal to workers in the industrial areas. Using Hammond's data on revivalism in upstate New York from 1825 to 1835, Richard Rogers found that revivalism flourished in manufacturing and commercial centres. Rogers concluded: 'Strong support has been found for the argument that the evangelical movement drew its strength from cities and towns specializing in manufacturing and commerce.'[27] By the beginning of the twentieth century, the Roman Catholic church (a sect when first arriving in America) had proved successful at appealing to the immigrant labourer and a close tie between Roman Catholics and the labour movement was becoming evident.[28] And in the 1970s, when Earle, Knudsen, and Shriver repeated Liston Pope's study of the industrial community of Gastonia, they concluded that 'mill churches, regardless of denomination, were frequently sectarian in character, and sect-type groups have continued to emerge especially amongst the poor and socially marginal of the city'.[29] For each of the time periods, the ever-emerging sectarian groups proved attractive to the working class.

A final component of the process of modernization, which is closely tied to the process of urbanization and the constantly emerging sectarian movements, is that of religious pluralism. As forcefully argued by Berger, modernity has led to pluralism, and pluralism undermines 'the authority of all religious traditions'.[30]

Yet this prediction has faced increased opposition and revision in the past decade.[31] In recent work Rodney Stark and I computed an index to measure the religious diversity of American cities in 1906.[32] The consequences of religious diversity are shown in Table 7.5. When we control for the proportion of Catholics in the population, the diversity index has a positive effect on the rate of church adherence. Unfortunately contemporary data are not well suited for testing this hypothesis but I have replicated this result for cities in 1890 and 1926.[33] The results are consistent. Religious diversity and the percentage of the population Catholic have positive effects on religious adherence rates and the rate of population growth has a negative effect. The diversity of religions in urban areas stimulated the growth of traditional religious institutions rather than stifling such growth.

However, the powerful impact of religious competition is not limited to large cities or to church membership. In the early 1920s the Institute of Social and Religious Research conducted a survey of 140 farming villages across the nation ranging in size from 250 to 2,500 residents.[34] The principal investigator, Edmund des Brunner, was adamantly opposed to small communities supporting a diversity of churches (especially small emotional sects) but he conceded that competition increased the involvement of the people. In the fifth and final volume published from this massive study, Brunner reports:

TABLE 7.5. *Regression coefficients for religious diversity, percentage Catholic, and population growth, with rate of church adherents as the dependent variable: 1890, 1906, and 1926*

	1890		1906		1926	
	B	β	B	β	B	β
Religious diversity	.26	.24*	.79	.72**	.29	.33**
Percent Catholic	.62	.62**	1.35	1.19**	.73	.69**
Population growth	−.33	−.03**	−.12	−.04*	−.23	−.03**
$R^2 =$	.39		.62		.38	

* $p < 0.05$
** $p < 0.01$

[an] increase in the relative number of churches was found to be associated with a progressive increase in the proportion of the population enrolled in the membership of local churches, in the proportion enrolled in the Sunday schools, in the number of resident ministers per 1,000 inhabitants, in the ratio of average attendance at church to the population, and in local expenditures by the churches per inhabitant.[35]

Thus, as Table 7.6 shows, when villages have a variety of churches, the people are more likely to join and more likely to become active in the church. In villages, towns and cities, diversity has stimulated institutional growth rather than decline.[36]

But two points should be clarified on the relationship between diversity and religious involvement. First, like commercial markets, religious markets are sometimes effectively dominated by one firm. For example, Catholics have effectively dominated many urban areas since the late nineteenth century and Mormons currently dominate all urban areas within Utah. This is why I controlled for the proportion of Catholics in the reported equations. The question is: how could the Roman Catholic church mobilize such a large portion of the population in the midst of a diversity of religious options?

TABLE 7.6. *Pluralism and religious involvment in rural communities**

| | Number of Churches per 1,000 Population | | | |
	One	Two	Three	Four or more
Percent who belong to a church	27.4	36.0	34.8	43.4
Percent enrolled in Sunday schools	15.8	22.3	25.2	37.4
Percent of population attending church*	24.1	29.9	36.5	65.9

Note: * These figures are based on the average attendance at the 'principal service'. Though Brunner does not explicitly state whether children are included in the membership and attendance counts, it appears that most denominations include only adult members, whereas adults and children are counted in the attendance figures.

Source: Adapted from Brunner, *Village Communities*.

A part of the answer is obvious: they were united by their minority status and their Catholic backgrounds. But this is not the whole story. They were also successful, because they tolerated diversity within their organization. Because the parishes were homogeneous by ethnicity and class, there was a wide range of variation across parishes. According to the 1916 Census of Religious Bodies, twenty-nine languages were being used for religious services in Catholic parishes, and approximately one half (49 per cent) of all parishes held services in a language other than English.[37] This diversity of languages also translated into a diversity of patron saints, style of worship, and choice of rituals. The Church Protestants viewed as a Roman monolith was, in fact, a mosaic of regional, ethnic, and national parishes. The local parish appealed to a specific immigrant group or social class, and the diversity of parishes appealed to a broad spectrum of the population.

A second issue that needs clarification is the relationship between denominational regionalism and diversity. Although several authors have identified the predominance of Catholics in the Northeast, Lutherans in the Midwest, and Baptists in the South, these broad generalizations should not distract from the diversity within these regions.[38] While the South might be dominated by an evangelical style of religion, it is not dominated by only one denomination. Not only are there a variety of Baptists (the *Yearbook of American and Canadian Churches* reported twenty denominations with the word 'Baptist' in their name), there is also a variety of evangelical and pentecostal sectarian groups with an affinity for the South, not to mention the long-established Presbyterian, Methodist, and Episcopal churches. In the Midwest the Lutherans have pared down from the twenty-one different denominational groupings reported in the 1926 census, but their share of the population has also been reduced. In 1980 the four largest Lutheran denominations represented only 13.7 per cent of the population in the West North Central and 6.5 per cent in the East North Central. The caricature of denominational regionalism is only partially accurate. There is a large number of Lutherans in the Midwest and Baptists in the South, but neither area is lacking for denominational diversity.

Urbanization, industrialization, and pluralism have all been cited as sources for the anticipated long-term process of secularization. Yet, in the USA, urban areas have held higher rates of involvement, the percentage of the labour force in manufacturing is positively associated with adherence rates, and pluralism has stimulated growth and involvement rather than decline. The sources for secularization, proposed by the traditional model of secularization, have all been associated with higher levels of religious involvement, rather than decline. But the trends I have reported on religion in the USA stand in sharp contrast with those found in Europe. In the final section, I turn my attention to explaining this variation.

REGULATION OF RELIGION AND RELIGIOUS CHANGE

As part of an evolutionary model of modernization, the traditional model of secularization was designed to explain decline, not variation. More specifically, it was designed to explain the decline of religion in western Europe. Yet religious change in Europe is not representative of all nations facing modernity and the USA is not the only case that fails to fit the model.[39] Explanations of religious change must recognize variations by countries and must be able to explain revivalism as well as secularization.

When explaining the growth of organized religion in the USA, one of the key variables of interest must be the regulation of religion. Whereas European countries have traditionally had a close tie between Church and State, and continue to regulate religion,[40] the USA has attempted to separate Church and State, and minimize regulation. The result: low start-up costs for new religions.[41]

Splitting from a church with ties to the State can be costly due to a loss of subsidies or a perceived increase in persecution; when there are no regulations to favour existing churches, the new movement must only garner the support of the people to survive.[42] Hence, whether the religious organization is an upstart sect, or a venerable church, the life of the organization relies upon the support of the people, not the State.

This lack of regulation in the USA leads to a proliferation of new sectarian movements each trying to meet the needs of some segment of the population. And though only a handful of the numerous movements ever become sizeable denominations, their presence forces all denominations to compete for adherents. Moreover, the lack of regulation allows sects to serve as a testing ground for religious innovation. Most will fail, but a few succeed.

Finally, a proliferation of new religious movements mobilizes segments of the population often alienated by the more 'respectable' churches. Since sectarian movements often flourish in the working classes, it is the working-class churches that benefit the most from the lack of religious regulation. Rather than joining a church that is led by educated clergy and politically aligned with their employer, the workers can support a church that addresses their needs and concerns.

In sharp contrast, when there is religious regulation, the start-up costs are higher and sectarian movements strive harder to reduce the tension with their environment—leading to more rapid secularization. A poignant example is offered in the divergent histories of American and English Methodism.

Whereas camp-meeting revivalism played a key role in the success of American Methodism, the Methodists of England feared the camp meetings because they threatened the 'fragile nature of religious toleration'.[43] When Lorenzo Dow first came to England to introduce the American camp meeting, he reports that 'they warned the Methodists against me, to starve me out . . . they offered to pay my passage home, if I would quit the country, and promise never to return, which in conscience I could not do.'[44] The camp meetings generated support from the laity, but the Methodist Conference quickly ruled against such meetings: 'It is our judgment, that even supposing such meetings to be allowable in America, they are highly improper in England, and likely to be productive of considerable mischief: and we disclaim all connections with them.'[45]

Regardless of the popularity of camp meetings, Methodist authorities in England did not want to risk the consequences of this uncontrolled evangelical fervour. Approximately a decade before Dow's arrival, a 'gentleman of rank' had called the 'constitutional loyalty of provincial Methodists' into question. Just a few years later, in 1811, Lord Sidmouth attempted to control the activity of itinerant preachers by proposing a bill that would limit preaching certificates to ministers attached to a specific congregation.[46] The bill was defeated, but the fear of regulation evoked responses of loyalty from Methodist leaders and led to a self-regulation of the evangelical itinerants.

The traditional model has often ignored these dramatic differences in religious regulation. Instead, secularization is treated as an inseparable companion of modernization and the trend of secularization in Europe is forecast as the inevitable trend for all. But not all countries have followed the trend of Europe and modernity has not been the only, or even the primary, cause of religious change.

CONCLUSION

The historical evidence on religion in the USA does not support the traditional model of secularization. Based on the evidence reviewed in this essay, modernization did not usher in a new era of secularization in America.

Instead, the evidence displays the vitality of religious organizations and the continuing commitment of individuals. Rather than declining, church adherence rates have shown a rapid increase in the nineteenth century and remarkable stability throughout the twentieth. Contributions have shown a steady increase, even when controlling for inflation. And though it is difficult to measure the thoughts and beliefs of individuals, it is clear that the growing denominations do not shy away from God-talk or religious experiences. Indeed, the most rapidly growing denominations hold a firm belief in the literal interpretation of the Bible and place strict demands on their members. The long forecasted decay of religion is not supported by the evidence.

The explanation offered for the anticipated decline is not supported by the evidence either. Whereas the model predicts that secularization will be closely tied to the process of modernization, the indicators of modernization reviewed in this essay show no support for the model. In fact, the results were contrary to the predictions. Adherence rates were higher in urban areas and positively correlated to the percentage of the population in manufacturing. Moreover, diversity has a positive impact on adherence rates, when a control is entered for the percent of the population Catholic. In the case of the USA, the advent of modernization has *not* been a source of religious decay.

Yet the traditional model offers no explanation of why modernization would have less impact on one society than another. If we are going to explain variations in religious change, we must look beyond modernization for the answer.

In this essay I have highlighted the importance of religious regulation in explaining the 'exceptionalism' of the USA. Without fear of penalty or the loss of privileges from the State, sectarian movements have formed quickly on the American religious landscape. These movements have served as a testing ground for religious innovation, have mobilized large segments of the population, and have held a special appeal to the working classes. Thus, the lack of religious regulation has had a major impact on the expression and organization of religion in the USA.

To explain religious change in the USA, we need to return to the question de Tocqueville asked about American religion over 150 years ago: 'I wondered how it could come about that by diminishing the apparent power of religion one increased its real strength.'[47]

NOTES

1. J. K. Hadden, 'Toward Desacralizing Secularization Theory', *Social Forces* 65 (1987), 588.
2. Greeley has expressed similar concerns about the strong belief in the decline of religion among academics: 'The problem is that . . . most academics are not religious themselves. Neither are their families or friends. Since many of them came from religious backgrounds, they naturally assume that their own biographies are typical. Scholarly restraint ought to incline them to skepticism about their own typicality. But on the subject of religion scholarly restraint is a notoriously weak quality' (A. M. Greeley, 'American Exceptionalism: The Religious Phenomenon', presented at a conference at Nuffield College, Oxford, 1988).
3. Martin, *The Religious and the Secular*.
4. B. Johnson, 'A Fresh Look at Theories of Secularization', in H. M. Blalock Jr. (ed.), *Sociological Theory and Research* (New York, 1970), 326.
5. Hadden, 'Toward Desacralizing', 598.
6. B. R. Wilson, *Religion in Sociological Perspective*, 149.
7. J. A. Reichley, *Religion in American Public Life* (Washington, DC, 1985).
8. Another problem in testing this thesis is defining the 'erstwhile activities and functions of religion'. B. R. Wilson proposes that the functions of religion are gradually shifted from 'religious to secular control' but defining the functions of religion is dependent on either a cultural specific or a value-laden judgement. The definition used will have a major impact on testing this thesis. E.g., if the functions of religion are restricted to the beliefs, traditions, and rituals related to the supernatural, then religion has regained sole control over its functions.
9. R. Finke, 'Religious Deregulation: Origins and Consequences', *Journal of Church and State* 32 (1990), 609–26.

10. E. S. Gaustad, *Historical Atlas of Religion in America* (New York, 1962).

11. R. Finke and R. Stark, 'Turning Pews into People: Estimating 19th-Century Church Membership', *Journal for the Scientific Study of Religion* 25 (1986), 180–92; R. Stark and R. Finke, 'American Religion in 1776: A Statistical Portrait', *Sociological Analysis* 49 (1988), 39–51.

12. R. T. Handy, 'The American Religious Depression, 1925–1935', in J. M. Mulder and J. F. Wilson (eds.), *Religion in American History* (Englewood Cliffs, NJ, 1978).

13. Using survey data from 1963 to 1983 Greeley has shown that church contributions, as a percentage of annual income, have remained unchanged for Protestants, but have declined for Catholics. See Greeley, *Religious Change*.

14. Ibid.

15. In a recent essay, Iannaccone revises Kelly's theory and makes the important point that the more demanding churches grow, but their demands cannot exceed the benefits members receive from the religion. Thus, demanding churches must also provide a wider range of rewards. See L. R. Iannaccone, 'Why Strict Churches are Strong', presented at the annual meeting of the Society for the Scientific Study of Religion, 1989.

16. R. Finke and R. Stark, 'How the Upstart Sects Won America: 1776–1850', *Journal for the Scientific Study of Religion* 28 (1989), 27–44.

17. E. T. Clark, *An Album of Methodist History* (Nashville, 1952).

18. Martin, *General Theory*, 2.

19. Ibid. 3.

20. The church adherence rates used throughout this essay are corrected for denominations not counting children.

21. The correlation between the size of the city and the adherence rate was as follows: $-\cdot 09$ for 1890, $-\cdot 08$ for 1906, $-\cdot 04$ for 1926, and $\cdot 00$ for 1980.

22. Finke and Stark, 'Religious Economies and Sacred Canopies', 41–9.

23. Yet another influence on the data used to compute the 1980 rates was the change in the definition used for 'urban area'. Some rural residents would be included in urban counties and many cities of greater than 25,000 would be included in 'rural areas' for 1980.

24. R. Stark, 'Correcting Church Membership Rates, 1971 and 1980', *Review of Religious Research* 29 (1987), 69–77.

25. C. S. Fischer, *To Dwell among Friends* (Chicago, 1982).

26. W. G. McLoughlin, *New England Dissent, 1630–1833* (Cambridge, 1971), 700.

27. R. Rogers, 'Revivalism and Manufacturing in Upper State New York', presented at the annual meeting of the American Sociological Association, 1987.

28. J. P. Dolan, *The American Catholic Experience* (New York, 1985).

29. J. R. Earle, D. D. Knudsen, and D. W. Shriver Jr., *Spindles and Spires: A Restudy of Religion and Social Change in Gastonia* (Atlanta, 1976), 115.

30. P. L. Berger, *The Heretical Imperative: Contemporary Possibilities of Religious Affirmation* (New York, 1979); *The Sacred Canopy* (New York, 1967).

31. See Brown in Ch. 3; L. R. Iannaccone, 'The Consequences of Religious Market Regulation', *Rationality and Society* 3(1991), 156–77; Finke and Stark, 'Religious Economies and Sacred Canopies', 41–9; T. Caplow, H. M. Bahr, and B. Chadwick, *All Faithful People: Change and Continuity in Middletown's Religion* (Minneapolis, 1983); Fischer, *To Dwell among Friends*.

32. The index we computed is commonly used to measure linguistic, ethnic, and market diversity. See F. M. Scherer, *Industrial Market Structure and Economic Performance* (Chicago, 1970); S. Lieberson, 'An Extension of Greenberg's Linguistic Diversity Measures', *Language* 40 (1964), 526–31; J. H. Greenberg, 'The Measurement of Linguistic Diversity', *Language* 32 (1956), 109–15. In recent work Iannaccone has proposed alternative equations for determining the consequences of religious competition; Iannaccone, 'Consequences of Religious Market Regulation'.

33. R. Finke and R. Stark, 'Evaluating the Evidence: Religious Economies and Sacred Canopies', *American Sociological Review* 54 (1989), 1054–6.

34. This massive study relied on two sources of data: 'unpublished census figures' and data gathered by 'trained fieldworkers'.

35. E. des Brunner, *Village Communities* (New York, 1927), 73.

36. In a recent article, Land, Deane, and Blau support our findings for urban counties, but report that religious pluralism 'retards church membership' for rural counties. See K. C. Land, G. Deane, and J. R. Blau, 'Religious Pluralism and Church Membership: A Spatial Diffusion Model', *American Sociological Review* 56 (1991), 237–49. I would suggest that their negative findings for rural counties are the result of an inappropriate unit of analysis. When

rural counties are used, and often merged, the diversity index fails to reflect the religious options *available* to residents. Rural counties do not represent a 'religious market', since residents do not have access to every church in the county and they do not choose their religious options based on county lines. Instead, they attend the most suitable local country church or one in a nearby village—regardless of the county line. For this reason some rural counties have membership rates exceeding 100 per cent of their population. Thus, I was not surprised to find that when data were collection on rural villages, as reported earlier, religious pluralism had a positive impact on religious involvement and membership—even in rural counties.

37. The mass was said in Latin, of course, but the sermon was given in the local language. In America the local language was whatever the people spoke.

38. See Bruce in Ch. 8; S. S. Hill, 'Religion and Region in America', in W. C. Roof (ed.), *The Annals: Religion in America Today* (Beverley Hills, Calif., 1985); W. M. Newman and P. L. Halvorson, *Patterns in Pluralism: A Portrait of American Religion* (Washington, DC, 1980); J. Shortridge, 'A New Regionalism of American Religion', *Journal for the Scientific Study of Religion* 16 (1977), 143–53; W. Zelinsky, 'An Approach to the Religious Geography of the United States: Patterns of Membership in 1952', *Annals of the American Association of Geographers* 51 (1961), 139–93.

39. W. H. Swatos Jr., 'Losing Faith in the "Religion" of Secularization: Worldwide Religious Resurgence and the Definition of Religion', in W. H. Swatos Jr. (ed.), *Religious Politics in Global and Comparative Perspective* (Greenwood Press, 1989); Greeley, 'American Exceptionalism'; Hadden, 'Toward Desacralizing'.

40. J. A. Beckford, *Cult Controversies: The Societal Response to New Religious Movements* (London, 1985); T. Caplow, 'Contrasting Trends in European and American Religion', *Sociological Analysis* 46 (1985), 101–8.

41. Iannaccone, 'Consequences of Religious Market Regulation'; R. Posner, 'The Law and Economics Movement', *American Economic Review* 77 (1987), 1–13; R. Finke, 'Religious Deregulation', 609–26.

42. Stark and Bainbridge, *Future of Religion*.

43. N. Hatch, *The Democratization of American Christianity* (New Haven, Conn., 1989), 50.

44. L. Dow, *Lorenzo Dow's Journal*, 6th edn. (New York, 1849), 256.

45. As quoted in Hatch, *Democratization*, 50.

46. See D. Hempton, *Methodism and Politics in British Society, 1750–1850* (Stanford, 1984). Also, in a later essay Hempton reports: 'How far Methodism should be allowed to shelter under the umbrella of the Church of England while developing its own style and structure became one of the most controversial legal problems of the period between 1740 and 1820'; see Hempton, 'Methodism and the Law', in A. Dyson and E. Barker (eds.), *Sects and New Religious Movements, Bulletin of the John Rylands University Library of Manchester* 70 (1988), 94.

47. A. de Tocqueville, *Democracy in America* (New York, 1969), 296.

8

Pluralism and Religious Vitality

STEVE BRUCE

In descriptions and explanations of secularization, the notion of religious or denominational pluralism is deployed by a number of scholars for competing purposes. In the sociology of knowledge perspective of Peter Berger and those influenced by him, pluralism threatens the plausibility of religious belief systems by exposing their human origins.[1] By forcing people to do religion as a matter of personal choice rather than as fate, pluralism universalizes 'heresy'. A chosen religion is weaker than a religion of fate because we are aware that we choose the gods rather than the gods choosing us.

In contrast, others such as Caplow[2] and Finke (in Chapter 7) have argued that the religious pluralism of the USA explains the continued popularity of religion. Where there is considerable diversity of religious expressions and organization, every social group can find something which suits its tastes and circumstances. With greater flexibility, major religious traditions continue to be relevant for larger numbers of people than is the case in societies, such as the Lutheran states of Europe, where there is less variety. As Martin describes the American case: 'An almost unqualified pluralism becomes associated with an almost universal popularized religious culture.'[3]

Caplow has reminded us of a second virtue of diversity in repeating de Tocqueville's judgment that the vitality of American religion owed a lot to the radical separation of Church and State.[4] Where there is a dominant religious 'establishment' (*de jure* or *de facto*), the lower classes and dissident regional and ethnic groups generalize their rejection of the politics of the establishment from the dominant Church to religion in general. That is, the political or class connections of the establishment threaten its legitimacy in the eyes of sections of the population (McLeod in Chapter 4 makes such a point about nineteenth-century Berliners). Where there is such religious diversity that there can be no establishment, most churches are not compromised by their links with the State or particular élites. Hence the plausibility of religion in general is not undermined. A similar case can be made from tone and taste.[5] Establishment churches will adopt the manner and mannerisms (and even accent) of the superior social groups and make the lower classes feel, if not positively rebellious, at least less than welcome.

To these 'demand' characteristics, one might add a 'supply' virtue for pluralism. Where there are a number of competing organizations, each is forced to work hard to gather resources and normally that means recruiting members. Purveyors of religious offices cannot live off their glebe lands or tax revenues; they have to work hard to entice and keep an audience. Religious adherence should remain high (or increase) because the suppliers work to cultivate their customers. Starting with Adam Smith's observations about religion, Iannaccone has argued that free markets in religion, like free markets in other goods, increase efficiency amongst suppliers and cause increased consumption.[6]

We thus have two competing views of the consequences of religious diversity for the plausibility of religion: THESIS 1: Religious competition weakens all religion by exposing its human origins; and THESIS 2: Religious competition strengthens the appeal of religion by (2a) ensuring that there is at least one version to suit every taste; (2b) by preventing the institution being compromised by associations with ruling élites; and (2c) by forcing suppliers to be more responsive to potential customers. Tied to these alternative expectations are differing interpretations of the same cases. The evidence most often produced to illuminate the argument is the contrasting fates of the Protestant churches in Europe and America, the old and new worlds. It is of course possible that both (1) and (2) might be right and both could be reconciled, as they are by Martin and Wilson, who both use the range of American alternatives to explain their popularity while also suggesting that the plausibility of religion has been reduced and that there has been considerable 'internal secularization'. In this case, secularization has taken the form of the churches themselves reducing what is distinctively 'religious' in their ethos. As Wilson puts it:

Whereas in England secularization has been seen in the abandonment of the Churches—as in other European countries—in America it has been seen in the absorption of the Churches by the society, and their loss of distinctive religious content.[7]

I do not want to argue with the Wilson–Martin resolution of the apparent tension between the two possible directions of effects of pluralism. They may well be right but I want to suggest that they explain too much. That is they too readily accept that the USA is a major anomaly.

The first contention of this essay is that the effects of pluralism cannot be considered until one makes legitimate comparisons. I will argue that the contrast of stagnant and bankrupt establishment in the old world and vibrant lively dissent in the new is an unhelpful caricature. The second contention is that the assumptions and methods of positivist sociology are distorting. I do not intend to address directly the issue of secularization in the USA; that has been done elsewhere.[8] In trying to assemble a more plausible picture of religion in Europe and the USA, I will raise a number of analytical problems with the conceptualization of 'pluralism' or 'diversity' as cause. The essay will raise more problems than it solves but it will hopefully clarify some issues.

RELIGION IN OLD AND NEW WORLDS

De Tocqueville 'proposed that the division of American Christianity into innumerable sects prevented any denomination from developing an alliance with the State and thereby protected the integrity of the faith'.[9] If this is going to be germane, it has to be the case that the USA was unlike Europe in possessing 'innumerable sects'. But there is an important point which has been overlooked in the enthusiasm for the observations of the peripatetic Frenchman: his view of the USA is a composite of impressions collected while travelling. The USA as a whole might have shown considerable religious diversity (and become more diverse since his day) but large parts of it were and are religious monopolies or hegemonies. Consider the South. While only six of every ten non-southern states Americans are Protestants, the figure for the South is nine out of ten.[10] Almost all of these are Baptist or Methodist and, as Hill argues, in the South the denominations are near identical; 'if anything, the religious homogeneity of most Southern communities is understated by these data, since Southerners not in the religious mainstream are geographically concentrated *within* the South'.[11] Or take the concentration of Lutherans in the corn belt. Gaustad's painstaking historical geography allows us some statistical description. Using as a measure of domination the point where 50 per cent of church members belong to one denomination, in 1906, twenty-two of forty-eight states—that is, close to half—were dominated by one denomination. By 1950 this concentration had increased so that (on the slightly more refined calculation of counties rather than states) just over half the counties of the USA were dominated by one denomination.[12]

This pattern should be no surprise if one considers how the diversity of religion in the USA was created. Most competing expressions were not schisms from a common stem but 'ethnic' churches brought with the various waves of immigrants. For European Lutherans and Catholics, or the Puritan English, or the Presbyterian Scots and Ulstermen, their religion was not one selected from a number of options but their national ethnic Church which they could no more consider leaving than they could consider ceasing to be Swedish or Scottish (and, of course, it is exactly when the heirs of the migrants have been in the USA so long that being Swedish or German is no more than a folk memory that they merge their ethnic churches into one pan-Lutheran organization).

Then the great waves of evangelical Protestant revival washed over the frontier areas of the West and the South and over the increasingly settled areas just behind the frontier. In some areas, revival brought greater fragmentation with denominations dividing over the 'new measures', but such divisions were usually along broad geographical lines so that in any one large area there was no increase in diversity but simply a change in the ethos of the dominant churches. In many places the result was greater homogeneity, not only because large numbers of people with nominal attachments to competing traditions were enrolled in Methodist or Baptist meetings, but also because the revival tradition itself smoothed out differences between denominations. Thus Presbyterians, Baptists, and Methodists became sufficiently alike to share united annual camp meetings on the frontier. Later divisions, for example over slavery, were also regional. The Baptists split into Northern and Southern branches but in any hamlet, town or city in either region there was still only the Baptists.

Scotland had a legally established national Church organized on a parish structure. Although for most of its post-Reformation history it differed from the Church of England in being presbyterian rather than episcopalian, prior to industrialization it usually resembled its southern neighbour in presenting a united front of local Church and State—minister and laird—to the populace. Indeed for parts of its history, its presbyterian nature was compromised by the major landowners having the legal right to impose their choice as minister on the congregation.

From the Reformation there were waves of 'Dissent'. Until the late seventeenth century, these took the form of arguments within the Kirk and periodic upheavals in its organization or doctrine. From the Williamite revolution of 1688, Dissent increasingly took the form of significant departures from the Kirk. Leaving aside old Catholics in parts of the lowland north-east and western highlands and islands (who had missed the Reformation) and Episcopalians in the north west (who had missed the *Presbyterian* bit of the Reformation), there were the Covenanters (extreme Presbyterians who regarded the post-1688 Kirk as a compromise) who were strong in the south-west and border areas. In the mid-eighteenth century, increasing social differentiation produced two defections from the Kirk which grew to offer alternatives in most of the lowlands of Scotland: the Secession and the Relief Presbytery. Then in 1843, the Kirk was split by the Disruption in which almost half the elders left to form the evangelical Free Church of Scotland. With a certain internal shuffling of schismatic elements to take account of new ideological and social developments, one has in the middle of the nineteenth century, three competing presbyterian organizations—the broad Kirk, the evangelical Free Church, and the more liberal United Presbyterian Church—each of which was well represented throughout lowland Scotland (that is the part which contained 80 per cent of the population). There were also Roman Catholic and Episcopalian congregations, Reformed Presbyterians (the heirs to the Covenanters), and scattered representations of all the English Dissenting movements. Although the Kirk remained the legally established State Church, this meant little after the growth of the Secession undermined its ability to organize education, administer social welfare, or arrange social discipline. The formation of the Free Church, although it did not occasion the divorce of Church and State, hastened their separation and reduced the marriage to a legal fiction.

As an indication of diversity we might note that in 1851, Aberdeen had fifty-two churches belonging to twelve competing denominations and three entirely independent religious meetings.

Contrary to the ethnocentric myths until recently popular with English and Scots scholars, the development of the Christian church in Scotland was not unique.[13] The history of the break-up of the Church of England follows the same pattern. There was a national reformation of the Church, from which small scattered groups dissented. There were then a series of major dissenting schisms, each related to a distinct episode of social differentiation. The last great wave was the 'revival' of the late eighteenth and early nineteenth century, which produced Methodism.

Contrary to the image presented by Caplow, England had considerable religious diversity. In Leeds in 1808, there were five Church of England churches, one Associate Presbytery Scottish church, three Independent chapels, a Quaker meeting house, two English Presbyterian chapels, three Methodist chapels, a Baptist chapel, a Roman Catholic church, and an Inghamite chapel. One of the Anglican churches had been a Countess of Huntingdon's Connection Methodist chapel before its congregation fell away and an Anglican clergyman bought it. Of the three Independents, one was initially

Unitarian and then 'Congregational', a second remained Unitarian, and the third was 'Calvinist'.[14]

The considerable problems of using the 1851 census of church attendance as an index of popular religious commitment are well known (see Gill in Chapter 5) but we can be reasonably confident that most places of worship were identified. If there is a pattern of mistakes we can expect it to be one of overlooking small independent groups and thus under-reporting evidence of diversity.[15] By 1851 Leeds had grown to 172,270 souls who, as we can see from Table 8.1, were served by 132 religious meeting places in 17 denominations and 6 isolated congregations:[16]

TABLE 8.1. *Places of worship, Leeds 1851*

Church of England	31
Independents	11
Particular Baptist	9
Scotch Baptists	1
General Baptists	2
Baptists (other)	1
Society of Friends	1
Unitarians	3
Wesleyan Methodists	26
Methodist New Connexion	7
Primitive Methodists	13
Wesleyan Association	10
Wesleyan Reformers	4
New Church	1
Brethen	2
Isolated congregations	6
Roman Catholic	2
Latter Day Saints	2
TOTAL	132

That this range of options was not just a feature of the cities can be seen from Table 8.2, which lists what was available in the county of Chester.[17] Of 820 places for worship, only 252—less than a third—were Anglican. Equally importantly from the point of choice, it is not easy to imagine some form of Protestantism which is missing from the county.

TABLE 8.2. *Places of worship, Cheshire 1851*

Church of England	252
Scottish Presbyterians	
United Presbyterians	2
Presbyterian Church	3
Independents	66
Baptists	
Particular Baptists	14
Scotch Baptist	1
General Baptists	4
Undefined	2
Society of Friends	10
Unitarians	14
Wesleyan Methodists	
Original Connexion	188
New Connexion	29
Primitive	135
Wesleyan Association	50
Calvinistic Methodists	
Welsh Calvinistic Methodists	4
Lady Huntingdon's Connexion	8
Brethren	5
Isolated congregations	7
Roman Catholic	17
Latter Day Saints	9
TOTAL	820

COMPARISONS OF BRITAIN AND THE USA

The above brief description allows us to develop some detailed comparisons and to clarify some of the assumptions made in various measures of diversity.

Religious establishment

Although Scotland and England still have legally established State churches, this is largely a matter of form. In England, the bishops have a privileged political platform (although no particular influence) in that some have seats in the House of Lords. At quite what point one places the transformation of establishment from fact to fiction is difficult. Does one take dates of legislative acts which are usually confirmations of

changes that have already occurred? One could defend 1843 for
Scotland (the Free Church Disruption) and 1827 (the Catholic
Emancipation Act) for England. Or perhaps 1744 as the date of
the first Methodist Conference could be taken as the start of the
movement which finally undermined the Anglican Church.

If one moves away from legal establishment to a more
general formulation of relations with the State, it is clear that
in some, mostly rural parts of the USA, evangelical Protestantism enjoys 'established' status in the dominance of its clergy
and members over matters of social policy. Witness the
increase in this century of local school boards introducing
public school prayer and bible reading in schools.[18]

The identification of religious establishment clearly depends
on the definition of the social unit which is thought to have
that characteristic. Where one puts the boundaries is vital. In
1820 England had a state church but then so did South
Carolina. The USA as a whole did not have a State Church
but then (a point often missed by people who confuse
England, Britain, Great Britain, and the United Kingdom)
nor did the United Kingdom. There was a Presbyterian
Church established in Scotland, an Episcopalian Church
established in England and Wales, and a theologically and
politically very different established Episcopalian Church in
Ireland (North and South), which was dis-established forty-
nine years later. If the correct unit for the USA is the nation–
state, why is the commonly used unit for this end of the
comparison only one part of a nation–state?

Religious diversity

As with the question of establishment, the measurement of
diversity first requires sensibly comparable units. Even at the
macro level one has to ask whether it is sensible to compare
the USA and Britain. Given the relative sizes, should not one
compare the USA with Europe or England with a clutch of
American states? In such comparison the difference would
disappear for the obvious reason that the diversity of American
religion resulted from it taking people from all over Europe.

There is also a problem of distortion which results from
insensitive comparisons of units of different size and popula-

tion density. Stark and Bainbridge have calculated a sect diversity rate for American religion at a state level. It ranges from a high of 5.48 sects per million population in Tennessee to a low of 0.17 sects per million in Massachusetts.[19] Whatever the value of that exercise for American states, if repeated for English counties it produces ridiculous figures. Even if we count its four isolated congregations as just one alternative and not four, Westmorland in 1851 had fifteen alternatives for 58,287 people or 257 sects per million! The county of Chester had twenty-one different bodies for just under half a million people. An interesting observation here is that the smaller the population of the county, the higher the rate because in any county there is at least one or two representatives of every denomination. Clearly, without new and time-consuming historical research we are confined to comparisons of British counties and towns and American states but the clumsiness of such units must be recognized.

But even if when we agree on the social units to be compared, there are major and to-date unrecognized problems with the measurement and conceptualization of religious diversity or pluralism. There are two quite different ways of thinking about this supposed variable: what people could choose and what they have chosen. First we can consider the *range of options available*. Since the late eighteenth century England and Scotland had a wide range of available alternatives. One particular 'firm' may have enjoyed State-supported privileges but that did not prevent considerable competition. The USA now has a larger number of discrete religious organizations than does Britain but the case can be made for arguing that since the 1750s England and Scotland have had *enough* religious diversity to satisfy the conditions of theses 2a and 2b: those who did not like one church could find another more suited to their tastes or station in life and there were sufficient dissenting organizations for most people to be able to distinguish 'religion' and the 'State Church' so that the latter could be rejected without the former also being abandoned. Apart from the large number of different language versions of the same religion found there, it is hard to think of any variant the USA had which Britain did not have. As we saw in the case of Chester, even the Mormons were in

Britain by 1851. Even some of the latter innovations which are often thought of as peculiarly American were found in Britain. Perfectionism and holiness were on offer at the Keswick Convention and there were modern pentecostal movements here as early as there were in the USA.

Although what I have called 'range of options' apparently meets the conditions of the de Tocqueville theses, many discussions of diversity refer not to what people *could* do but to what they *have* done. That is, they refer to the distribution of a population across the alternatives. There are two different ways in which this is expressed. Gaustad uses the measure of *domination*: the frequency with which 50 per cent or more of the population of a given social unit belongs to the same denomination. On this measure we find that England and Wales show a degree of domination similar to that of the USA. Of the USA, Gaustad says:

> there were in 1950 amazingly few counties that were not dominated by one or another ecclesiastical bodies . . . in approximately one-half of the counties of the nation, a single religious body accounts for at least 50% of all the membership in the county.[20]

Furthermore the uniformity is reinforced by the contiguity of hegemonic counties. In almost all of the many counties dominated by Baptists, the neighbouring counties are also dominated by Baptists.

In England and Wales, of forty-three counties in 1851, 25 or 52 per cent were homogeneous. In the towns and cities, where more than half the population lived, only sixteen of fifty-nine had half or more of those who attended church on the census day in the Anglican Church. Where the Anglican Church was not dominant, no other denomination reached 50 per cent.

An alternative measure of diversity is used by Finke and Stark.[21] They use church-membership data from the 1906 census of American churches to test the propositions that 'Urbanization increases levels of religious mobilization' and that 'Pluralism increases levels of religious mobilization'. They conclude that religious participation was higher in the cities than in the surrounding villages and hinterlands.[22] Where the national rate of church adherence was 51 per cent of the population, for small cities (between 25,000 and 50,000 people) it was 60 per cent and for big cities, it was 55 per cent. The explanations offered concern practicalities: 'it was much easier to attend church in an urban area than in a rural area'; pluralism: 'Americans in cities always had a much greater range of available choices, and urbanites have always been exposed to more intensive recruitment efforts'; and the presence of Catholics.[23]

For Finke and Stark the key to increased participation is the Sunday school movement. Pluralism increases the number of Sunday-schools competing for pupils and the presence of Catholics stimulates Protestants into greater evangelistic activity.

I will concentrate on the pluralism issue and leave aside for the time being the variables of urbanism and presence of Catholics. First, it is worth noting a failing which is common to all snapshot comparisons. We are told that there was more religion in the cities than in the surrounding rural areas and this is offered as evidence about the effects of characteristics of those cities. It might well be but it might also be a story about the greater religiosity of *foreign* rural areas. Given the impact of Catholics on the overall figures, it is worth noting that a large proportion of these people were first- and second-generation migrants from traditional societies such as southern Ireland, Poland, and Italy, places with monopolistic religious cultures.

As I have already implied, there is a possibility that two importantly different things are being confused in the diversity index. Let us consider just what the index does. The index is $[1-1(a/z)^2 + (b/z)^2 + (c/z)^2 \ldots]$ where z is the total number of religious adherents and a, b, c, etc. are the numbers in any particular denomination. The closer the number is to 1, the greater the diversity. Although this measure is more sensitive than Gaustad's notion of domination, there is the problem that it elides what it explains (the popularity of religion) and what it offers as an explanation (religious diversity) by producing a higher diversity score when a number of competing organizations are successful in recruiting than when a wide range of options are relatively unsuccessful. Imagine a city whose population is divided in five equally large denominations. That gives an index of 0.80.

Now imagine a city in which one denomination accounts for half the population, three each have 10 per cent, and four others each have 5 per cent. This gives an index of diversity of only 0.61. That is, on Finke's measure, the second city has less 'diversity' than the first, although it actually has a wider variety of options: eight different denominations as against five. Thus the Finke index actually builds into its measure some element of 'success'. A range of options is only measured by the index when a number of them have been successful in picking up roughly similar numbers of adherents. A city such as Leeds in 1808, which has a wide variety of churches but where most of the options remain unpopular, scores low on diversity even though it is high on one aspect of pluralism: the range of options. If the second city in my example has a lower rate of religious adherence than the first, its comparative 'irreligiosity' will be explained by its lack of diversity and the case will be offered as proof of a correlation between pluralism and adherence when it actually offered a wider variety of options than the first city.

DIVERSITY AND ATTENDANCE IN 1851 ENGLAND

With the above misgivings, I decided to use the Finke index to correlate diversity and church attendance in the 1851 census data for England and Wales. Given the different speed of industrialization of England and the USA, 1851 seems an appropriate enough point of comparison with the American data for 1906 (and Brown in Chapter 3 argues a similar case).

Church attendance figures for sixty-six major towns and cities were correlated with (1) size of town (which seems as good an index of urbanism as any), (2) the Finke index of diversity, and (3) the percentage Catholic.[24] The results of the regression analysis are given in Table 8.3. All three variables make a significant contribution to church attendance and in all cases that contribution is *negative*. For reasons that are not at all clear to me, the strongest predictor is the percentage of Roman Catholics and the direction is negative. That is the more Catholics, the lower the rate of church attendance,

TABLE 8.3. *Church attendance in England and Wales 1851 (Standard multiple regression of town size, Roman Catholic population, and religious diversity with church attendance)*

Variables	Attendance	Diversity	% RC	Size	B	β	T
Diversity	−.44	1.00			−42.62	−0.29750	−2.82**
% RC	−.48	.29	1.00		−58.97	−0.32594	−3.02***
Size	−.39	.21	.29	1.00	−8.69	−0.23209	−2.20*
Means	52.652	0.736	7.2%	1.673			R = 0.61
Standard Deviations	13.657	0.095	0.075	0.365		Adjusted	R² = 0.35
							R² = 0.38

* p<0.05
** p<0.01
*** p<0.005

which is quite different to Finke and Stark's result. Further, the correlation is not reducible to the effects of size. It also goes against the common wisdom that the Catholic Church succeeded where others failed in retaining the urban working class. The second strongest relationship is between diversity and attendance and again it is statistically significant and negative: the more diversity, the less attendance. The weakest of the three variables is size but even this is statistically significant. Brown argues that the 'religious census of 1851 showed no statistically significant relationship between church-going rate and population size or growth for towns and cities'.[25] Although I have not the data to test the population-growth hypothesis, I can report that I find a significant relationship between church-going and size in the same data.

There may be a number of explanations for this divergence in results. It is easy for the debate to become bogged down in statistics but we must appreciate that 'results' in statistical analysis owe a great deal to the procedures used to produce them.[26] If one treats London as one unit, the sample is massively skewed. Most towns and cities in the sample are much of a muchness in size, there are a few big ones, and then there is London, a massive 'outlier'. Most statistical tests are designed to analyse cases that are similar or 'normally distributed' and produce unreliable results when applied to badly skewed samples. So that the usual tests could be applied I used a standard technique to 'normalize' the sample for size.[27] To insist as Brown does that London be treated as one unit and then fail to 'normalize' the data set is to make it certain that conventional statistical tests will produce unstable results. To further explore the role of size and the impact of London, I ran a simple correlation of size and church attendance without the London boroughs and produced a stronger correlation than in the Table 8.3 regression. Taking the sizes untransformed, one gets an R^2 of ·10, a beta of −·32 and a T of −2.7, which is significant. Using a LOG 10 transformation to normalize the sample for size, produces an R^2 of ·14, a beta of −·38 and a T of −3.3, which is significant at the level of 0.005. In English: leave out London and the corrosive effect of town size on attendance is even greater.

There is also a problem of multi-collinearity. Put most simply, when one places in a regression equation a number of independent variables which are themselves closely linked, one loses definition. It seems extremely likely that Brown's results are distorted by placing town size, rate of growth from 1801–51 and rate of growth from 1841–51 in the same equation.[28]

Far more could be said, and at some stage needs to be said, about the different ways of identifying patterns in statistical data sets but my application of the Finke index of diversity to the 1851 census data (which is as appropriate as others' use of the same index) produces a result entirely at variance with the new 'revisionism' and entirely at one with the orthodox views of British social historians: size and diversity are associated with less and not more church attendance.[29]

EXPLAINING CHOICES

The above discussion has either introduced or implied a number of analytical points about pluralism and religious diversity which will now be made explicit. Correlation (even at the unlikely point of constant concomitance) is not itself explanation. One cannot stress enough the point that if we are to move from general observation to explanation, then we must also move from the big picture to the details of plot. If we are to use differences in degree and extent of religious diversity to explain the degree and extent of popular support for the churches, we have to 'unpack' the supposed connection between these two variables into a story which is plausible and sensible at the level of the individual actor who either stays in a church or leaves it. That is, we have to be able to tell some sensible story about why pluralism might erode or strengthen the religious commitment of an individual actor.

Both the sociology of knowledge de-legitimation position (Thesis 1) and the de Tocquevillian strengthening view (Thesis 2) suppose that the religious diversity of the largest social unit impinges on the individual actor. Pluralism can only undermine faith if one knows about it and one could sensibly argue that pure knowledge is not enough. One would actually have to have frequent contact with representatives of other denominations or religious traditions in order for one's own faith to cease to be 'taken for granted'.

Whether the de Tocquevillian non-establishment argument (Thesis 2b) requires diversity at local level will depend on what one supposes to be the operative causal mechanisms. Suppose I am a freehold farmer in Yorkshire in 1750. In a parish where the squire and vicar are in cahoots, I might well show my rejection of this local combination by helping to found a Methodist congregation. But what if there is no resident squire and the vicar is an independent-minded sort of chap? Should the Church's links at nation–state level still offend me enough to drive me out? Anyway, Thesis 2b requires something further: that I express my dissatisfaction, not by religious dissent but by withdrawal from religion altogether. Even if the dominant religion does discredit itself in my eyes by supporting oppressive social élites, why not form my own church? The Methodists did it. If the gradual rise in social status of the Methodists discourages many working-class people from staying in that wave of dissent, why do they not form a new wave of dissent? This is a question which is not asked let alone answered by those such as Caplow or McLeod (in Chapter 4), who wish to explain a decline in adherence or commitment by the political associations of the dominant religious tradition. The answer Finke gives is that the 'costs' of religious dissent are inflated in a regulated religious economy but this would only be relevant if church history showed a general reluctance of believers to make sacrifices for their beliefs. In fact, it shows quite the opposite. As Finke himself notes, many sects throve on adversity.

The Horace Mann position, which is taken up by Callum Brown, is that lack of financial resources prevents continued religious adherence. Mann uses shortages of 'seats' as an explanation of declining church attendance and Brown uses the high price of pew rents in explaining why the working classes of Glasgow were alienated from the Free Church.[30] Yet this can only work as an explanation for the actions of those people whose religious commitment is already weak. Nothing stopped people from holding services in their own rooms. When the people of Strontian, who left the Church of Scotland in 1843, were denied land for a Free Church building by their landlord, they had a floating church built in a Clyde shipyard, sailed it into Loch Sunart, and worshipped there.[31] Although there were petty obstacles, British people who wished to do religion and were alienated from the dominant form in their area could pursue religious activity outside the established churches, and some did so. That many did not provide their own offices and had little interest in consuming the dissenting offices already provided, needs to be explained by something other than alienating aspects of the establishment.

To return to the ecological issue of how the characteristics of the large social unit bear upon the decision-making individual, it is clear that Thesis 2a—that diversity allows greater choice which reduces alienation—requires that the religious diversity of the nation-state be repeated at local levels. One cannot explain the strength of religious adherence in *Lake Wobegon* by talking about alternatives if there is nothing or nothing within reasonable travelling distance of *Lake Wobegon* which is not Lutheran. But the theoretical availability of options has an element of mechanical insensitivity about it. Adding a Swedish-language Lutheran church to an American county with a large number of Germans increases the options for Swedes but does little or nothing for Germans. Adding a black Baptist church in a Tennessee county does not increase alternatives for disaffected Methodists if they are white.

Here we come to the problems of positivism. Finke's essay and related work supposes that pluralism is a unitary phenomenon with an impact that will vary in proportion to the 'amount' of diversity and that diversity is to be measured by some objective method, as an analyst's concept. The problems of what Herbert Blumer called 'variable analysis' should be well known but the cautions are still ignored.[32] That a situation can be described by the remote outsider as having property X does not mean that the actors who have to define that situation in order to act in it will see the situation as having X. The simple presence of a Methodist chapel in upper Weardale does not mean that Methodism is available to the farm-workers of the surrounding hills if they are too poor to make what they believe to be the expected contribution to the support of the enterprise, or to the workers in an early industrial enterprise if they feel obliged to follow the religion of the master. Or to take Brown's point about Glasgow Free Church pew rents: working people might want to be part of a dissenting movement but feel prevented from exercising their choice. Economic and political pressure do not exhaust the list of barriers. The new religion may be devalued by its association with some despised subordinate group. The building of Catholic chapels in the west coast of Scotland in the nineteenth century did not increase the options for the vast majority of Scots who saw Catholicism as the religion of the ignorant and poor Irish.

Reasoning along those lines a version of the de Tocquevillian point can be salvaged by saying that, although in many parts of Britain there were alternatives, many people were prevented from moving from a formal attachment to the established Church to an enthusiastic attachment to a more suitable alternative by the political and social power of the establishment. But for the reasons already given, this sounds unconvincing. It requires a separate explanation of why the alienated poor did not organize their own offices. One cannot assert that they lacked the skills or the initiative to do so because they managed quite well to organize their own friendly societies, guilds, sporting associations, and trade unions.

To summarize my argument thus far, I believe that the contrast between the extent of religious diversity of old and new worlds has been exaggerated, that there were plenty of options available in the UK for those who wanted them, and that the failure of the options to recruit and maintain numbers of adherents on the US scale cannot be explained by the absence of choice. I have also raised a number of questions about the nature of religious diversity, our measures of it, and their implied models of human action. To respond to the challenge to sociology made by Brown in Chapter 3, it is certainly the case that sociology loses historical detail and sometimes plausibility in its search for general explanations, but it is no less the case that historians assume but rarely state general socio-psychological principles. In the above I have identified some of these so that they can be further debated.

None of this is to say that there is nothing at all in the contrast between the structure of religion in old and new worlds. I have no doubt that the State support of the clergy found in the old world with its established churches removes a major incentive to missionize and to respond to the demands of potential memberships, but the increased striving for sales characteristic of a free market does not explain why anyone buys the product. The limits of economic analysis are very clearly given by one of the doyens of the application of economic models to the market for ideas, Gary Becker, when he says:

Since economists generally have little to contribute . . . to the understanding of how preferences are formed, preferences are assumed not to change substantially over time, not to be very different between wealthy and poor persons, or even between persons in different societies and cultures.[33]

Precisely. In the case of religious behaviour we have to recognize that preferences change a great deal (and include the preference not to do any religion) and it is exactly the change in preference that we are trying to explain. What remains unexplained by the kind of assumptions used by Finke is why some people respond to the missionary work of competing religious organizations and others do not. Or, to borrow the economist's metaphor, why do those who have an unmet preference for religion of a certain kind not provide it for themselves in the United Kingdom when they do exactly that in the USA?

DIVERSITY AS A RESOURCE FOR SUB-CULTURE FORMATION

Although the positivist view of diversity as an objective stimulus which has a uniform impact on all people in 'objectively similar' circumstances is convenient for measurement and regression analysis, it fails to do justice to the complexities of real life. Counting spires is just not good enough. The proponents of Theses 1 and 2 have to come to terms with the idea that diversity describes circumstances that the actors whose behaviour we wish to explain have to *interpret*. I have already offered criticisms of the de Tocquevillian story on that ground but it applies also to the Bergerian Thesis 1. We know that it is possible to cope with threats to one's world-view by employing a number of strategies of denial. We can always deflate the challenge of alternative cultural expressions by employing invidious stereotypes of the carriers. Missionaries are not deflected from their faith by discovering that the heathen do not share it; they are no-account heathen after all. There is clearly a qualitative difference in the threat to one's world-view posed by a low-status ethnic or occupational group and by one's own people defecting to some alternative religion. We might suppose that day-to-day contact with people of another church, provided it is amicable and does not form part of a wider range of points of conflict, will reinforce the impression that good people can differ about God and increase the likelihood that the Lutheran will develop some sort of relativistic position. But how can one quantify this? Do we suppose that there is a regular relationship between the number of alternatives and the extent of threat? Should four competing denominations be more eroding than just two?

If one adopts the more active model of the actor as choice-maker, one discovers a radical alternative reading of the consequences of diversity: people may use 'objective' pluralism as a resource for creating or maintaining 'inter-subjective' hegemony.[34] The argument can be simply illustrated with a comparison of the presentation of religion in the British and American media. There are only four television channels in Britain and two of these are operated by the British Broadcasting Corporation (BBC). Both the BBC and the Independent Television (ITV) companies (who run the other two channels) air weekly worship programmes. The opportunity to broadcast such services is rotated around the British denominations according to their relative size. The religious broadcasting of both the BBC and ITV is produced in accordance with the advice given by a Joint Advisory Committee of clergymen and interested lay people. The result is that anyone who watches religion on British television can hardly avoid diversity (except in so far as all the denominations tend to slant their performances towards an ecumenical middle ground). American television is much more open. The greater diversity takes the form of a much wider variety of sources but viewers need not be confronted with diversity. Instead they may select from a large number of shows those which most closely represent their position. Fundamentalists do not have to watch Robert Schuler; they can stay with Jerry Falwell. Pentecostalists do not have to watch Falwell; they can tune to Pat Robertson. The same point applies across all mass media and extends to schooling, a wide range of voluntary associations, and even colleges and universities. Fortunately situated Americans can use the openness of the American context to carefully select only those products, performances, associations, and activities which they find congenial. That is, they can create sub-cultures and sub-societies in which, far from being confronted with diversity, they live a large part of their lives in a world that is religiously homogeneous. We have the irony that the larger, more open society with the more diverse culture gives its citizens greater freedom to avoid those characteristics. Jerry Falwell's followers can actually believe that they are a 'moral majority' because, except when they switch into apocalyptic thinking and suppose that the USA consists largely of coke-crazed, homosexual secular humanists, they are able to select the lenses through which they will view the USA. In the UK, the centralized and paternalistic nature of the organization of the media, social administration, government, and political parties has the effect of making the lesser cultural diversity all the more pressing because we have less opportunity for selecting only some social and cultural products with which to build a world in which our culture is hegemonic. To present an example flippantly, we have fewer and smaller ethnic minorities than does the USA but we have a far greater number of television and radio programmes about 'multi-cultural Britain'.

In summary, I want to suggest that religious diversity has to be reconceptualized in active terms so that we concentrate on the availability (in the sense of being plausibly available rather than the mechanistic notion of present in the environment) and avoidability of options.

CONCLUSION

There are many other difficulties with the notion of pluralism which could have been discussed. A glaring one is that, counter to de Tocqueville's argument about the de-legitimating effects of establishment, in the old world it is those churches which retain a monopoly or near monopoly within one ethnic or racial group that have retained greatest popular support. De Tocqueville travelled briefly in Ireland in 1835 and met a number of Catholic priests. He asked one if he would like to be supported by the State and recorded the reply that it would cost him his flock. De Tocqueville missed the point that it was the *British* Establishment which was the problem. Once home rule had been achieved the Irish hierarchy had no problem at all with the reality of establishment and there has been no major decline in public support since the Church went from being the Church of the oppressed to the Church of the Irish Free State.[35]

I am not concerned here to explain the difference in church membership and attendance in Britain and the USA. I doubt if my account would be very different from those of Wilson or Martin, except in so far as they subscribe to widely held views that (1) America is much more religiously diverse than Britain and (2) that the greater diversity explains the greater religiosity. My argument in this chapter is that the first is not true and hence the second cannot follow. If we are to get any further in understanding its effects on religious observance and belief, we need to become considerably more sophisticated in our conceptualization of diversity than the present state of the debate shows us to be.

NOTES

1. Berger, *Heretical Imperative*; J. D. Hunter, *American Evangelicalism: Conservative Religion and the Quandary of Modernity* (New Brunswick, NJ, 1983) and *Evangelicalism: The Coming Generation*; Bruce, *A House Divided*.
2. Caplow, 'Contrasting Trends', 101–8.

3. Martin, *General Theory*, 5.
4. de Tocqueville, *Democracy* (New York, 1969).
5. Martin, *Sociology*.
6. For details of Iannaccone's work, see notes in Ch. 7.
7. B. R. Wilson, *Religion in Secular Society*, 114.
8. Bruce, *A House Divided*.
9. Caplow, 'Contrasting Trends'.
10. S. S. Hill, *Southern Churches in Crisis* (New York, 1966), 34–9.
11. J. Reed, *The Enduring South: Subcultural Persistence in Mass Society* (Lexington, Mass., 1972), 58.
12. Gaustad, *Historical Atlas*.
13. C. G. Brown, *Social History of Religion* and in Ch. 3 argues persuasively that English and Scottish religion developed in very similar ways.
14. C. Cayley, *The Leeds Guide: Giving a Concise History of that Rich and Populous Town . . .* (Leeds, 1808).
15. G. Patterson, 'The Religious Census: A Test of Its Accuracy in South Shields', *Durham County Local History Society Bulletin* (April 1978), 14–17 and I. Beckwith, 'Religion in a Working Men's Parish', *Lincolnshire History and Archaeology* 4 (1969), 29–38 are typical in identifying the omission of small organizations' churches as the major mistake of the census.
16. Details taken from British Parliamentary Papers *1851 Census*.
17. Ibid.
18. On this and other aspects of church–state relations in the US, see Bruce, *Rise and Fall*; R. S. Alley, *The Supreme Court on Church and State* (New York, 1988); and T. Robbins and R. Robertson (eds.), *Church–State Relations: Tensions and Transitions* (New Brunswick, NJ, 1987).
19. Stark and Bainbridge, *The Future of Religion*, 145.
20. Gaustad, *Historical Atlas*, 159.
21. Finke and Stark, 'Religious Economies and Sacred Canopies', 41–9.
22. Ibid. 42.
23. Ibid. 44.
24. I am grateful to Dr Fiona Alderdice of the Department of Social Studies, The Queen's University of Belfast, for assistance in the preparation and analysis of these data. In the regression equation 'Attendance' is the index of attendance calculated by Inglis, 'Patterns'.
25. C. G. Brown, 'Urbanization', 1–14.
26. To say this is not to endorse the radical view that one can never meaningfully quantify, or having quantified use statistical

analyses. Even if statistics are not used, all sociological comparison implicitly quantifies.

27. I am grateful to Dr Alderdice for pointing out the deleterious effects of the lack of 'normality' in the sample. For further discussion of the problem, see B. G. Tobacknick and L. S. Fidell, *Using Multivariate Statistics* (New York, 1983). The data were examined with the Komogorov–Smirnov 'goodness of fit' test and transformed using a Log 10 transformation.

28. There also appears to be a problem of multi-collinearity in the equations presented in Finke and Stark, 'Religious Economies and Sacred Canopies'; see K. D. Breault, 'New Evidence on Religious Pluralism, Urbanism and Religious Participation', *American Sociological Review* 54 (1989), 1048–53. For a general discussion, see Tobacknick and Fidell, *Multivariate Statistics*.

29. Inglis, *Churches*; Wickham, *Church and People*.

30. C. G. Brown, 'Costs of Pew-Renting, 347–61.

31. G. N. M. Collins, *The Heritage of Our Fathers* (Edinburgh, 1976), 66.

32. H. Blumer, *Symbolic Interactionism* (Englewood Cliffs, NJ, 1969), Ch. 7.

33. G. Becker, 'The Economic Approach to Human Behavior', in J. Elster (ed.), *Rational Choice* (Oxford, 1986), 110. I offer a detailed critique of the rational-choice approach to the explanation of religion in 'Religion and Rational Choice', *Sociological Analysis* (forthcoming).

34. The following argument is made at length in Bruce, *Pray TV*.

35. A. de Tocqueville, *Travels to England and Ireland* (New Brunswick, NJ, 1988).

9
Reflections on a Many Sided Controversy

BRYAN R. WILSON

REFLECTING on the essays gathered in this volume, I cannot but think that it would be tedious for the reader were I to attempt to pick up the minutiae of debate on every point which I might want to dispute. Even at the risk of reiterating (and, one hopes, more fully justifying) facets of the discussion that have been aired elsewhere, it seems more sensible to take the issues in the broad. There is, indeed, one particular broad topic that, with one or two honourable exceptions, has failed to command the attention of most of the contributors and that is the question of definition. Secularization is readily discussed as if everyone were agreed on what was meant by that term. Religion, too, is taken for granted as a self-understood phenomenon. At times, one has the impression (particularly in Brown's chapter) that religion is equated exclusively with Christianity (is Christianity also equated with Protestantism?). My own usage—and this is perhaps more typically the stance of a sociologist than of a historian—is to adopt a much more encompassing concept of just what constitutes religion: Christianity is regarded as just one species of the genera; and Protestantism a sub-species. They chance, of course, to be the species and sub-species with which these writers are primarily acquainted and concerned but, in its broader application, the secularization thesis relates to more general propositions than those which in the nineteenth and twentieth centuries are held specifically to apply to western Christianity, and more narrowly to its American and British manifestations.

The contributors identify secularization with decline, but some of them proceed to take a rather narrow view of just *what* has declined. In the main their preoccupation (almost exclusively) is with the figures for those who go to church.

Church attendance gives all the appearance of being an objective indicator of spontaneous religious commitment, but, as Gill notes (although he does not allow the point to hinder his analysis), there may be different motivations prompting church attendance. They may include everything from assertions of group solidarity to the local assumption that 'going to church' is required of those who would make claim to social standing. Of course, contributors are aware that, traditionally at least, 'going to church' meant something very different for a Catholic from what it meant to an Anglican, and again something quite different from what it implied for a Nonconformist. Not to take into account these very different assumptions is to endorse an old-fashioned behaviouristic idea about what appears—but only appears—to be a uniform item of social action. The act, however, is not a common unit at all, and this fact alone must cast a long shadow over arguments that rely unduly on comparative attendance statistics for different denominations, for different countries, and even for different historical periods. The statistics, seductive as they are because of their apparent objectivity, do not carry the same weight or tell an unambiguous story.

If secularization implies decline, then one might expect other aspects to be invoked in addition to church attendance. Gill certainly looks at the ratios of church sittings to local populations, which is an innovative and interesting variant on the usual tendency to look only at attendance figures. There are, however, other indices worthy of consideration, even if some of them are not entirely free from difficulty or ambiguity of interpretation. Church membership where it applies, is one. Others include the statistics for confirmation—allowing again that the social meaning of such a rite differs profoundly as between, say, an otherwise apparently very secular country like Sweden, where confirmation rates are very high, and England, where they have been in sharp decline in recent decades. There may be no statistics for confirmation in the Roman Catholic or (High) Anglican churches, but the diminution of this form of religious practice is a subject of commonplace comment readily acknowledged by (older) priests. For baptisms, there are figures, however, and they surely tell one something about the extent to which a solemn rite of passage at a crucial time of life when the individual is particularly vulnerable, has, for increasing numbers, ceased to mean very much. One might leave aside the churching of women—once so important but so secularized has society become, today its purpose is scarcely remembered. It would be difficult to get figures for households in which grace is still said at meal times (let alone collective morning prayers). Indeed, even to mention such items might be said to be trivializing the debate but this reflects the secularizing of the modern mind, at the cost of discounting the meaning with which, at least in the past, such rituals were endowed.

If private devotions are likely to be ruled out as being of little account, the same cannot be said for the economic aspects of church life. One does not have to be an economic determinist to suggest that the financial support for religion is a salient indicator of just how important that religion is, not merely for individual contributors, but also for society at large. In some countries church taxes persist as a leftover from the days when a policy of religious obligation was enforced, and this despite decline in church attendance and belief in God; Belgium and Germany furnish examples. In others, of which England is a prime instance, the established Church depends on historical possessions. In Europe, free-will offering as the major financial underpinning of the dominant churches is the exception rather than the rule. Even so, religious bodies are often experiencing financial crises. As I write, the Church of England is cutting the stipends of its clergy, which were, in any case, already at a sub-professional level. The Methodist Church in England has appealed for more generosity from the people in the pews if the Church is to make ends meet. The Vatican is reported to stagger from one year of deficit to another. And in the USA, where the demand for more giving is one of the more insistent messages of the churches, even the Catholic diocese of Chicago reports severe financial stringency. The failure of individual donations to church collections to keep pace with expenditure is one thing but any realistic appraisal of religion would need to assess more than the rate of individual giving, despite the evidence advanced by Finke. It would require that examination be made of the proportion of income received by religious bodies *relative to the gross national product* (GNP). One might hypothesize that, since the time of primitive tribalism, the relative amount of wealth devoted to supernatural concerns (taking religion at its widest) had very much declined. The same trend might be revealed if an appraisal could be made of the capital and income of churches and clergy in, say, the fifteenth century and today, relative to the wealth of each particular society.

Despite their almost exclusive preoccupation with well-established church religion, the contributors in this volume pay no attention to the decline in the number (relative to the population) of religious professionals. This has been a long-term process but the trend has been very much in evidence in recent decades. I have already alluded to the income of clergy, which is one indicator of decline. It should be possible to make some assessment of social standing (and income would be one indicator of the maintenance of status). Certainly as far as Anglican clergy in England are concerned, it can readily be shown that the educational levels of the clergy have been in decline. To make up numbers, the profession has been relying increasingly on 'late entrants'—migrants disenchanted by their experiences of other professions. In consequence partly of that development, the average age of Anglican and Catholic clergy has been rising in England and in Europe. The work-load in respect of servicing more churches has grown for Anglican clergy and ministers of Nonconformist denominations, not because churches have been growing in numbers. Indeed, in England exactly the reverse has been true; these denominations have been closing churches and selling them off. Workloads have been going up because of the decline in the number of ministers and, it appears, the inability of the churches to employ more, even were they available.

All these foregoing points are made as items of common knowledge. I produce no statistics since this is not a research paper so much as a series of reflections but I do not believe the points contentious. The indicators that I have mentioned, together with the attendance statistics—which are the principal interest of most of the contributors—suggest a process of decline in the social significance of religion. It should not pass unnoted, however, that apart from my reference to the proportion of GNP devoted to the supernatural, all of these items pertain primarily to the popular and voluntary support of religion. Even taken together, these factors might be considered as not wholly adequate data for assessing social significance. By that I mean that while they might reveal the extent of popular commitment (to church institutions if not to religious truths) they do not indicate what significance religion has for the operation of the social system. This, I believe, is a much more central aspect of secularization and one which is not merely a matter of the measure of popular support for religious agencies or religious practices but which raises the essential question of just what part religion plays in the functioning of society.

In his essay Brown makes various assertions concerning the continuing significance of religion; 'religion', he avers, 'can and has retained social significance across the change from pre-industrial to industrial society. . . . The power of religion in some of the most advanced economies of the world is manifestly apparent in the late twentieth century.' These are assertions; what is the evidence? Do the churches influence big business? Do business corporations regularly consult the will of God in planning their commercial strategies or in determining the appropriate levels of profit to be sought? Is trades-union policy forged only after prayerful religious counselling? Are we to assume that the moral fibre of the Nixon, Reagan, and Bush administrations was reinforced by the White House breakfasts with Billy Graham or the televangelists? Does the British government consult the Archbishop when devising social policy or does a contemporary prime minister devote to episcopal affairs even a fraction of the time which (as revealed by their correspondence) was the habit of prime ministers in the late nineteenth century? Has *Humane Vitae* given pause to any government with respect to the availability of birth-control appliances (Ireland, of course, always excepted)? Where is this continuing power—a power which once could define secular laws in usury, regulate the conditions of production in the guilds, and prohibit what today are normal business and commercial practices? Such was the power of religion in pre-industrial society, when monarchs were brought cringing for forgiveness to religious shrines and matters of personal morality were effectively dictated by pontifical pronouncements. Where is such power 'manifestly apparent' today?

As measured by figures for church attendance, there are obviously still sizeable—if reduced—bodies of religious votaries in western populations. Yet it is conceivable that many of those who are religiously committed, who attend church, make donations, have their children baptized and confirmed, their weddings celebrated, their funerals conducted, and who say their prayers regularly, none the less do not seek a larger role for religion in the organization and operation of society nor indeed seek to restore to the Church the role which once it played. There are other areas of voluntaristic commitment, some of which elicit response no less fervent that that of most churchpeople; which command larger audiences; which pay their professionals vastly higher stipends; but which none the less exert no great influence on the social system. Football would be one of them. Even were the numbers of church attenders actually increasing (and none of the contributors have actually suggested that) it would not follow that, by virtue of that fact alone, religion was retaining the significance it once had for the operation of the social system.

It is not necessary here to rehearse yet again the functions, now lost, which religion once fulfilled for other social institutions, save to recall that religion once provided legitimacy for secular authority; endorsed, at times even sanctioned, public policy; sustained with a battery of threats and blandishments the agencies of social control; was seen as the font of all 'true learning'; socialized the young ; and even sponsored a range of recreative activities. The loss of these functions is the core of the secularization thesis, much more so than the church-attendance figures which receive so much more attention. Although they were once vital to the functioning of earlier social systems, we have also lost sight of the societal dimensions of religion. There is now an almost exclusive concentration on the voluntaristic commitment of individuals, who seek benefit from religious performance. Of course, the fact that the debate has narrowed in this way is in itself not so surprising—that is what religion has so largely come to be about. In concentrating on these private religious predilections, the contributors unwittingly endorse the contentions of the secularization thesis. They have nothing to say about the social functions of religion because they have come to terms with the actual reality of an increasingly secularized society within which the role of religion has markedly shrunk.

Part of this loss is referred to by Hornsby-Smith as the loss of 'political clout', although he appears to oscillate in his appraisal, saying that English Roman Catholicism has lost political clout, but also saying that 'one should be cautious about assuming that there was a time when English Catholics had greater political clout'. Of course, since the Reformation, as a minority in England, Roman Catholics as such could never have expected their Church to play a central role in the political arena. When we examine such influence as Catholics have been able to exert, it becomes clear that this is not the exercise of societal functions but is predominantly activity as a pressure group pursuing sectional interest such as the best financial terms available from government for support of Catholic schools, or the promotion of sectarian concerns about housing and social welfare for its own people. Catholics or other separate denominations might mobilize their following for the pursuit of such goals but such claims are inspired less by religious impulses than by the demand for the maintenance of quasi-ethnic group identity.

Even in those countries in which Catholics were successful in creating separate facilities and institutions of their own, the specifically religious influence in those organizations has been gradually eroded. Dobbelaere's studies of 'pillarization' in Belgium, the Netherlands, and elsewhere, document the process by which religionists of a particular persuasion created their own agencies replicating those of the State, and did so initially on the assumption that there was a distinctive religious ethos and ideological orientation that must be preserved. Yet his findings were that, in Belgium, Catholic hospitals and Catholic universities were very little differentiated from their secular equivalents. In each case, personnel came increasingly to conform to secular professional and technical norms, took the staff of secular institutions rather than the Church hierarchy as their appropriate reference groups, and served institutions that differed from those of the State principally in name and to some extent in the

discriminatory practices by which they recruited their personnel and clientele. Of course, the promotion of sectional
facilities of this kind is one way of reminding adherents of their
religious identity and a way of recruiting them for instrumental activities to be pursued in the name of their creedal
commitment, even if (or perhaps because) the content of that
creed has itself become somewhat eviscerated. Loyalty to a
specific religious group, even if commitment to its creed has
become largely notional, may continue to evoke response, and
these generalized, perhaps at times nostalgic, dispositions
might continue to provide the basis for voluntary associations
to promote particular causes in the field of social welfare, but
they do not in themselves show sustained religiosity as such.

Hornsby-Smith also alludes to the endorsement by religious
groups of political goals, expressing opposition to the dualism
between religion and politics, and suggesting that the
concerns of social justice are scripturally rooted. It is not my
concern to contest this proposition (which is not in the realm
of an empirical social science) but one might observe that it
has taken the Catholic Church a long time to discover some of
these scriptural roots, and it might be suspected that some
priests have espoused such causes because of their dissatisfaction with their traditional religious roles or perhaps even from
the boredom which is said to beset many religious professionals. The social causes that are espoused, however, are by
no means exclusively endorsed by scripture—there are other
sources of ethical concern, some of them manifestly secular,
and some that might be described as secularist. Nor is
scripture an unequivocal guide to political and moral action.
This is no place in which to trade bible texts but one recalls
that the New Testament virtually endorses civil strife ('father
against son'), acceptance of poverty as permanent human
condition ('the poor you have always with you'), exhorts
obedience to secular authorities ('render unto Caesar' and
'obey the magistrates'), tells Christians 'to be separate', and
gives marriage at best only a qualified sanction (Luke 20: 34–
5; I Cor. 7: 8–9). The religious groups newly concerned with
social justice can rely only selectively on scripture. Much
more to the point respecting the new fashions in moral
theology is the fact that religion has been 'liberated' from its

erstwhile function of providing legitimacy for secular authority. Hence, it has become free to criticize action in the political sphere. The English Nonconformists met this circumstance somewhat earlier but now it has become possible for Catholics and Anglicans to challenge the social and moral premisses of contemporary state societies and to do so whilst claiming religious justification.

Yet, if the heightened religious concern about these political issues is now held up as evidence of the continued power of religion, one must ask further questions. The issues are themselves secular and in so far as religious agencies are active in these areas, is that not in itself a radical shift of concern from the supernatural, from devotional acts, to what are largely secular goals being pursued by secular means? May it not be an evidence that even very committed religionists no longer believe quite so much in the power of prayer to accomplish things, when compared to secular action, whether the goals be the rescue of refugees or the change of governmental policies? Choosing to act as pressure groups rather than as prayer groups, religious bodies, even so, have not been particularly effective. Governments pursue policies with little heed to specifically religious injunctions or interdictions. To take an extreme case, the high attendances at church in pre-war Germany did nothing effective to hinder the rise, or to change the policies of, the Nazis. But even in far less central matters, it is not easy to see just what influence religious lobbies exercise on any but a very limited range of social policies in advanced societies. The Moral Majority effected little in the US, whether the issues were open (and by no means exclusively religious) as in the case of abortion, or were narrower attempts to defend religion (as in the promotion of 'creation science').

None of the critics of the secularization thesis address these issues or the extent to which religion in western societies has undergone the process sometimes described as 'internal secularization'. Certainly Brown declares that religion is 'not a human failing that was born in ignorance and . . . is dying in knowledge'. Discounting the implicit value commitments of this statement, the question remains not whether religion is true—a question with which a dispassionate consideration of secularization need not and should not be concerned—but more empirically, whether people continue to believe what religious agencies have declared to be true. The evidence is that, in one case after another, what religion has held to be true has been relinquished, not only by ordinary laymen but also, implicitly or explicitly, in the overt and covert premises on which our pattern of social organization rests. On every side, we see that what people were required to believe they now tend not to believe or to believe much less, or only with reservations and qualification. Opinion polls have established that belief in God has steadily declined in recent decades and belief in a personal God even more so; fewer people accept the idea of a personal evil, or the reality of the afterlife; whilst the virgin birth, the resurrection, and many biblical miracles are disavowed even by theologians. Natural causes are offered to account for the many biblical episodes in which the supernatural was held to have intervened in human affairs, since empirically untestable claims apparently become less and less credible to men living in a society in which empirical–rational procedures are relied upon to solve an increasing range of both intellectual and practical problems.

In such practical matters, the same abandonment of religious precepts is no less discernible. For centuries, the Church regarded illness and affliction as the will of God, to which resignation, fortitude, and prayer were the appropriate responses for the devout Christian. Who believes that now? Certainly, in modern societies vast sums of money are deployed in direct contravention of such a proposition. If illness is the will of God then mankind, distributively and organizationally, is busy resisting and confuting that will. Our social policy implicitly declares that the world is less God-given than man-made and is subject to man's further amendment. People may still pray for clement weather, for protection from catastrophe, for sufficiency of food, and for the experience of health and well-being, but fewer people believe that prayer has objective effects in influencing supernatural agencies to undertake beneficent man-regarding action, whatever beneficial consequences it may have on the psyche of those who engage in it. The very phrase 'pious hope' indicates the measure of scepticism that is commonly accepted with respect to the extent to which man's petitions and supplications are thought to issue in objective consequences other than those of people's own making.

To turn to another facet of internal secularization, official Christian teaching is that man is inherently sinful and in need of redemption. This is the keystone text on which the structure of Christian theology rests. Yet this fundamental element of Christian faith is now much less emphasized than it was and is often disregarded, and this, it might be suggested, because in the light of contemporary social conditions, people find themselves much less the subject of what was for long taken to be God's punitive dispensation. God as judge, whether in daily life or at Judgement Day, has been largely replaced in contemporary religion by images of the loving son. The stern authority of the father has been very largely displaced by what was once merely the countervailing brotherly love of the son. Is the change only coincidental with the shift from a paternalistic society to one in which fraternity is more stressed? Hellfire, once so powerful a concept in religious teaching, has been steadily abandoned. If the message of salvation is still accepted—as it is by many—the preconditions and post-conditions have become largely neglected. The current mood, reflecting secular experience of a society in which there has been increasing affluence and heightened living standards and expectations, is one wholly at odds with what religion was once considered to be all about. Of course, apologists for religion and those committed to the proposition that religion is a constant in social organizations, will interpret such radical processes of abandonment of traditional teaching as evidence of the remarkable capacity of religion to adapt to change. In doing so, they concede (even if unwittingly) that the character of religion is in large part dependent on existing social structure.

The question is raised whether religious pluralism promotes secularization by relativizing faith or whether by widening choice it stimulates commitment to competing religious bodies. The difficulties of isolating plurality of religion as a variable and of dissociating its influence from that of other cultural circumstances may preclude any satisfactory answer to such a question. A multiplicity of religions may offer free choice. On the other hand, where different religious persuasions serve as badges of identity for distinct ethnic constituencies there can be no 'market situations' for religions and no effective free choice. The effect of pluralism may change over time. As people become aware that alien religionists are also capable of what they regard as civilized behaviour, decency, and integrity, there may be a diminution of the sense of distinctive superiority which in origin (and often long thereafter) each religion claims for itself.

It is certainly likely to be the case that manifestations of secularization in countries with a tradition of more or less coercive religious conformity will differ from those of countries such as the USA with a history of religious voluntarism. Secularization, after all, is a many sided phenomenon affecting different aspects of the social and cultural structures of society in diverse ways and in different sequence. Religious coercion in European countries was seen as essential for the maintenance of social cohesion; religious dissent and diversity were perceived as a threat to social solidarity. In the USA, the inheritor of divergent strands of European religion, exactly the opposite perception necessarily came to prevail. Religious toleration was the only guarantor of social cohesion in a society inheriting such diverse religious traditions, all of which had to be tolerated and accommodated. Coercion or obligation in societies without (or with few) plural opportunities may, once these constraints are relaxed, be a likely precondition for religious indifference. The dominance of one State-supported faith and the suppression of alternatives has the effect of inducing those opposed to the State and its government to become anti-clerical and thus stimulates secularist ideology. The evidence is there from France, Belgium, Spain, and Italy. In contrast, where plural religious expression was permitted, the political debate pro- and anti-State remained within the confines of the wider ultimate religious discourse, and although in the narrower sense, State-supported religion was challenged, the challenge was less radical and was fought on shared religious ground. Such was the case with the toleration of Nonconformist groups in Britain, which may be said without entirely endorsing the Halevy thesis. It is in this situation that one might expect the effects of relativism to become evident. As old causes of dissent and divisions were forgotten, as they lost significance for subsequent generations, as religious ardour cooled and lost its political connotations, so might accommodation occur between religious groups, eventually facilitating a pusillanimous ecumenism and a measure of the type of internal secularization of the churches that we have already discussed.

One of the not uncommon arguments against the secularization thesis, and one which can be found in the foregoing pages, is that since the thesis contends that there has been a decline in religion (a decline in the social significance of religion, as I should prefer to put it), then it follows that there must have been an earlier time when religion was more vigorous and more socially influential than it is today. It is then asked when exactly was that time. Hornsby-Smith declares that there never was a 'golden age' of English post-Reformation Catholicism. One can readily concur, since the thesis does not apply to one particular minority denomination. One may concede more. As has sometimes been pointed out, episcopal records for many different points of time in foregoing centuries document frequent and recurrent complaints about laxity in religious practice, absence from communion, the persistence of folk practices, the growth of heretical movements, and even (less in England than in Catholic countries) the appearance of anti-clericalism. The flaw in the argument is that those who point to these matters implicitly assume that there was only one religion at issue, that 'religion' meant Christianity and often meant only the one established or State-supported Church. The secularization thesis is concerned with much more than this one manifestation of religiosity. Past ages were generally times of intense religiosity, which included a wide variety of supernaturalist orientations. It is only the consequence of the trenchant exclusivism of Christianity that other manifestations of religion were conceptually ruled out of court as 'unbelief' or 'irreligion'. It took the Church a long time to eradicate paganism and local magic, and before these were extinguished, heresy and dissent were rampant. Times past may not present to us an age of faith in the narrow Christian sense, but they were times of vigorous, albeit promiscuous, religiosity, and the secularization thesis has to do with the diminution of the significance of the whole gamut of these variant manifestations of supernaturalist belief, practice, and institutions.

It is in this sense that it is sometimes suggested that Christianity was itself an agency of secularization, as was Judaism in its contention with the immanentist magical practice of the indigenous populations of the territory in which the Jews took up occupation. In suppressing the multiform local manifestations of supernaturalism, in disciplining procedures for the invocation of divine power, in organizing a regulated public cult to replace private and individual attempts to harness the spiritual forces supposedly operative in the world, the great religions were incipient agencies of secularity. Through the unified organizations which they evolved, the sphere of the sacred was distinguished from that of the profane, a secular realm became recognizable and the legitimate area for supernaturalist operations became defined and demarcated. Under the rationalizing spirit of Christianity, the world full of spirits, demons, fairies, nymphs, goblins, and necromancers became an outlawed world, reference to which was marginalized in Christian teaching, despite the significance which scripture at some points accords to such supposititious entities. Increasingly, Christianity itself became the vehicle for more rational orientations to the supernatural, with manifest leaps forward into a more secular frame of mind as illustrated in the Reformation, and subsequently by a variety of more secularized religious bodies, including Quakers, Baptists and, above all, Unitarians. If each movement embraced more of the rationalistic spirit of the age of their early development, each also tried to 'hold the line' by sustaining entrenched religious tenets. Yet popular belief (or disbelief) regularly outstripped the creedal position adopted by these movements, most evidently in the widespread disbelief in the charter articles of the Anglican Church, even by those who had formally declared their belief in them.

If one seeks to transcend the insularity of approach which identifies Christianity as the only and exclusive brand of religion, one may, I think, recognize that there was in times past (whether one calls it 'a golden age of faith' or not) a much wider acceptance of supernaturalism of one sort or another (or perhaps simultaneously of several sorts). The reality of spiritual things was accepted and men lived in fear of supernatural intervention in everyday life, and regulated their conduct by a variety of nostrums and superstitions, prayers, charms, intercessions, masses, and pilgrimages, to manipulate the supernatural in ways propitious to the supplicant and his community. Nor was this all. In its more formal aspects, the institutions of religion (in western Europe for centuries the institutions of the Christian Church) were closely integrated with the other institutional orders of society, which they may at times have dominated and which—in economics, in the polity, in judicial affairs, in education, even, in some respects, in the maintenance of health, and certainly in the superinten-dence of birth and death—were infused with religious legitimations, prescriptions, and interdictions. It seems to me not difficult to dispel the objections that are mounted by those who ask when it was that religion was so pervasive in society.

It may not be altogether inappropriate, in conclusion, to address the issue which is raised by Finke, although it is somewhat external to the actual merits of the arguments concerning secularization. If one looks at those who are actively engaged in discussion of the subject, one sees that the list appears to be remarkably tilted. The majority are undoubtedly disposed to reject the secularization thesis. Some do so on the grounds advanced twenty-five years ago by David Martin, that secularization is a 'counter-religious' ideology that betrays a Marxist orientation. The point is endorsed by Finke. Martin, let it be said, apparently recanted for having demanded in that same article that the word 'secularization' should be expunged from the sociological dictionary; a dozen years later he wrote a book entitled *A General Theory of Secularization*. The source of this particular charge appears to lie in a confusion of secularism with secularization. Whilst the former is certainly an ideology and one which seeks to minimize, if not to eliminate, the role of religion in social affairs, secularization is merely the description, for which empirical evidences can be advanced, of a process of social change in which religion loses social significance. No one, I imagine, charged Owen Chadwick with covert Marxism or counter-religious ideology when he wrote *The Secularization of the European Mind* nor says this of the clergy when—as they not infrequently do—they lament the loss of religious moral influence in social life and dilate on the problems of redundant churches and the superintendence by one clergyman of three, four, or even five, once-thriving but now ill-attended, rural churches. Yet despite acknowledgement of such actualities, when the issue is given a measure of theoretical conceptualization and broadly discussed as a long-term social process, it appears to arouse passions and to give rise to the charge that the concept is the pure and fictive creation of a counter-religious ideology.

For some circumstances, the secularization thesis appears to be regarded almost as a moral affront, as assault on their faith, a betrayal of a latent belief in the inevitable progress of Christianity, and the Christianization of the world. Yet, it should be possible for academics to appraise this issue dispassionately and without the intrusion of any religious (or anti-religious) dispositions and extraneous value-commitments which, as private individuals, they might entertain.

When, outside the confines of the relatively small circles of those who have involved themselves with it, one raises this subject with historians, sociologists, economists, or psychologists, one sees how readily those engaged with other aspects of the social system and its culture take secularization for granted. Their overwhelming tendency, as I have observed it, is to regard religion as a peripheral phenomenon in contemporary social organization, and one which, in their studies of the broad contours of social change, productivity, economic growth, or human psychology, they rarely find need to consider. Not infrequently they express some amusement that religion should be given the serious attention which I and others in the sociology of religion devote to it. Of course, these various and numerous social scientists could be overlooking a social force of paramount importance in the operation of those facets of the social system in which they are expert, but I doubt it.

Bibliography

ALLEY, R. S., *The Supreme Court on Church and State* (New York, 1988).

ANDERSON, A. L., *Divided We Stand: Institutional Religion as a Reflection of Pluralism and Integration in America* (Dubuque, 1978).

ARCHER, A., *The Two Catholic Churches: A Study in Oppression* (London, 1986).

ARGYLE, M., *Religious Behaviour* (London, 1958).

BAKER, D. (ed.), *Religious Motivation* (Oxford, 1978).

BALLARD, R., and BALLARD, C., 'The Sikhs: The Development of Southern Asian Settlements in Britain', in J. L. Watson (ed.), *Between Two Cultures* (Oxford 1977), 21–56.

BARTLETT, A., 'The Churches in Bermondsey 1880–1939', Ph.D. thesis (Birmingham, 1987).

BECK, G. A., 'Today and Tomorrow', in Beck, G. A. (ed.), *The English Catholics 1850–1950* (London, 1950), 585–614.

BECKER, G., 'The Economic Approach to Human Behavior', in J. Elster (ed.), *Rational Choice* (Oxford, 1986).

BECKFORD, JAMES A., *Cult Controversies: The Societal Response to New Religious Movements* (London, 1985).

—— *Religion and Advanced Industrial Society* (London, 1989).

BECKWITH, I., 'Religion in a Working Men's Parish', *Lincolnshire History and Archaeology* 4 (1969), 29–38.

BERGER, P. L., *The Noise of Solemn Assemblies: Christian Commitment and the Religious Establishment in America* (New York, 1961).

—— 'A Market Model for the Analysis of Ecumenicity', *Social Research* 30 (1963), 77–93.

—— *The Sacred Canopy* (New York, 1967).

—— *A Rumour of Angels: Modern Society and the Rediscovery of the Supernatural* (New York, 1969).

—— *The Social Reality of Religion* (Harmondsworth, 1973).

—— *Facing Up To Modernity* (Harmondsworth, 1979).

—— *The Heretical Imperative: Contemporary Possibilities of Religious Affirmation* (New York, 1979).

Berlin und die Berliner: Dinge, Sitten, Winke (Karlsruhe, 1905).

BIBBY, R., 'Religious Encasement in Canada', *Social Compass* 32 (1985), 287–303.

—— and WEAVER, H. R., 'Cult Consumption in Canada: A Further Critique of Stark and Bainbridge', *Sociological Analysis* 35 (1985), 189–200.

BIGLER, R. M., *The Politics of German Protestantism* (Los Angeles, 1972).

BLACK, A., 'London Church and Mission Attendances', The *British Weekly*, 23 Feb. 1928, 1 Mar. 1928, and 8 Mar. 1928.

BLOTH, P., 'Zum Verhaltnis von Religionsunterricht und Konfirmandenunterricht unter seelsorgerisch-diakonischem Aspekt', in Elm, K., and Loock, H.-D. (eds.), *Seelsorge und Diakonie in Berlin* (Berlin, 1990), 329–39.

BLUMER, H., *Symbolic Interactionism* (Englewood Cliffs, NJ, 1969).

BOOTH, C., *Life and Labour of the People in London: Third Series: Religious Influences* (London, 1902).

BREAULT, K. D., 'New Evidence on Religious Pluralism, Urbanism and Religious Participation', *American Sociological Review* 54 (1989), 1048–53.

BRIERLEY, P. (ed.), *Prospects for the Eighties* (London, 1980).

—— 'Religion', in Halsey, A. H. (ed.), *British Social Trends Since 1900* (London, 1990), 518–60.

—— (ed.), *UK Christian Handbook (1985/86 Edition)* (London, 1984).

—— *UK Christian Handbook (1989/90 Edition)* (London, 1988).

BRITISH PARLIAMENTARY PAPERS, *1851 Census, Great Britain, Report and Tables on Religious Worship, England and Wales*, 1852–3, (reprinted Irish University Press 1970) and *Religious Worship and Education, Scotland, Report and Tables* (London, 1854).

—— *The Royal Commission on the Church of England and Other Religious Bodies in Wales and Monmouthshire 1905–6* (London, 1911).

BROWN, C. G., 'The Costs of Pew Renting: Church Management, Church-Going and Social Class in Nineteenth-Century Glasgow', *Journal of Ecclesiastical History* 38 (1987), 347–61.

—— *The Social History of Religion in Scotland Since 1730* (London, 1987).

—— 'Did Urbanization Secularize Britain?' *Urban History Yearbook* (1988), 1–14.

—— 'Religion and Social Change', in Devine, T. M., and Mitchison, R. (eds.), *People and Society in Scotland: i, 1760–1830* (Edinburgh, 1988) 143–62.

—— 'Religion, Class and Church Growth', in Fraser, H., and Morris, R. J. (eds.), *People and Society in Scotland: ii, 1830–1914* (Edinburgh, 1990).

—— 'Religion and Secularization', in Dickson, T. M., and Treble, J. (eds.), *People and Society in Scotland: iii, 1914 to the Present* (Edinburgh, forthcoming).

BROWN, T. N., *Irish-American Nationalism 1870–1890* (Philadelphia, 1966).

BRUCE, S., *God Save Ulster! The Religion and Politics of Paisleyism* (Oxford, 1986).

—— *The Rise and Fall of the New Christian Right: Conservative Protestant Politics in America 1978–1988* (Oxford, 1988).

—— *A House Divided: Protestantism, Schism and Secularization* (London, 1990).

—— 'Modernity and Fundamentalism: The New Christian Right in America', *British Journal of Sociology* 41 (1990), 477–96.

—— *Pray TV: Televangelism in America* (London, 1990).

—— 'Religion and Rational Choice', *Sociological Analysis* (forthcoming).

BRUNNER, E. DES, *Village Communities* (New York, 1925).

BUDD, S., *Varieties of Unbelief* (London, 1977).

BUKOWCZYK, J. J., 'The Transforming Power of the Machine: Popular Religion, Ideology and Secularization Among Polish Immigrant Workers in the United States 1880–1940', *International Labor and Working Class History* 34 (1988), 22–38.

CAPLOW, T., 'Contrasting Trends in European and American Religion', *Sociological Analysis* 46 (1985), 101–8.

—— BAHR, H. M., and CHADWICK, B., *All Faithful People: Change and Continuity in Middletown's Religion* (Minneapolis, 1983).

CARWARDINE, R., 'The Religious Revival of 1857–8 in the United States', in Baker, D. (ed.), *Religious Motivation* (Oxford, 1978), 393–406.

CAYLEY, C., *The Leeds Guide: Giving a Concise History of That Rich and Populous Town . . .* (Leeds, 1808).

CHRISTIANO, K. J., *Religious Diversity and Social Change: American Cities 1890–1906* (Cambridge, 1987).

CLARK, E. T., *An Album of Methodist History* (Nashville, 1952).

COLLINS, G. N. M., *The Heritage of Our Fathers* (Edinburgh, 1976).

COLLINSON, P., *The Religion of Protestants: The Church in English Society 1559–1625* (Oxford, 1982).

—— *Godly People: Essays on English Protestantism and Puritanism* (London, 1985).

COMAN, P., *Catholics and the Welfare State* (London, 1977).

COX, J., *The English Churches in a Secular Society: Lambeth 1870–1930* (Oxford, 1982).

CROSSICK, G. (ed.), *The Lower Middle Class in Britain 1870–1914* (London, 1977).

CURRIE, R., *Methodism Divided* (London, 1968).

—— GILBERT, A. D., and HORSLEY, L., *Churches and Churchgoers: Patterns of Church Growth in the British Isles Since 1700* (Oxford, 1977).

DANIELL, A. E., *London City Churches* (London, 1895).

DAVIE, G., '"An Ordinary God": The Paradox of Religion in Contemporary Britain', *British Journal of Sociology* 41 (1990), 395–421.

DE TOCQUEVILLE, A., *Democracy in America* (New York, 1969).

—— *Travels to England and Ireland* (New Brunswick, NJ, 1988).

DOBBELAERE, K., 'Secularization: A Multi-Dimensional Concept', *Current Sociology* 29 (1981), 3–213.

—— 'Secularization Theories and Sociological Paradigms: A Reformulation of the Private–Public Dichotomy and the Problem of Societal Integration', *Sociological Analysis* 46 (1985), 377–87.

—— 'Some Trends in European Sociology of Religion: The Secularization Debate', *Sociological Analysis* 48 (1987), 107–37.

—— 'The Secularization of Society? Some Methodological Suggestions', in Hadden, J. K., and Shupe A. (eds.), *Secularization and Fundamentalism Reconsidered* (New York, 1989), 27–44.

DOLAN, J. P., *The American Catholic Experience* (New York, 1985).

DOUGLAS, M., *Natural Symbols: Explorations in Cosmology* (Harmondsworth, 1973).

DOW, L., *Lorenzo Dow's Journal*, 6th edn. (New York, 1849).

EARLE, J. R., KNUDSEN, D. D., and SHRIVER Jr., D. W., *Spindles and Spires: A Restudy of Religion and Social Change in Gastonia* (Atlanta, 1976).

ELM, K., and LOOCK, H.-D. (eds.), *Seelsorge und Diakonie in Berlin* (Berlin, 1990).

ERMEL, H., *Die Kirchenaustrittsbewegung im Deutschen Reich 1906–14* (Cologne, 1971).

FINKE, R., 'Religious Deregulation: Origins and Consequences', *Journal of Church and State* 32 (1990), 609–26.

—— and STARK, R., 'Turning Pews into People: Estimating 19th-Century Church Membership', *Journal for the Scientific Study of Religion* 25 (1986), 180–92.

—— —— 'Religious Economies and Sacred Canopies: Religious Mobilization in American Cities, 1906', *American Sociological Review* 53 (1988), 41–9.

—— —— 'How the Upstart Sects Won America: 1776–1850', *Journal for the Scientific Study of Religion* 28 (1989), 27–44.

—— —— 'Evaluating the Evidence: Religious Economies and Sacred Canopies', *American Sociological Review* 54 (1989), 1054–6.

FISCHER, C. S., *To Dwell among Friends* (Chicago, 1982).

FLORA, P., *et al.*, *State, Economy and Society in Western Europe 1815–1975*, ii. (Frankfurt, 1987).

FOSTER, P., 'Secularization in the English Context: Some Conceptual and Empirical Problems', *Sociological Review* 20 (1972), 153–68.

FRANCIS, L., *Rural Anglicanism* (London, 1985).

FULTON, J., *The Tragedy of Belief* (Oxford, 1991).

GALLUP Jr., G., and POLING, D., *The Search for America's Faith* (Nashville, 1980).

—— and CASTELLI, J., *The People's Religion* (New York, 1989).

GALLUP ORGANIZATION, THE, *Religion in America*, Report No. 259 (Princeton, NJ, 1987).

GAUSTAD, E. S., *Historical Atlas of Religion in America* (New York, 1962).

GIBSON, R., *A Social History of French Catholicism 1789–1914* (London, 1989).

GIDDENS, A., *Consequences of Modernity* (London, 1991).

GILBERT, A. D., *Religion and Society in Industrial England: Church, Chapel and Social Change 1740–1914* (London, 1976).

—— *The Making of Post-Christian Britain* (London, 1980).

GILL, R., *Competing Convictions* (London, 1989).

—— *The Myth of the Empty Church* (London, forthcoming).

GILLEY, S., 'Vulgar Piety and the Brompton Oratory', in Swift, R., and Gilley, S. (eds.), *The Irish in the Victorian City* (Beckenham, 1985), 255–66.

GLAZER, N., and MOYNIHAN, D. P., *Beyond the Melting Pot*, 2nd edn. (Cambridge, Mass., 1970).

GLOCK, C. Y., and STARK, R., *Religion and Society in Tension* (Chicago, 1965).

GOODRIDGE, R. M., '"The Ages of Faith": Romance or Reality?', *Sociological Review* 23 (1975), 381–96.

GOUDSBLOM, J., *Dutch Society* (New York, 1967).

GRAY, R. Q., *The Labour Aristocracy in Victorian Edinburgh* (London, 1976).

GREELEY, A. M., *Religious Change in America* (Cambridge, 1989).

—— 'American Exceptionalism: The Religious Phenomenon'. Presented at a conference at Nuffield College, Oxford, 1987.

GREENBERG, J. H., 'The Measurement of Linguistic Diversity', *Language* 32 (1956), 109–15.

GRIFFEN, C., 'An Urban Church in Ferment: The Episcopal Church in New York City 1880–1900', Ph.D. thesis (Columbia, 1960).

HADDEN, J. K., 'Toward Desacralizing Secularization Theory', *Social Forces* 65 (1987), 587–611.

HAMMOND, P. E., 'Religion and the Persistence of Identity', *Journal for the Scientific Study of Religion* 27 (1988), 1–11.

HANDY, R. T., 'The American Religious Depression, 1925–1935', in Mulder, J. M., and Wilson, J. F. (eds.), *Religion in American History* (Englewood Cliffs, 1987).

HARRIS, H. W., and BRYANT, M., *The Churches and London* (London, 1914).

HATCH, N., *The Democratization of American Christianity* (New Haven, 1989).

HAY, D., and MORRISEY, A., 'Reports of Ecstatic, Paranormal and Religious Experience in Great Britain and the United States: A Comparison of Trends', *Journal for the Scientific Study of Religion*, 17 (1978), 255–68.

HEMPTON, D., *Methodism and Politics in British Society, 1750–1850* (Stanford, 1984).

—— 'Methodism and the Law', in Dyson, A., and Barker, E. (eds.), *Sects and New Religious Movements, Bulletin of the John Rylands University Library of Manchester* 70 (1988), 93–107.

HERBERG, W., *Protestant-Catholic-Jew* (New York, 1959).

HERVIEU-LÉGER, D., *Vers un nouveau christianisme? Introduction à la sociologie du christianisme occidental* (Paris, 1986).

HERZFELD, H. (ed.), *Berlin und die Provinz Brandenburg im 19. und 20. Jahrhundert* (Berlin, 1968).

HICKEY, J., *Urban Catholics: Urban Catholicism in England and Wales from 1829 to the Present Day* (London, 1967).

HICKMAN, M. J., 'A Study of the Incorporation of the Irish in Britain with Special Reference to Catholic State Education: Involving a Comparison of the Attitudes of Pupils and Teachers in Selected Catholic Schools in London and Liverpool', Ph.D. thesis (London, 1990).

HILL, S. S., *Southern Churches in Crisis* (New York, 1966).

—— 'Religion and Region in America', in Roof, W. C. (ed.), *The Annals: Religion in America Today* (Beverley Hills, Calif., 1985).

HOBSBAWM, E. J., *Industry and Empire* (Harmondsworth, 1977).

HÖLSCHER, L, *Weltgericht oder Revolution?* (Stuttgart, 1989).

—— 'Die Religion des Bürgers: Bürgerliche Frömmigkeit und Protestantische Kirche im 19. Jahrhundert', *Historische Zeitschrift* 256 (1990), 595–630.

HORNSBY-SMITH, M. P., 'Catholic Accounts: Problems of Institutional Involvement', in Gilbert G. N., and Abell, P. (eds.), *Accounts and Action* (Aldershot, 1983), 132–52.

—— 'The Immigrant Background of Roman Catholics in England and Wales: A Research Note', *New Community* 13 (1986), 79–85.

—— *Roman Catholics in England: Studies in Social Structure Since the Second World War* (Cambridge, 1987).

—— 'Into the Mainstream: Recent Transformations in British Catholicism', in Gannon, T. M. (ed.), *World Catholicism in Transition* (London, 1988), 219–31.

—— *The Changing Parish: A Study of Parishes, Priests, and Parishioners After Vatican II* (London, 1989).

—— *Roman Catholic Beliefs in England: Customary Religion and Transformations of Religious Authority* (Cambridge, 1991).

—— and Dale, A., 'The Assimilation of Irish Immigrants in England', *British Journal of Sociology* 39 (1988), 519–44.

—— Fulton, J., and Norris, M., 'Assessing RENEW: A Study of a Renewal Movement in a Roman Catholic Diocese in England', in

Fulton, J., and Gee, P. (eds.), *Power in Religion: Decline and Growth?* (London, 1991), 101–14.

—— and Lee, R. M., *Roman Catholic Opinion: A Study of Roman Catholics in England and Wales in the 1970s* (Guildford, 1979).

—— —— and Reilly, P. A., 'Social and Religious Change in Four English Roman Catholic Parishes', *Sociology* 18 (1984), 353–65.

—— —— —— 'Common Religion and Customary Religion: A Critique and a Proposal', *Review of Religious Research* 26 (1985), 244–52.

—— —— and Turcan, K. A., 'A Typology of English Catholics', *Sociological Review* 30 (1982), 433–59.

—— Turcan, K. A., and Rajan, L. T., 'Patterns of Religious Commitment, Intermarriage and Marital Breakdown Among English Catholics', *Archives de sciences sociales des religions* 64 (1987), 137–55.

HOUTART, F., 'Conflicts of Authority in the Roman Catholic Church', *Social Compass* 16 (1969), 309–25.

HUNTER, J. D., *American Evangelicalism: Conservative Religion and the Quandary of Modernity* (New Brunswick, NJ, 1983).

—— *Evangelicalism: The Coming Generation* (Chicago, 1987).

IANNACCONE, L. R., 'The Consequences of Religious Market Regulation', *Rationality and Society* 3 (1991), 156–77.

—— 'Why Strict Churches are Strong'. Presented at the annual meeting of the Society for the Scientific Study of Religion, 1989.

INGLIS, K. S., 'Patterns of Religious Worship in 1851', *Journal of Ecclesiastical History* 11 (1960), 74–87.

—— *Churches and the Working Classes in Victorian England* (London, 1963).

IRELAND, R., *The Challenge of Secularization* (Melbourne, 1988).

JACQUET, C. H., *Yearbook of American and Canadian Churches* (Nashville, 1988).

JOAD, C. E. M., *The Present and Future of Religion* (London, 1930).

JOHNSON, B., 'A Fresh Look at Theories of Secularization', in Blalock Jr., H. (ed.), *Sociological Theory and Research* (New York, 1970).

JONES, C. C., *The Social Survey of Merseyside*, 3 vols. (London, 1934).

JONES, I. G., and WILLIAMS, D. (eds.), *The Religious Census of 1851: A Calendar of the Returns Relating to Wales*, 2 vols. (Cardiff, 1976 and 1981).

KELLEY, D. M., *Why Conservative Churches are Growing: A Study in the Sociology of Religion* (New York, 1972).

KNIFFKA, J., *Das kirchliche Leben in Berlin-Ost in der Mitte der Zwanziger Jahre* (Munster, 1971).

KOOPMANSCHAP, T., 'Transformations in Contemporary Roman Catholicism: A Case Study', Ph.D. thesis (Liverpool, 1978).

KUPISCH, K., 'Christlich-kirchliches Leben in den letzten hundert Jahren', in Herzfeld, H. (ed.), *Berlin und die Provinz Brandenburg im 19. und 20. Jahrhundert* (Berlin, 1968).

LADOURIE, E. LeR., *Montaillou: Cathars and Catholics in a French Village 1294–1324* (Harmondsworth, 1980).

LAND, K. C., DEANE, G., and BLAU, J. R., 'Religious Pluralism and Church Membership: A Spatial Diffusion Model', *American Sociological Review* 56 (1991), 237–49.

LANNON, F., *Privilege, Persecution and Prophecy: The Catholic Church in Spain 1875–1975* (Oxford, 1987).

LASLETT, P. W., *The World We Have Lost* (London, 1971).

LAWRENCE, B. B., *Defenders of God: The Fundamentalist Revolt Against the Modern Age* (London, 1990).

LEES, L. H., *Exiles of Erin: Irish Migrants in Victorian London* (Manchester, 1979).

LEINENWEBER, C., 'The Class and Ethnic Bases of New York City Socialism 1904–15', *Labor History* 22 (1981), 29–56.

LEIXNER, O. VON, *Soziale Briefe aus Berlin* (Berlin, 1891).

LEVENSTEIN, A., *Die Arbeiterfrage* (Munich, 1912).

LIDTKE, V. L., 'August Bebel and German Social Democracy's Relationship to the Christian Churches', *Journal of the History of Ideas* 27 (1966), 245–64.

LIEBERSON, S., 'An Extension of Greenberg's Linguistic Diversity Measures', *Language* 40 (1964), 526–31.

LISCO, F. G., *Zur Kirchengeschichte Berlins* (Berlin, 1857).

LODGE, D., *How Far Can You Go?* (London, 1980).

LUCKMANN, T., *The Invisible Religion: The Problem of Religion in Modern Society* (London, 1970).

McILHINEY, D. B., 'A Gentleman in Every Slum: Church of England Missions in East London 1837–1914', Ph.D. thesis (Princeton, NJ, 1977).

MACINTYRE, A., *Secularization and Moral Change* (London, 1967).

McLEOD, H., 'Class, Community and Religion: The Religious Geography of Nineteenth-Century England', in Hill, M. (ed.), *Sociological Yearbook of Religion in Britain*, vol. vi (London, 1973).

—— *Class and Religion in the Late Victorian City* (London, 1974).

—— 'White Collar Values and the Role of Religion', in Crossick, G. (ed.), *The Lower Middle Class in Britain 1870–1914* (London, 1977).

—— *Religion and the People of Western Europe 1789–1970* (Oxford, 1981).

—— 'Protestantism and the Working Class in Imperial Germany', *European Studies Review* 12 (1982), 323–44.

—— 'New Perspectives on Victorian Working-Class Religion: The Oral Evidence', *Oral History Journal* 14 (1986), 31–49.

—— 'Religion in the British and German Labour Movements', *Bulletin of the Society for the Study of Labour History* 51 (1986), 25–35.

—— 'Catholicism and the New York Irish 1880–1920', in Obelkevich, J., Roper, L., and Samuel, R. (eds.), *Disciplines of Faith* (London, 1987), 337–51.

—— 'The Culture of Popular Catholicism in New York City in the Later Nineteenth and Early Twentieth Centuries', in von Voss, L. H., and van Holthoon, F. (eds.), *Working Class and Popular Culture* (Amsterdam, 1988), 71–82.

McLOUGHLIN, W. G., *New England Dissent, 1630–1833* (Cambridge, 1971).

MARTIN, D., 'Towards Eliminating the Concept of Secularization', in Gould, J. (ed.), *Penguin Survey of the Social Sciences* (Harmondsworth, 1965), 169–82.

—— *A Sociology of English Religion* (London, 1967).

—— *The Religious and the Secular: Studies in Secularization* (London, 1969).

—— *A General Theory of Secularization* (Oxford, 1978).

MATZERATH, H., 'Wachstum und Mobilitat der Berliner Bevölkerung im 19. und frühen 20. Jahrhundert', in Elm, K., and Loock, H.-D. (eds.), *Seelsorge und Diakonie in Berlin* (Berlin, 1990).

MAY, H. F., *The Protestant Churches in Industrial America* (New York, 1949).

MERTON, R. K., *The Sociology of Science: Theoretical and Empirical Investigations* (Chicago, 1973).

—— and KENDALL, P. L., *The Focused Interview* (Glencoe, 1956).

MOORE, D. D., *At Home in America: Second-Generation New York Jews* (New York, 1981).

MUDIE-SMITH, R. (ed.), *The Religious Life of London* (London, 1904).

MURPHY, J., *Church, State and Schools in Britain: 1800–1970* (London, 1971).

NEUHAUS, R., *The Naked Public Square: Religion and Democracy in America* (Grand Rapids, Mich., 1984).

NEWMAN, W. M. and HALVORSON, P. L., *Patterns in Pluralism: A Portrait of American Religion* (Washington, DC, 1980).

NIEBUHR, H. R., *The Social Sources of Denominationalism* (New York, 1962).

NIPPERDEY, T., *Religion im Umbruch: Deutschland 1870–1914* (Munich, 1988).

NUGENT, W. T. K., *From Centennial to World War: American Society 1876–1917* (Indianapolis, 1977).

OBELKEVICH, J., *Religion and Rural Society: South Lindsey 1825–1875* (Oxford, 1976).

OBELKEVICH, J., ROPER, L., and SAMUEL, R. (eds.), *Disciplines of Faith* (London, 1987).

ORSI, R., *The Madonna of 115th Street* (New Haven, Conn., 1985).

PATTERSON, G., 'The Religious Census: A Test of Its Accuracy in South Shields', *Durham County Local History Society Bulletin* (Apr. 1978), 14–17.

PAUL, L., *The Deployment and Payment of the Clergy* (London, 1964).

PERRY, F., 'The Working Man's Alienation from the Church', *American Journal of Sociology* 4 (1898–9), 621–9.

PHAYER, M., *Sexual Liberation in Nineteenth-Century Europe* (London, 1977).

POLLMANN, K. R., *Landesherrliches Kirchenregiment und Soziale Frage* (Berlin, 1973).

POMIAN-SRZEDNICKI, M., *Religious Change in Contemporary Poland: Secularization and Politics* (London, 1982).

POSNER, R., 'The Law and Economics Movement', *American Economic Review* 77 (1987), 1–13.

PRYCE, K., *Endless Pressure* (Harmondsworth, 1979).

QUINN, B., ANDERSON, H., BRADLEY, M., GOETTING, P., and SHRIVER, P., *Churches and Church Membership in the United States, 1980* (Atlanta, 1982).

RAVITCH, D., *The Great School Wars: New York City 1805–1973* (New York, 1974).

REED, J. S., *The Enduring South: Subcultural Persistence in Mass Society* (Lexington, Mass., 1972).

REICHLEY, A. J., *Religion in American Public Life* (Washington, DC, 1985).

REX, J. and MOORE, R., *Race, Community and Conflict: A Study of Sparkbrook* (Oxford, 1967).

RIBBE, W., *Geschichte Berlins*, 2 vols. (Munich, 1987).

—— 'Zur Entwicklung und Funktion der Pfarrgemeinden in der evangelischen Kirche Berlins', in Elm, K., and Loock, H.-D. (eds.), *Seelsorge und Diakonie in Berlin* (Berlin, 1990), 233–64.

RICHMAN, G., *Fly a Flag for Poplar* (London, 1976).

ROBBINS, T., and ROBERTSON, R. (eds.), *Church–State Relations: Tensions and Transitions* (New Brunswick, NJ, 1987).

ROBERTSON, R., *The Sociological Interpretation of Religion* (Oxford, 1970).

—— and CHIRICO, J.-A., 'Humanity, Globalization and Worldwide Religious Resurgence: A Theoretical Exploration', *Sociological Analysis* 46 (1985), 219–42.

ROCHON, T. R., 'The Creation of Political Institutions: Two Cases From the Netherlands', *International Journal of Comparative Sociology* 25 (1984), 173–88.

ROGERS, R., 'Revivalism and Manufacturing in Upper State New York'. Presented at the annual meeting of the American Sociological Association, 1987.

ROOF, W. C., and McKINNEY, W., *American Mainline Religion: Its Changing Shape and Future* (New Brunswick, 1987).

ROSENBERG, C. S., *Religion and the Rise of the American City* (Ithaca, NY, 1971).

ROSENWAIKE, I., *Population History of New York City* (Syracuse, NY, 1972).

ROSS, E., 'Survival Networks: Women's Neighbourhood Sharing in London Before World War One', *History Workshop* 15 (1983).

ROWNTREE, B. S., *Poverty: A Study of Town Life* (London, 1901).

—— *Poverty and Progress: A Second Social Study of York* (London, 1941).

—— and LAVERS, G. R., *English Life and Leisure: A Social Study* (London, 1951).

RYAN, W., 'Assimilation of Irish Immigrants in Britain', Ph.D. thesis (St Louis, 1973).

SCHERER, F. M., *Industrial Market Structure and Economic Performance* (Chicago, 1970).

SCHNABEL, F., *Deutsche Geschichte im 19. Jahrhundert*, 4 vols. (Freiburg im Breisgau, 1937).

SCHNEIDER, L., and DORNBUSCH, S. M., 'Inspirational Religious Literature: From Latent to Manifest Functions', *American Journal of Sociology* 62 (1957), 476–81.

SCOTT, G., *The RCs: Report on Roman Catholics in Britain Today* (London, 1967).

SHORTRIDGE, J., 'A New Regionalism of American Religion', *Journal for the Scientific Study of Religion* 16 (1977), 143–53.

SIMON, W., 'Katholische Schulen, Religionsunterricht und Katechese in Berlin', in Elm, K., and Loock, H.-D. (eds.), *Seelsorge und Diakonie in Berlin* (Berlin, 1990), 341–84.

SMITH, J. T., *The Catholic Church in the Archdiocese of New York*, 2 vols. (New York, 1905).

SPENGLER, O., *Das deutsche Element von New York* (New York, 1913).

SPERBER, J., *Popular Catholicism in Nineteenth-Century Germany* (Princeton, NJ, 1984).

SPUFFORD, M., 'Can We Count the "Godly" and the "Conformable" in the Seventeenth Century?', *Journal of Ecclesiastical History* 36 (1985).

STARK, R., 'Must All Religions Be Supernatural?', in Wilson, B. R. (ed.), *The Socialist Impact of New Religious Movements* (New York, 1981), 159–78.

—— 'Correcting Church Membership Rates, 1971 and 1980', *Review of Religious Research* 29 (1987), 69–77.

STARK, R., *Sociology*, 3rd edn. (Belmont, Calif., 1989).

—— and BAINBRIDGE, W. S., 'Towards a Theory of Religion: Religious Commitment', *Journal for the Scientific Study of Religion* 19 (1980), 114–28.

—— —— *The Future of Religion: Secularization, Revival, and Cult Formation* (Berkeley, 1985).

—— —— *The Theory of Religion* (New York, 1987).

—— and FINKE, R., 'American Religion in 1776: A Statistical Portrait', *Sociological Analysis* 49 (1988), 39–51.

STODDART, J. T., 'The *Daily News* Census of 1902–3 Compared With the *British Weekly* Census of 1886', in Mudie-Smith, R. (ed.), *The Religious Life of London* (London, 1904).

SWATOS JR., W. H., 'Losing Faith in the "Religion" of Secularization: Worldwide Religious Resurgence and the Definition of Religion', in Swatos Jr., W. H. (ed.), *Religious Politics in Global and Comparative Perspective* (Greenwood, 1989).

SWIFT, R., and GILLEY, S. (eds.), *The Irish in the Victorian City* (Beckenham, 1985).

THOMAS, K., *Religion and the Decline of Magic* (London, 1973).

THOMPSON, D. M., 'The 1851 Religious Census: Problems and Possibilities', *Victorian Studies* 11 (1967), 87–97.

THOMPSON, K., 'Religion: The British Contribution', *British Journal of Sociology* 41 (1990), 531–7.

THOMPSON, P., *Socialists, Liberals and Labour: The Struggle for London 1885–1914* (London, 1967).

TOBACKNICK, B. G., and FIDDELL, L. S., *Using Mutivariate Statistics* (New York, 1983).

TOWLER, R., *Homo Religiosus: Sociological Problems in the Study of Religion* (London, 1974).

TURNER, B. S., *Religion and Social Theory* (London, 1983).

U.S. BUREAU OF THE CENSUS, *Historical Statistics of the United States: Colonial Times to 1970, Bicentennial Edition* (Washington, DC, 1975).

VRIJHOF, P. H., and WAARDENBURG, J., *Official and Popular Religion: Analysis of a Theme for Religious Studies* (Hague, 1979).

WALKER, R. B., 'Religious Changes in Cheshire, 1750–1850', *Journal of Ecclesiastical History* 17 (1966), 77–93.

—— 'Religious Changes in Liverpool in the Nineteenth Century', *Journal of Ecclesiastical History* 19 (1968), 195–211.

WALLIS, R., *The Elementary Forms of the New Religious Life* (London, 1984).

—— 'The Caplow–De Toqueville Account of Contrasts in European and American Religion: Confounding Considerations', *Sociological Analysis* 47 (1986), 50–2.

—— and Bruce, S., *Sociological Theory, Religion and Collective Action* (Belfast, 1987).

—— —— 'Religion: The British Contribution', *British Journal of Sociology*, 40 (1989), 493.

—— —— 'Secularization: Trends, Data and Theory', *Research in the Social Scientific Study of Religion* 3 (1991), 1–31.

WARD, C., *Priests and People: A Study in the Sociology of Religion* (Liverpool, 1965).

WEBER, M., *Ancient Judaism* (New York, 1967).

WELTY, W., 'Black Shepherds: A Study of Leading Negro Clergymen in New York City 1900–1940', Ph.D thesis (New York University, 1989).

WENDLAND, W., *Siebenhundert Jahre Kirchengeschichte Berlins* (Berlin, 1930).

WHITE, J. G., *The Churches and Chapels of Old London* (London, private circulation, 1901).

WICKHAM, E. R., *Church and People in an Industrial City* (London, 1957).

WILLOWS, H. (ed.), *A Guide to Worship in Central London* (London, 1988).

WILSON, B. R., *Sects and Society* (London, 1955).

—— *Religion in Secular Society* (London, 1966).

—— *Contemporary Transformations of Religion* (Oxford, 1976).

—— *Religion in Sociological Perspective* (Oxford, 1982).

—— 'Morality in the Evolution of the Modern Social System', *British Journal of Sociology* 36 (1985), 315–32.

—— 'Secularization: The Inherited Model', in Hammond, P. E. (ed.), *The Sacred in a Secular Age: Toward Revision in the Scientific Study of Religion* (Los Angeles, 1985), 9–20.

—— *The Social Dimensions of Sectarianism: Sects and New Religious Movements in Contemporary Society* (Oxford, 1990).

WILSON, J., *Religion in American Society* (Englewood Cliffs, NJ, 1978).

WOLFE, J. N., and PICKFORD., M., *The Church of Scotland: An Economic Survey* (London, 1980).

WUTHNOW, R., *The Restructuring of American Religion: Society and Faith Since World War II* (Princeton, NJ, 1988).

YATES, N., 'Urban Church Attendance and the Use of Statistical Evidence, 1850–1900', in Baker, D. (ed.), *The Church in Town and Countryside* (Oxford, 1979).

YEO, S., *Religion and Voluntary Organizations in Crisis* (London, 1976).

ZELINSKY, W., 'An Approach to the Religious Geography of the United States: Patterns of Membership in 1952', *Annals of the American Association of Geographers* 51 (1961), 139–193.

Index